KU-536-548

High Performance Mobile Web

Maximiliano Firtman

WITHDRAWN

Beijing · Boston · Farnham · Sebastopol · Tokyo

LIVERPOOL JMU LIBRARY

3 1111 01505 4776

High Performance Mobile Web

by Maximiliano Firtman

Copyright © 2016 Maximiliano Firtman. All rights reserved.

Printed in the United States of America.

Published by O'Reilly Media, Inc., 1005 Gravenstein Highway North, Sebastopol, CA 95472.

O'Reilly books may be purchased for educational, business, or sales promotional use. Online editions are also available for most titles (*http://safaribooksonline.com*). For more information, contact our corporate/institutional sales department: 800-998-9938 or *corporate@oreilly.com*.

Editors: Brian Anderson and Virginia Wilson	**Indexer:** WordCo Indexing Services, Inc.
Production Editor: Colleen Cole	**Interior Designer:** David Futato
Copyeditor: Rachel Head	**Cover Designer:** Karen Montgomery
Proofreader: Jasmine Kwityn	**Illustrator:** Rebecca Demarest

September 2016:   First Edition

Revision History for the First Edition

2016-09-01:   First Release

See *http://oreilly.com/catalog/errata.csp?isbn=9781491912553* for release details.

The O'Reilly logo is a registered trademark of O'Reilly Media, Inc. *High Performance Mobile Web*, the cover image, and related trade dress are trademarks of O'Reilly Media, Inc.

While the publisher and the author have used good faith efforts to ensure that the information and instructions contained in this work are accurate, the publisher and the author disclaim all responsibility for errors or omissions, including without limitation responsibility for damages resulting from the use of or reliance on this work. Use of the information and instructions contained in this work is at your own risk. If any code samples or other technology this work contains or describes is subject to open source licenses or the intellectual property rights of others, it is your responsibility to ensure that your use thereof complies with such licenses and/or rights.

978-1-491-91255-3

[LSI]

For my lovely wife Ani
and Matías,
who came into our lives while writing this book;
being your dad is the best new job I've ever had.

Table of Contents

Preface

Many web designers and web developers are not paying enough attention to their mobile websites' performance. And we as users are paying for that. Lots of mobile and responsive websites have performance problems today, so I think there is still much room for discussion on this topic.

With this book, I hope to help mobile website creators to understand what things are harming performance and what other things might increase performance. When I talk about performance, I'm also talking about another important metric: conversion. It's well known that better performance leads to an increase in conversions, and—in the end—that means more money for you.

A lot of interesting data has appeared in the last few years about how performance may be impacting conversion rate. For example:

- Shaving 2.2 s off load time increased downloads for Mozilla by 15%
- A 60% faster website led to a 14% increase in donations to Barack Obama's US presidential campaign
- A 50% faster website led to 15% more revenue for AutoAnything
- Cutting 100 ms off load times meant 1% more revenue for Walmart

Who Should Read This Book

This book is for web developers and web designers who are ready to optimize the performance of their mobile websites and web apps to the extreme. I'm expecting that you have medium-level knowledge of and experience working with HTML, CSS, JavaScript, and HTTP. Having previous experience with web performance optimization will help, but it's not required.

A Word on "Mobile Web" Today

In this book, we will explore the current ecosystem and why the mobile web needs special attention in terms of performance. We'll see the differences in cellular networks and what the latest versions of mobile browsers are offering to improve the user experience and performance.

Navigating This Book

This book is organized as follows:

Chapter 1, The Mobile Web World
    Discusses the current ecosystem of the mobile world. I strongly suggest reviewing this chapter, even if you think that you know what the world looks like. You might find some surprises.

Chapter 2, Where to Measure Performance
    Describes the usage of different tools to measure performance, such as emulators, simulators, and real devices.

Chapter 3, Web Performance Basics
    Covers all the basic web performance concepts, including metrics, charts, and what they mean.

Chapter 4, Measurement Tools
    Reviews the tools that are available to get real data from your mobile browsers.

Chapter 5, Performance APIs
    Gets into the world of APIs and specs, analyzing the options we have available to measure and improve performance.

Chapter 6, Optimizing for the First Visit
    Gives you all the insights and tricks you need to start optimizing the first-view experience.

Chapter 7, Optimizing After First Load
    Describes how to take advantage of the first view to improve user perception and performance for future visits.

Chapter 8, Optimizing Responsiveness and the Post Loading Experience
    Gets into the experience and responsiveness of our web content after it has been loaded.

Chapter 9, Responsive Web Design
    Discusses responsive web design and web performance.

Chapter 10, Extreme Mobile Web Performance
> Provides lots of useful tips for extreme performance that will get great results, but with greater effort.

Chapter 11, The Native Side of the Web
> Discusses what you can do for performance when you are working with the native side of the web, such as web views or hybrid applications.

Chapter 12, Mobile Web Performance Checklist
> We will recap everything in this book with a Mobile Web Performance Checklist.

Online Resources

In this book, I will share dozens of online resources based on different topics. If you want to get updated information on the mobile web performance field, I suggest you follow the website of this book at *https://www.highperfmobile.com*.

Conventions Used in This Book

The following typographical conventions are used in this book:

Italic
> Indicates new terms, URLs, email addresses, filenames, and file extensions.

`Constant width`
> Used for program listings, as well as within paragraphs to refer to program elements such as variable or function names, databases, data types, environment variables, statements, and keywords.

`Constant width bold`
> Shows commands or other text that should be typed literally by the user.

`Constant width italic`
> Shows text that should be replaced with user-supplied values or by values determined by context.

 This element signifies a tip or suggestion.

This element signifies a general note.

 This element indicates a warning or caution.

Safari® Books Online

 *Safari Books Online* is an on-demand digital library that delivers expert content in both book and video form from the world's leading authors in technology and business.

Technology professionals, software developers, web designers, and business and creative professionals use Safari Books Online as their primary resource for research, problem solving, learning, and certification training.

Safari Books Online offers a range of plans and pricing for enterprise, government, education, and individuals.

Members have access to thousands of books, training videos, and prepublication manuscripts in one fully searchable database from publishers like O'Reilly Media, Prentice Hall Professional, Addison-Wesley Professional, Microsoft Press, Sams, Que, Peachpit Press, Focal Press, Cisco Press, John Wiley & Sons, Syngress, Morgan Kaufmann, IBM Redbooks, Packt, Adobe Press, FT Press, Apress, Manning, New Riders, McGraw-Hill, Jones & Bartlett, Course Technology, and hundreds more. For more information about Safari Books Online, please visit us online.

How to Contact Us

Please address comments and questions concerning this book to the publisher:

O'Reilly Media, Inc.
1005 Gravenstein Highway North
Sebastopol, CA 95472
800-998-9938 (in the United States or Canada)
707-829-0515 (international or local)
707-829-0104 (fax)

We have a web page for this book, where we list errata, examples, and any additional information. You can access this page at *http://bit.ly/high-performance-mobile-web*.

To comment or ask technical questions about this book, send email to *bookquestions@oreilly.com*.

For more information about our books, courses, conferences, and news, see our website at *http://www.oreilly.com*.

Find us on Facebook: *http://facebook.com/oreilly*

Follow us on Twitter: *http://twitter.com/oreillymedia*

Watch us on YouTube: *http://www.youtube.com/oreillymedia*

Acknowledgments

It's difficult to write a book on web performance without offering thanks to Steve Souders. Author of the first book on the matter, *High Performance Web Sites* (O'Reilly), and performance advocate for years, he is definitely the guy we should all thank for bringing to light the importance of web performance. More importantly, Steve is a great person. I'm grateful to him for allowing me to add my point of view at many Velocity Conferences (*http://conferences.oreilly.com/velocity*).

Several other members of the mobile web community have helped in many ways with this book, writing blog posts, delivering talks, and spending time doing tests on dozens of devices. The list includes Ilya Grigorik, Jake Archibald, Scott Jehl, Nicole Sullivan, Tim Kadlec, Paul Irish, Guy Podjarny, Paul Kinlan, Jason Grigsby, Dion Almaer, Christian Heilmann, Stoyan Stefanov, and many more. Their work is inside this book, and if you are not already following them on Twitter, stop reading for a minute and add them to your list.

A big thanks to the technical reviewers, María Evangelina Ferreira, Luca Passani, Anselm Hannemann, Hogel Bartel, and Jonathan Barbero. Their comments and ideas were really useful for making this the book I wanted.

Also thanks to the great O'Reilly team who worked in this project: Virginia Wilson, Brian Anderson, and Simon St. Laurent. Thanks, Simon, for trusting me on every new project!

Finally, and really importantly, thanks to my family, who let me take time out for writing, speaking, and teaching. To my parents, my brother, my lovely wife Ani, and my son Matías, who came into our lives while writing this book—being your dad is the best new job I've ever had :).

CHAPTER 1

The Mobile Web World

The topic of performance on the mobile web might seem confusing at first. Isn't the mobile web the same web as the one we already know?

The answer is not so simple. Yes, it's the same web; but the context in which it's being accessed—from a variety of browsers, devices, screens, and networks—is very different. Those differences play a big role in determining performance—or the lack of it—and that's why we need to pay special attention to the mobile web.

Fortunately, following the idea originally stated by Luke Wroblewski (*http://www.lukew.com*) in *Mobile First*, if you first apply performance techniques for mobile devices, your website will also perform well and faster on other kinds of devices, including desktops and TVs.

Mobile Performance First

If you have a multidevice web solution, starting to optimize the mobile web performance will also help with other devices, such as when using desktop browsers. While most techniques in this book can be applied to both the classic and mobile web, some of them are specific to mobile devices' problems and therefore it's easier if we start with them.

Don't get me wrong, I'm not pushing the idea of having a separate web. Ultimately, we are still talking about the same content and the same services, accessed from different devices. In this chapter, we'll cover the differences from the desktop web, which we will call from now on *the classic web*—that is the web from the main browsers on typically desktop-based operating systems, such as Windows, macOS, or Linux.

We'll define the mobile web as web content being accessed from a feature phone, smartphone, tablet, or wearable device. I know there are some hybrid devices that can fit into the classic web definition, but I think we all know where the line is.

Before getting into the performance side of the mobile web, we need to establish and clarify the differences between classic web platforms, such as on desktop PCs, and web platforms running on mobile devices.

Form Factors

Several form factors are available on the market, but if we focus just on mobile devices with web platforms we can divide them into:

- Tablets
- Phablets (phones with screens bigger than 5.5″)
- Smartphones (phones using a *big OS* such as Android, iOS, or Windows)
- Social devices (cheap phones with web access using operating systems like Firefox OS, Nokia Ashas, or feature phones—these are starting to disappear these days)
- Smartwatches

In this book, we'll focus on smartphones, phablets, social phones, and tablets, but some techniques and tools might also be useful for other form factors.

Mobile Hardware

In the future, there might come a point when mobile devices will be more powerful than desktops and laptops (mostly because the technology is going in that direction), but we are not there yet. Mobile devices have less RAM available and less-powerful CPUs.

I know you might think this is not true, in an age of octa-core mobile devices, but the reality is that the average mobile device out there is not the most expensive device. And this is particularly true in certain regions in the world, such as Asia, Africa, and Latin America.

If you are reading this book, you probably don't have an average phone in terms of hardware and network access. When thinking about performance, always think about average users and test on those devices.

There are dozens of differences between mobile devices and classic desktop devices, such as screen resolutions, screen densities, and hardware sensors, but the ones that might affect web content's performance are:

- CPU, where the parsing, rendering, and execution happens
- Memory, where the DOM tree, image buffers, and decompression data are stored
- GPU, where, when available, some rendering happens (usually known as *hardware accelerated*)
- GPU memory, where, when a GPU is available, some image buffers and layers are stored

We can roughly say that in terms of CPU, an average mobile device will be about five times slower than an average desktop device acquired at the same time. In terms of RAM, the difference is around three times smaller.

Mobile Phones Are Still Behind Desktop Hardware

You might say that because the screen is also smaller having less power and memory won't make a big difference, but if you think about it, that's not really true.

The desktop computer I'm using to write this book (a high-end laptop) has 8 GB of RAM, 1.5 GB of GPU memory, and 1.3 million pixels on the screen. My current phone—a high-end Android phone bought at the same time as my laptop—has 2 GB of RAM and 2 million pixels on the screen. In terms of CPUs, they have different architectures (Intel versus ARM), so it's difficult to compare them by their specs, but based on CPU Boss Comparison (*http://cpuboss.com/compare-cpus*), my laptop's CPU is 2.7 times faster than my phone's CPU.

Therefore, just in my own example, my phone has 53% more pixels to draw on the screen with a quarter of the RAM and roughly a third of the CPU power when compared to my laptop acquired at the same time. And remember, I don't have an average device. This means that web content on a mobile device suffers in terms of performance.

Mobile Networks

> We have 4G now! We don't have performance problems on the network anymore.
>
> —A random web developer

Mobile devices connect to the network in different ways, usually using a WLAN (WiFi) connection or a cellular connection.

WiFi access can be reliable (such as a home or office connection) or unreliable (such as at a coffee shop or on a plane or a bus, where it usually goes through a cellular connection).

Cellular connections are far less reliable compared to WiFi access because of the nature of the system. We are connecting wirelessly through radio waves, to a remote wired connection (in a cell tower up to a couple of miles from us). The connection changes cells, availability, and connection type frequently—more frequently if we are on the move.

Cellular connections today are usually known by popular names, such as 2G, 3G, and 4G. However, those names are used as a shorthand to refer to several different underlying connection types, such as:

- GPRS (2G)
- EDGE (2G, 2.5G, or 3G)
- UMTS (3G)
- WCDMA (3G)
- HSPA (3G)
- EVDO (3G)
- HSPA+ (3G or 4G)
- Mobile WiMax (4G)
- LTE (4G)

Distribution

Although it's easy to assume that 4G is now everywhere, particularly for those in urban areas, in reality, that's far from the case.

At the end of 2015, according to GSMA Intelligence (*https://gsmaintelligence.com*), 58% of the world was connected through 2G, 32% through 3G, and only 9% through 4G.

The values change when talking about developed countries, including the United States, but still 20% of the users were on 2G, 55% of the users on 3G, and just 25% on 4G.

5G Americas also has a chart of 4G penetration as of 1Q 2016 (*http://www.4gameri cas.org/en/resources/statistics/statistics-global*) that shows that North America accounted for 20% of connections, Western Europe 11%, and all other regions outside of Oceania and Eastern and Southeastern Asia just under 13% combined.

The other important data here is that even when you have a 4G device and you have a 4G carrier, 30% of the time you might not be using that connection but downgrading to 3G or 2G. Open Signal has great deep information on this problem (*https://opensig nal.com/reports/2015/09/state-of-lte-q3-2015*); it states that US 4G users are not using 4G 23% of the time while in Germany it can be up to 50%.

Also, on unlimited plans, most carriers have a data limit. When you reach that limit, you are mostly downgraded to 2G, even if you are in a big US city with the latest iPhone or Android device.

All this data means that we will be living with 2G and 3G connections for a while, and we need to pay special attention to this when we are providing mobile services.

Bandwidth

The first thing that comes to mind when talking about 3G or 4G is *bandwidth*. And it's true: better connections mean higher bandwidth.

The bandwidth available on average in each type of connection is shown in Table 1-1.

Table 1-1. Mobile network speeds in Megabits/second (Mbps)

Network	Minimum	Maximum	Average[a]
2G (EDGE)	0.1	0.4	0.1
3G	0.5	5	1.8
4G	1	50	3.2 (HSPA+), 12.6 (LTE)
WiFi[b]	1	100	5

[a] Data by Open Signal State of LTE Report (*https://opensignal.com/reports/2015/09/state-of-lte-q3-2015*)
[b] Measured by Open Signal on mobile apps

However, the question for us is: how important is the bandwidth when we are delivering mobile web content? More bandwidth is usually better, but the difference will not be huge because we are transferring just a bunch of small files. If you are doing video streaming, then bandwidth will be more important.

Latency

And here comes the biggest problem on mobile networks: the *wireless network latency*. The latency is the time it takes for the mobile device to send a data packet to the server. Usually we measure the *round-trip time* (RTT) latency—that is, the time it takes to get the first byte from the server after making a request.

Latencies can be up to 1 second on 2G networks—that means the browser will wait 1 second per request before starting to receive any actual data. Even on 4G (which, remember, accounts for just a small percentage of users worldwide), the RTT can be up to 180 milliseconds. Just to make a comparison with your home wired connection, a DSL in the United States has an RTT latency of 20 to 45 milliseconds.

Table 1-2 shows you the latencies we can find today in mobile networks.

Table 1-2. Mobile network latencies in milliseconds

Network	Minimum	Maximum	Compared to average home
2G (EDGE)	300	1000	+20x
3G	150	450	+9x
4G	100	180	+4x

 RTT latency is a big problem for the mobile web, because a typical mobile website or web app is composed of a group of small files that travel through the network as several requests, each one with RTT overhead.

If you are wondering why we have the RTT latency, it's caused by the network architecture involving:

1. The travel time from the phone to the cell tower (wireless)
2. The travel time from the cell tower to the carrier gateway (wired or wireless)
3. The travel time from the carrier gateway to the Internet (mixed)
4. The same travel time (1 to 3) in reverse order

When you are connecting to the web using a home or office connection, you are skipping travel times 1 and 2 from this list.

Radio state

The final characteristic of a mobile network is *radio state changes*. Your mobile device has a radio, the one used to send and receive data to and from the cell tower. That radio consumes battery, so the mobile operating system usually tries to save its usage to reduce battery consumption.

That means that if no app is using the network, the mobile device will switch the radio from *active state* to *idle state*. As a user, you don't know the current radio state. When any app or website tries to gather some data from the network, the device will restart the radio, and that usually involves time. On 3G connections, the time can be up to 2.5 seconds, while on 4G connections, it's usually less than 100 milliseconds.

Therefore, if the radio was in idle state, the first RTT latency will also have an overhead.

You might be thinking: I'm not a network operator, what can I do from a web point of view about this? Throughout this book, we'll see techniques and best practices to improve performance and perception thanks to having an understanding of these network problems.

Mobile Operating Systems

For the purposes of this book, we'll focus our attention on the main mobile operating systems based on current market share. Most of the explanations and techniques will also be useful for other operating systems, and I'll make some comments when something might be different.

The main operating systems are:

- iOS
- Android
- Windows

For Windows, we'll focus on the versions available on phones (formerly known as Windows Phone), with some comments on Windows for tablets.

Fire OS is an operating system created by Amazon that powers the Kindle Fire series and the Fire Phone. Fire OS is a UI layer on top of Android, so from an OS perspective we'll be considering it as Android. Nokia took a similar approach for one year with Nokia X, an Android-based platform that was discontinued by Microsoft in mid-2014. Both projects use different web runtimes and web browsers compared to the original standard Android flavors, meaning different techniques to test and debug for performance.

Besides the main operating systems, in the mobile space today we can also find a small number of devices using:

- BlackBerry 10
- Firefox OS
- Tizen
- Sailfish
- Ubuntu

There are also other obsolete operating systems that we won't cover in this book, as they have less than 0.5% market share at the time of this writing and don't have any future. These include:

- Symbian
- MeeGo
- webOS
- Nokia Series 40

 While most techniques in this book will also be useful on desktop devices, we will not focus here on Windows for desktop, macOS, Linux, or Chrome OS.

Engines

Before getting into the analysis of the current state of the mobile web, let's do a quick review of web rendering engines and execution engines that will be useful to understand some references in the rest of this book.

Rendering Engines

The *rendering engine* (also known as the *layout engine*) is the code that will be downloading, parsing, and rendering your HTML and CSS code on the screen, as well as other related content, such as SVG or images.

With regard to mobile devices, for years the king of rendering engines was WebKit, powering browsers on iOS, Android, BlackBerry, Symbian, and many others.

Today, in the mobile space we can find the following rendering engines available:

- WebKit
- Blink
- Trident
- Gecko
- Presto

Created by Apple in 2001, *WebKit* is an open source project based on KHTML (another engine available for Linux-based browsers created in 1998) to support the Safari browser. The component related to layout and rendering is known as WebCore. Many companies have been using WebKit in the mobile space for years, including BlackBerry, Nokia, Google, Samsung, and Palm. It's today the most used rendering engine in the mobile space.

 When we talk about WebKit, we are usually talking about WebCore, the part of WebKit that is responsible for parsing and rendering HTML and CSS.

The great thing about WebKit is that most web platforms in the mobile world are using it. This means that even on very different mobile devices we can expect very similar web rendering with simple markup and styles, which is good news for developers. However, it isn't perfect—as we'll see in later chapters, many differences do exist between WebKit implementations, as well as in HTML5 compatibility.

Google Chrome was using WebKit until 2013, when it decided to fork it and continue it in a separate path with the name *Blink*. Today, in terms of performance Blink and WebKit are different even though they share the same source. Blink powers Google Chrome and Opera.

Trident is the proprietary engine inside Internet Explorer, while Gecko is an open source engine managed by the Mozilla Foundation. Neither of them has gained much traction in the mobile space yet, but they have enough market share to pay attention to them. From Windows 10, a new engine was born on Microsoft Edge; while it was originally based on Trident, it was rewritten almost entirely.

Finally, Opera used Presto—its own proprietary engine—for years on its mobile browsers, but as of Opera 12, switched to Blink, ceasing future updates of Presto. However, even today there are still users browsing the web with older versions of Opera using this engine. The Presto engine is still being used on Opera proxy-based solutions, such as Opera Mini, where the rendering happens server-side.

Execution Engines

When you have JavaScript code, the *execution engine* comes into action. It's the run-time that interprets your code, manages the memory for your variables and objects, and interacts with the platform behind it—usually, a browser.

We need to separate the life of JavaScript execution engines into two eras: classic and just-in-time (JIT) compilers. Classic engines interpret JavaScript while executing, while JIT engines precompile the JavaScript code into native code before executing it, with a big improvement in terms of performance.

The first of the new engines was *Carakan*, created by Opera for its desktop browser; this was followed by *V8*, an open source JavaScript engine developed by Google that is currently used in Google Chrome and other projects such as *Node.js*. Other modern JavaScript engines include *JägerMonkey* (Mozilla Foundation), *IonMonkey* (Mozilla Foundation, since 2013), *Nitro* (also known as SquirrelFish), and *Chakra* (Internet Explorer).

 Execution engines with JIT compilers can run JavaScript code between three and five times faster on the same device.

Older engines with no precompilation features include the original JavaScriptCore—part of the WebKit project—and SpiderMonkey (originally used in Netscape, later in Firefox). As of 2016, JavaScriptCore includes the FTL JIT compiler B3 (*https://webkit.org/blog/5852/introducing-the-b3-jit-compiler*).

Web Platforms

A *web platform* is the scope where our web content is being executed and parsed. We can start categorizing the mobile web platforms today into:

- Web browsers
- Web apps
- Web view–based content
- Ebooks

Ebooks are out of the scope of this book, but I will say for now that latest versions of EPUB (the standard format for publishing ebooks) and MOBI (the Amazon proprietary format) are using HTML5-based content. Therefore, interactivity comes in the form of JavaScript running inside the ebook reader.

While I'm pretty sure you already know what a web browser is, you might have some doubts about the exact definitions of the other platforms. Let's talk about them before we get into the world of web browsers on mobile devices.

Web Apps

While the definition is not 100% written in stone, at least from this book's perspective, a *web app* is web content that is installed in the Applications menu or the home screen of a device and has a Chromeless user interface in the operating system.

You can think on of a web app as a website on steroids; from a user's perspective it looks like an installed app, but from our perspective we are talking about web content in HTML5, CSS, and JavaScript.

Web App Synonyms

Web apps are sometimes known as *home screen web apps* or *full screen web apps*. Also, a new name has appeared lately: *progressive web apps*, including similar solutions but with new techniques.

From a performance point of view, a web app includes:

- A server that is hosting the files
- A possible local resource installation
- A declaration of metadata for the installation process
- A web rendering engine and a JavaScript execution engine loading the content, with or without the context of a browser process

There is no compilation or package process. Web apps can be installed from a browser or from an app store.

While on some operating systems a web app runs on exactly the same engine as a website, on others the engine might differ, meaning different performance measurements and techniques.

At the time of this writing, the web app platforms available are:

- iOS home screen web apps
- Progressive web apps (available at the time of this writing mostly on Android using Chrome, Firefox, Opera, or Samsung Internet, with Windows support coming in 2017 with Edge)

There were some other platforms supporting web apps that today are considered obsolete, such as Series 40 web apps and MeeGo web apps, both from Nokia, before Microsoft's acquisition.

Native Versus Website Versus Web App Versus Hybrid

In this book I'm not getting into the discussion of which approach is the best one per case. I will cover techniques applicable to all the options but native. Table 1-3 shows you the features unique to each approach.

Table 1-3. Mobile approaches

Approach	Distribution	Usage	Development	Full native access
Website	Browser	URL, Social sharing and search engine	HTML5 and web	No
Web app	Browser	Icon	HTML5 and web	No
Hybrid	App store	Icon, Custom URI (web and other apps)	HTML5 and web	Yes (through native code)
Native	App store	Icon, Custom URI (web and other apps)	Native code	Yes

---

iOS Home Screen Web Apps

On iOS—the operating system behind iPhones, iPod touches, and iPads—Safari has an option to "Add to the Home Screen" any website. By default, when the option is activated, Safari adds a shortcut to the website on the home screen, as we can see in Figure 1-1.

If the website has the proper declaration through `<meta>` tags, when the user adds the website to the home screen, the icon becomes a web app. A web app runs in full-screen mode, it appears as a full app from the operating system's perspective, and it doesn't run under Safari, as we can see in Figure 1-2.

Figure 1-1. On Safari, we can add a website to the home screen to get an icon as an application. Here, we add forecast.io to illustrate the process.

Figure 1-2. When a web app has the right metadata, it runs in full-screen mode, outside of the scope of Safari. From an operating system's point of view, it's a separate app from Safari.

For the purposes of this book, we won't get into too much detail about how to create these web apps. If you want more insights, check out my book *Programming the Mobile Web* (*http://firt.mobi/pmw*) (O'Reilly). However, let's say that the main reason for getting a homescreen web app is using the following <meta> tag:

```
<meta name="apple-mobile-web-app-capable" content="yes">
```

 If you have never seen a web app on iOS, you can try these examples from Safari iOS: Financial Times (*http://app.ft.com*), AliExpress (*http://aliexpress.com*), or Forecast (*http://forecast.io*).

Web apps on iOS run under a process known as *Web*. This process uses the same WebCore and Nitro engine as Safari but it also adds its own set of features and bugs.

iOS web apps didn't have the JIT Nitro engine for a couple of versions when this faster engine appeared on Safari. This absence led to several criticisms in the press about Apple not pushing web technologies. From version iOS 5.0, the home screen web apps are using the much faster engine instead of the older JavaScript code.

 On iOS, home screen web apps are usually the target of several bugs when a new version appears. If you are creating these kinds of solutions, keep in mind that you should retest your app after each iOS release.

Chrome Home Screen Web Apps

Google Chrome for Android (since version 33) also supports home screen web apps using the same mechanism: the user can select the option from the menu and a new icon will appear on the home screen, as shown in Figure 1-3.

As in iOS, the web app appears from an OS point of view as a different document, and in terms of performance and engines, it is using the Chrome you have installed on your phone. That means that if you update Chrome from the Play Store, the web app's engine will also be updated.

Remember that a website is not a web app by default after adding it to the home screen. The website has to declare a manifest file for Chrome to consider it as a web app. Without the manifest, the icon on the home screen will just open Chrome, as for a normal website.

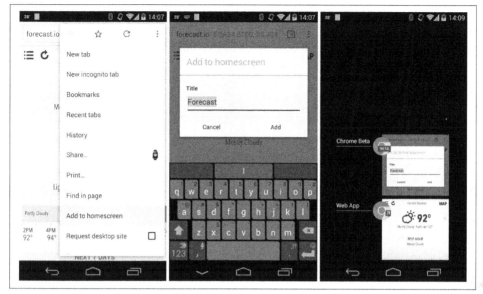

Figure 1-3. Chrome for Android has the ability to install a web app through the drop-down menu. Here, forecast.io installation is illustrated step by step.

If you want to learn more about Chrome home screen web apps, visit the Chrome Developer's Guide (*https://developer.chrome.com/multidevice/android/installtoho mescreen*).

 While sharing an engine and code from Android 4.4, home screen web apps and web views have different compatibility and performance when running on the same device.

Progressive Web Apps

After Chrome added support for home screen web apps, the team evolved the concept, adding more features to what is now known as a *progressive web app* (PWA). A PWA is a website running in a browser that will progressively add more features based on compatibility. The features involve using service workers for offline usage, optional web push notifications, and letting the user install the web app in the home screen through the manifest.

On compatible browsers, if you meet some conditions, the browser will ask the user if she wants to install the PWA into the home screen, creating a fully offline-capable app experience on the device.

PWAs are compatible at the time of this writing with Chrome, Firefox, Opera, and Samsung Internet browsers on Android. Microsoft has announced PWA support coming to the Edge browser on all their platforms starting in 2017. In terms of web rendering engine, a PWA will use the engine from the browser from which it was installed. Therefore, you can have several icons on the home screen pointing to the same PWA but running on different web engines if you install it from several browsers.

The installation part of a progressive web app is available thanks to the Web App Manifest (*https://www.w3.org/TR/appmanifest*).

> PWA Rocks (*https://pwa.rocks*) is a progressive web app gallery maintained by the Opera team.

When you update the browser, it will automatically update the web rendering engine for all the PWAs installed on that device.

> Firefox has created an open platform for web apps for Android and Firefox OS (an operating system that was available for mobile devices for a while). The Open Web Apps platform was deprecated in favor of progressive web apps in 2016, and it won't have any further development.

Summary of Web Apps

Web apps are a way to install apps without the need for native compilation and store distribution, based 100% on web content. Table 1-4 provides information on the engines available.

Table 1-4. Web app engines

OS	Devices	Versions	Rendering	Execution	Process
iOS	All	2.0–4.3	WebKit	JavaScriptCore	Web.app
iOS	All	5.0+	WebKit	Nitro	Web.app
Android with Chrome	All	4.0+	Blink	V8	Chrome
Android with Firefox	All	2.3+	Gecko	SpiderMonkey	Firefox
Android with Opera	All	4.0+	Blink	V8	Opera
Android with Samsung	All	4.1+	Blink	V8	Internet

Remember, when we are talking about web apps we are not packaging the contents in a ZIP file or similar container, such as APKs (Android packages) or IPAs (iPhone applications). We are using just a normal web server to host the files, and those files will run in a full-screen environment.

Web Views

A *web view* is a native control available on most platforms (similar to buttons, labels, and text inputs) that allows a native app to include and run web content. The web view can use the entire screen or just a small portion of it.

While most of the techniques in this book will apply to web view–based content, later on we'll focus specifically on web view–based platforms. We need to consider web views separately because while they sometimes share the same engine as the default browser on the device, performance techniques will vary.

Web views can be used for different purposes, including to:

- Show rich content
- Execute JavaScript code
- Show animations or ads
- Show an in-app browser
- Create a pseudo-browser
- Create the entire user interface and logic with web content (usually known as a *native web app* or a *hybrid app*), such as an app using Apache Cordova or Phone-Gap
- Create a native shell for a web app

 While working with web view–based solutions, we need to understand that the same code on different devices might run on different engines. Even on the same device, after an OS update the engines will be updated, meaning that our code is not guaranteed to run in exactly the same way. If we follow good practices, we will reduce the risk of incompatibilities in the future.

Native Web Apps

On some platforms, we have an official set of tools to create native apps from web content without creating a native project and adding a web view. These platforms are using the web view inside.

Some platforms that will use the web view in the background are:

- Apache Cordova (also known as PhoneGap), including if you build using the PhoneGap Build service from Adobe
- JavaScript Windows apps
- BlackBerry WebWorks
- Amazon Web Apps for Fire OS and Android
- Tizen apps

Compared to the web apps we covered before, a native web app or hybrid involves:

- Packaging the web content into a ZIP file or platform-specific container
- Creating a manifest declaration
- Signing the package
- Distributing the app as a native app on app stores

 We shouldn't confuse a native web app platform running web content on the fly on the device with cross-platform solutions that might start with web content but precompile it into native code before publishing it. No web view is involved in these cases. Appcelerator, ReactNative, and NativeScript are examples of these tools; you write JavaScript but it is compiled into native code.

In native web apps, we are not hosting the files on a web server but inside the app's package. This will be a big difference when talking about performance.

In-App Browsers

Some native applications have the need to show you a website, but don't want you to leave the app. This happens mostly on iOS, where before iOS 9 you didn't have a back button to quickly go back to the app after opening the browser. Even with a small back button available since iOS 9 in the status bar, most apps still want to have in-app browsers. Great examples here are Facebook (see Figure 1-4), Twitter, and Flipboard.

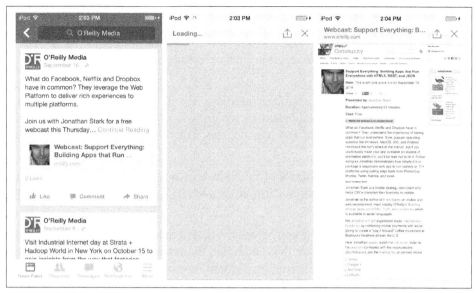

Figure 1-4. Some iOS apps include an in-app browser mechanism, such as Facebook, which allows you to browse a friend's suggested website without opening Safari

According to ScientiaMobile's Mobile Overview Report (MOVR) (*http://www.scientia mobile.com/page/movr-mobile-overview-report*), from October 2015 to April 2016, 33% of the web traffic coming from iOS and 40% from Android was received from inside a native app that is not marketed as a browser, Facebook being the most prominent app (accounting for 95% and 86% of this traffic, respectively).

 When you see an app with an ad on iOS or Android there is a good chance that it's using a web view, because both iAd from Apple and AdSense from Google are using this control for in-app advertisements.

Pseudo-Browsers

I'm pretty sure you've never heard about *pseudo-browsers*. It's really a new category that I defined a couple of years ago. A pseudo-browser is a native application marketed as a web browser that, instead of providing its own rendering and execution engines, uses the native web view.

From a user's point of view, it's a browser. From a developer's point of view, it's just the web view with a particular UI. Therefore, we have the same rendering engine as in the preinstalled browser, but with a different UI. These pseudo-browsers are mostly available for iOS and Android, and they offer the same service as the native browsers but with different services on top of them.

On iOS, the web view is upgraded with the operating system. There is no way to update or change it as a separate component. Because of an App Store rule, we can't provide our own web engine inside an iPhone native app, as in other operating systems.

This can lead to some philosophical questions about what a browser is. From a developer's perspective, it's important to understand that pseudo-browsers are not adding fragmentation—they're not new engines, but simply the web view from the operating system.

Chrome on iOS is the best example of a pseudo-browser; because Apple has a restriction on using third-party engines, Chrome uses the iOS web view instead of a Blink-based engine.

The main difference with an in-app browser is that in that case, the app is not marketed as a browser—you can't say that Facebook, for example, is a web browser, even though it now has an in-app browser on iOS and Android.

Other examples on iOS are Firefox and Brave.

The Web View on iOS

The web view available on iOS is WebKit-based, and while some people will consider the web view as an embedded Safari, the reality is different.

First, on iOS since version 8.0, we have two web views available: the old one (known as *UIWebView*) and the new one (known as *WKWebView*). While we will talk more about this later in this book, from our point of view it's important to understand that performance on both web views will be different.

To clarify the engines behind iOS, take a look at Table 1-5.

Table 1-5. iOS web engines

Type	Versions	Rendering	Execution
Safari and Safari View Controller	1.0–4.2	WebKit	JavaScriptCore
Safari and Safari View Controller	4.3+	WebKit	Nitro JIT
Web app	2.0–4.3	WebKit	JavaScriptCore
Web app	5.0+	WebKit	Nitro JIT
UIWebView	All	WebKit	JavaScriptCore
WKWebView	8.0+	WebKit	Nitro JIT

On iOS, the difference between using JavaScriptCore and Nitro with the JIT compiler is a factor of 3. That is, on the same device, JavaScript code running on UIWebView will be at least three times slower than the same code running on WKWebView or Safari. However, we will see later that JavaScript execution time is just one part of the total time a page takes to load, so this doesn't mean your website loads three times slower.

The Web View on Android

For years, the web view on Android was the cause of many companies not using HTML5 for creating native apps. The web view was extremely slow on Android 2.x; it got better on 4.0 but wasn't really good enough until 4.4.

Until Android 4.3, the web view was based on WebKit, and from 4.0 to 4.3 it was pretty much the same version without any changes or updates in terms of performance or compatibility.

Because of this problem, some Android manufacturers, including Samsung and HTC, have decided to replace the default web view with a modern version of WebKit or Chromium (the open source version of Chrome with Blink and V8, much faster and compatible with modern HTML5 features). The problem is that on each device and version of the operating system, the version of WebKit or Chromium (as well as the features and abilities enabled) might be different.

Amazon for Kindle Fire has kept the original Android web view but also added a second web view, known as *Amazon Web View* (based on Chromium 18), from the Kindle Fire 2nd Generation. Finally, on the Fire Phone, Amazon has decided to just replace the default web view on Android 4.2 (the version it uses) with its Amazon web view.

From Android 4.4 (KitKat), Google has decided to replace the web view on Android with Chromium to keep everything under one umbrella again, starting with Chromium 30 (equivalent to Chrome 30) and following with version 33 in the small 4.4.1 update.

Even if they have installed Chrome, or Chrome came pre-installed, users on Android 4.0–4.3 will execute web view–based code on WebKit and a non-JIT JavaScript engine by default.

Since Android 5.0, the web view is based on Chromium 39, and it has become—for the first time—updatable from the Google Play Store, meaning that the user can install new versions of the Chromium-based web view without waiting for the next version of the operating system. Therefore, now web view–based solutions can keep up to date with Chrome's new features.

 Some people are treating Android Browser as a modern Internet Explorer 6: a slow, noncompatible browser that is difficult to get rid of from the market and that we need to still support. In July 2013, I wrote about this issue in the article "Android and the Eternal Dying Mobile Browser" (*http://www.mobilexweb.com/blog/android-browser-eternal-dying*).

Table 1-6 provides a summary of what the web view world on Android looks like today.

Table 1-6. Android web view engines

Devices	Versions	Rendering	Execution
All[a]	1.0–4.3	WebKit	JavaScriptCore
All	4.4	Chromium 30	V8 JIT
All	4.4.1	Chromium 33	V8 JIT
All	5.0+	Chromium 37+ (updatable via store)	V8 JIT
Samsung	4.1–4.3 (some devices, such as S3 and S4)	WebKit	V8 JIT
Samsung	4.1–4.3	Chromium (Blink)	V8 JIT
HTC	4.1–4.3	WebKit	V8 JIT
Amazon Kindle Fire (using alternative web view)	4.0+	Chromium (Blink)	V8 JIT
Amazon Fire Phone	4.2+	Chromium (Blink)	V8 JIT

[a] Not including Samsung, HTC, and Amazon devices with custom web views.

 Intel has created an open source project based on Chromium called Crosswalk that offers us an injectable web view for Android 4.0+, supporting the latest versions of Chrome. If we use it, we will be normalizing all the web views on Android but delivering a bigger Android app file.

The Web View on Windows

The web view on Windows (formerly also known as Windows Phone), such as on Microsoft Lumia devices, is far simpler than that on Android or iOS. It uses Trident and Chakra, the engines behind Internet Explorer, which up to Windows 8.1 differ depending on the version of Windows.

For example, on Windows 8 the engine is the same as in IE10, and on Windows 8.1 it is the same as in IE11. From Windows 10 in all versions (mobile and desktop), the engine was replaced by Edge, removing all the old IE stuff.

While technically you can inject your own web view in a native desktop Windows app, there are no options to do that for mobile phones at the time of this writing.

Summary of Web Views

We now know that web view engines can be pretty different on different devices—even on the same version of the operating system. Table 1-7 shows the current state of web views with their rendering and execution engines.

Table 1-7. Web view engines

OS	Devices	Versions	Rendering	Execution
iOS UIWebView	All	All	WebKit	JavaScriptCore
iOS WKWebView	All	8.0+	WebKit	Nitro
Android	All	2.x	WebKit	JavaScriptCore
Android	All[a]	4.0–4.3	WebKit	JavaScriptCore
Android	All	4.4+	Blink	V8
Android	Amazon Kindle Fire	4.0+	WebKit	JavaScriptCore
Android	Fire Phone	4.0+	Blink	V8
Android	Some Samsung devices	4.0–4.3	WebKit	JavaScriptCore
Android	Some Samsung devices	4.0–4.3	Blink	V8
Android	Some HTC devices	4.0–4.3	Blink	V8
Windows	All	7.5–8.1	Trident	Chakra
Windows	All	10	Edge	Edge
Windows	All	Android Runtime	Blink	V8
BlackBerry	All	7.0–10.2	WebKit	JavaScriptCore
BlackBerry	All	10.3+	Blink	V8
Tizen	All	All	WebKit	JavaScriptCore

[a] Excluding Amazon, Samsung, and HTC devices with custom web views.

Web Browsers

When talking about the classic web, usually web browsers are the only platform we care about. In the mobile web, it's for sure the most important category but not the only one, as we've just seen.

Now that we have looked at the web view and web app platforms, it's time to discuss browsers. I won't make a big list of mobile browsers here, but will provide just enough information to help you understand where users are browsing the mobile web, as that might affect our performance analysis and techniques.

We have already covered the most important operating systems that we will follow in this book, such as iOS, Android, and Windows. And maybe you are thinking that in terms of browsers it's easy: Safari, Chrome, and Internet Explorer/Edge. That's a typical mistake—in reality, it's a bit more complex.

Stats

Instead of just guessing, we can check different sources that will give us some hints on the current state of affairs. Unfortunately, there are several sources with different measurement methods.

 If you are using an analytics tools such as Google Analytics, you can check information about your own website and compare it with the global data from these sources.

The sources available for checking information on mobile browsers are:

- StatCounter Global Stats (*http://gs.statcounter.com*): select mobile browsers
- Akamai IO Dataset (*http://www.akamai.com/html/io/io_dataset.html*): select mobile browsers
- Mobile Overview Report (MOVR) (*http://wurfl.io/MOVR*) by ScientiaMobile
- Adobe Digital Index (ADI) Mobile Browser Share (*http://www.cmo.com/articles/2014/6/2/adi_2014_browser_war.html*)
- Market Share Reports (*http://www.netmarketshare.com*): select device type as mobile
- Wikimedia Stats (*http://stats.wikimedia.org/archive/squid_reports*), public stats from Wikipedia and other websites

I processed all those sources to reach some conclusions. Table 1-8 shows what the market share in terms of browsers looked like at the end of 2015. The table does include web views when used for browsing the web, such as in-app browsers (e.g., inside Facebook) and pseudo-browsers (e.g., Chrome on iOS).

Note that the data will change radically depending on whether you count tablets as contributing to mobile browser share, as Safari for the iPad accounts for a lot of traffic.

Table 1-8. Mobile web browsers global market share

Browser	Operating systems	Engines	%
Safari and web view	iOS	WebKit	45%
Chrome	Android	Blink	23%
Android Browser	Android	WebKit	15%
Samsung Browser	Android	Blink	7%
Opera[a]	Mixed	Presto	3%
Internet Explorer	Windows	Trident	3%
UC Browser	Mixed	U3 (proprietary engine)	3%
Firefox	Android and Firefox OS	Gecko	1%
Nokia Browser	Symbian	WebKit	<1%
Nokia Browser	Series 40	Gecko	<1%
Nokia Browser	Android (Nokia X)	Chromium	<1%
BlackBerry Browser	BBOS	WebKit	<1%
Samsung Dolfin	Samsung	WebKit	<1%
Amazon Silk	Fire OS	Blink	<1%

[a] Mostly Opera Mini.

 If your website or web app is targeting specific countries or regions, you should be aware that mobile browser market share might change a lot based on the region. In Asia, you will see more than 30% of users using UC Browser, while the old Nokia and Black-Berry Browsers with Internet Explorer might account for 10% and iOS for only 15% in Latin America.

Cloud Versus Direct Browsers

Direct browsers get content directly from the website server, and *cloud browsers* (also known as proxied browsers) go through a proxy server in the cloud. The proxy server usually does many of the following actions on the fly:

- Reduces the content, eliminating features that are not mobile-compatible
- Compresses the content (images included)
- Prerenders the content, so it can be displayed in the browser faster

- Converts the content, so we can see Flash video on devices with no Flash support
- Encrypts the content
- Caches the content for quick access to frequently visited sites
- Potentially blocks ads

Cloud-based browsers, such as Opera Mini, consume less bandwidth, increasing performance and reducing total navigation time at the same time. From a developer's perspective, the main difference is that the device is not directly accessing our web server; it's the proxy server in the cloud that is requesting all the files from our server, rendering those files in the cloud, and delivering a compressed, proprietary result to the browser. Usually there is no client-side interaction happening in these browsers.

Tim Kadlec did a great job analyzing proxy-based browsers in his article "Understanding Proxy Browsers: Architecture" (*https://timkadlec.com/2015/07/understanding-proxy-browsers-architecture*).

Google Chrome, Opera Mobile, Internet Explorer, and Amazon Silk offer a cloud compression mechanism as an optional feature to their direct browsers, as we can see in Figure 1-5. The feature needs to explicitly be enabled by the user (choose "Reduce data usage" in Chrome, "Off-Road mode" in Opera, "DataSense" in IE, and "Compression in Silk") and there is no data available on how many users are currently enabling the option.

Figure 1-5. Because performance is a top priority in mobile web browsing, some browsers, including Chrome, Opera, IE, and Silk, offer you an option to enable a proxy compression option

Stock Browsers

Practically every mobile device on the market today has a preinstalled browser (also known as the *stock browser*). The average user typically doesn't install a new web browser; therefore, on each device the preinstalled browser is the most-used one. One main disadvantage of preinstalled browsers is that sometimes there is no way to update the browser independently from the operating system. If your device doesn't get operating system updates, usually you will not get browser updates.

iOS Browsers

In iOS, there is a simple and single answer: Safari. We saw that nearly half of the mobile web traffic comes from iOS, and fortunately all the traffic uses the same engine.

If you are not browsing the web on iOS with Safari, it's because you are using a pseudo-browser, such as Chrome, Firefox, or Brave, or an in-app browser, such as when clicking on a link inside Facebook. In any case, you are using the same Web-Core. The JavaScript runtime might differ, though, as in different versions of the web view (UIWebView or WKWebView) we have JavaScriptCore or Nitro with the JIT compiler.

According to Mobile Overview Report (*http://wurfl.io/MOVR*), 33% of iOS traffic comes from Facebook's in-app browser, 5% from Twitter and other apps, and 3% from Chrome on iOS and other pseudo-browsers. Therefore, around 41% of iOS traffic is being executed in a web view and not inside Safari.

Android Browsers

Some developers and designers think that if we are talking about "the Android browser" we are talking about Google Chrome. Unfortunately, that's not exactly the reality.

Android, as an open source operating system, doesn't include Chrome, which is a non–open source browser. It has included a Chromium-based web view version since 4.4, and up to 4.3 it included a browser based purely on WebKit. This browser is usually known as *Android Browser*, the *Stock Browser*, or *Android WebKit*. The browser, while sharing roots with Chrome on WebKit, is a very different app in terms of performance and web compatibility, as you can see in Figure 1-6.

Figure 1-6. Here we can see HTML5test.com results on Android Browser 2.3, 4.0, and 4.3 compared with Google Chrome

From Android 4.4, Google has decided to remove support for that browser, but it didn't replace it with Chrome (at least not technically). I know you've seen several Android 4.4+ devices with Chrome preinstalled. That is because the manufacturer (Samsung, HTC, Motorola, Sony, etc.) signed a separate agreement with Google to include Play Services and Google apps that are not part of the Android OS, such as Maps, Gmail, Inbox, Play Store, and Google Chrome.

 Because Google Chrome is not really part of the Android Open Source Project (AOSP) and it's part of Play Services, it can be uninstalled, reinstalled, and updated from the Google Play Store by the user at any time. That's not true of preinstalled browsers.

Because the default Android Browser wasn't good enough, some vendors using Android as an operating system, including Samsung, Amazon, HTC, Nokia, and Barnes and Noble, have created their own custom versions of the default browser, sometimes WebKit-based (but more modern than the one used by Android), sometimes Chromium-based (using the Blink engine). Figure 1-7 shows a few examples.

And that's not all, because some manufacturers and some carriers around the globe have made agreements with Opera or Firefox to replace the default browser with those versions.

 Some devices, such as the Samsung Galaxy series, include two different browsers preinstalled, such as Chrome—thanks to a Google Play agreement—and the Samsung Internet Browser (with *Internet* as the name of the icon; also Chromium-based on modern devices). The user has the choice to use one or the other.

Figure 1-7. Some manufacturers, such as LG and Samsung, include a preinstalled browser that is not Android Browser or Chrome. They are today usually based on Chromium, but as you can see here, with different compatibility with the original Chrome.

Table 1-9 gives us an idea of how complicated the preinstalled browser situation looks on Android. Remember, most users will use just that browser.

Table 1-9. Preinstalled browsers on Android

Browser	Devices	Version	Engine	Updatable
Android Browser	All[a]	1.0–4.3	WebKit	no
Google Chrome	Manufacturers with a Play Services agreement	4.2+	Blink	Yes
Samsung Internet	Galaxy S3 and others	4.2+	WebKit	No
Samsung Internet	Galaxy S4 and others	4.2+	Blink	No
Nokia Browser	Nokia X, X+	4.1, 4.3	Blink	Yes
HTC Browser	Some	4.2+	Blink	No
LG Browser	Some	4.2+	Blink	No
Silk	Kindle Fire	4.2+	WebKit or Blink	No
Silk	Fire Phone	4.2+	Blink	No
Opera	Based on carrier	4.0+	Blink	Yes
Firefox	Kobo, Gigabyte devices	4.0+	Gecko	Yes

[a] Except those whose manufacturer replaced it by a custom browser.

Samsung and Web Runtimes

Because the Android web view and browser were old and slow before Android 4.4, Samsung decided to change them. However, there is no single or simple rule here.

To give you some examples, on the Galaxy S3 the web view and the browser are WebKit-based, but not the ones provided by the AOSP. On the Galaxy S4, the same WebKit-based web view is still used, but the browser was upgraded to a Chromium engine (version 18, upgraded to 28). Other devices that were shipped after the Galaxy S4 were still on WebKit.

Even when Samsung is using a version of Chromium, that doesn't mean that features and bugs are the same as in Chrome on that same version, because Samsung enables and disables different experimental features.

All the new Android phones, phablets, and tablets shipped from 2014 have a Chromium-based Samsung Internet Browser.

Android users have several options from the Google Play Store in terms of downloading browsers, as we can see in Figure 1-8, including Firefox (Gecko), Opera Mobile (Blink), Opera Mini (cloud-, Presto-based), UC Browser (cloud-based), and Dolphin (Blink). Unfortunately, stats show that few users actually use additional browsers.

Figure 1-8. On Android, the user has the option to install several browsers on the same device from the Play Store

According to the Mobile Overview Report (*http://wurfl.io/MOVR*), 34% of Android traffic comes from Facebook in-app browser and 5% from other in-app browsers. Therefore, around 39% of Android traffic is being executed in a web view and not inside a browser.

Windows Browsers

On Windows mobile devices, Internet Explorer (different versions based on the OS version) was the only browser available by default up to Windows 8.1. As of Windows 10, it was replaced by Microsoft Edge.

Some cloud-based browsers are available to download from the Windows Store, including Xpress Browser and UC Browser.

The Mobile Web Is Not Just a Narrow Viewport

In this chapter, we've covered the main differences of the mobile web as compared to classic web engines. It's important to not underestimate these differences or the diversity of the mobile web—and to test, debug, and measure with multiple devices and scenarios in mind, in order to account for the variety of mobile devices, cellular networks, and browsers currently in use.

As a review, we've covered in this chapter:

- Different engines in the mobile world, such as WebKit, Trident, and Blink
- Different platforms, such as the browser, web apps, and web views
- How different platforms and web views can define the performance of your solution
- How the web browser market share looks on the mobile side

In the next chapter, we will analyze where to measure web performance before getting into the necessary tools and metrics and how to improve perception.

CHAPTER 2

Where to Measure Performance

Measuring speed is critical if we want to detect problems and improve performance. The first question to consider when talking about measurement is the target. Where should we measure?

Your first thought may be to measure on a desktop. There are several tools available for classic web performance optimization. However, as we saw in Chapter 1, mobile browsers, hardware, and networks are different. Therefore, measuring in a classic browser will lead to false ideas of performance.

When measuring web performance on mobile devices, sometimes it's not the absolute values that are the most important data, but the comparisons with different techniques and the relative differences when you are applying web performance optimization techniques. Because of all the differences in devices and environments, saying that your website can be loaded in 2 seconds on a cellular phone means nothing—it might be much slower on 2G networks, on unreliable 3G networks, or in some different mobile browsers.

Simulators and Emulators

Generally speaking, an *emulator* is a piece of software that translates compiled code from an original architecture to the platform where it is running. It allows us to run an operating system and its native applications on another operating system. In the mobile development world, an emulator is a desktop application that emulates mobile device hardware and a mobile operating system, allowing us to test and debug our applications and see how they are working. The browser, and even the operating system, is not aware that it is running on an emulator, so we can execute the same code that we would execute on the real device.

In Chapter 5, we'll analyze some HTML5 APIs that will help us measure and log performance on real users' devices and connections. Those cases will help us in getting real-world data.

In terms of performance measurement, because there is a translation between the original code and our host machine, the measurements won't be accurate. However, we can definitely use them for comparisons and to get accurate waterfall charts of how the browser is rendering our pages.

Emulators are created by manufacturers and offered to developers for free, either standalone or bundled with the Software Development Kit (SDK) for native development.

There are also operating system emulators that don't represent any real device hardware (e.g., a Galaxy S5), but rather the operating system as a whole. These exist for Windows Phone and Android.

 The definitions of *emulator* and *simulator* in this book are based on majority opinion. However, some vendors are mixing those names. For example, BlackBerry Simulators are real virtual machines, so they fall under our definition of emulator.

On the other hand, a *simulator* is a less complex application that simulates some of the behavior of a device, but does not emulate hardware and does not work over the real operating system. These tools are simpler and less useful than emulators. A simulator may be created by the device manufacturer or by some other company offering a simulation environment for developers.

In mobile browsing, there are simulators that create a skin over a typical desktop browser (such as Firefox, Chrome, or Safari) without these browsers' rendering engines.

 For performance purposes, simulators—as tools that look like X but are not really using the code of X—are not interesting. They are usually running in a classic desktop browser and don't exhibit all the same behavior as their real counterparts. They are just meant to make a quick check on how websites look in different situations.

Android

As we covered in Chapter 1, there are several browsers and web views available on the Android OS, and that means that there are different techniques to measure performance on emulators and simulators.

Android Browser

The default Android Browser available until version 4.3 can be emulated through the official Android OS emulator. Because this emulator is based on Android Open Source Project (AOSP), it included the standard Android Browser until version 4.3. From version 4.4, the Android Browser was no longer distributed on real devices, but the emulator still included it. The emulated browser uses web view with a Chromium engine, but is not reliable for testing because it is neither the older browser nor a browser on real phones.

The Android Emulator is available in conjunction with the SDK to create native applications for Android. You can download it for free from the Android Developer page (*http://developer.android.com/sdk/installing/index.html*); the base SDK and the different Android OS versions are available separately.

The Android Emulator is available for Windows, macOS, and Linux. Once you've downloaded it, create a folder for the contents on your hard drive and unzip the package. On Windows, there is an installer version that will do the work for you.

In the folder where you extracted the package, there is an `android` terminal command on macOS and Linux systems, and an *SDK Setup.exe* application for Windows that opens the Android SDK Manager shown in Figure 2-1, where you can download and configure Android platforms (known as *packages* or *targets*) after installing the base SDK.

 The Android Emulator is really slow in some situations, which might affect your perception of performance. You can increase performance if you have an Intel-compatible CPU in your host computer using a free tool known as the Intel Harware Acceleration Execution Manager (HAXM) (*https://software.intel.com/en-us/ android/articles/speeding-up-the-android-emulator-on-intel- architecture*), or by switching to a third-party emulator, such as Genymotion or Microsoft's Android Emulator.

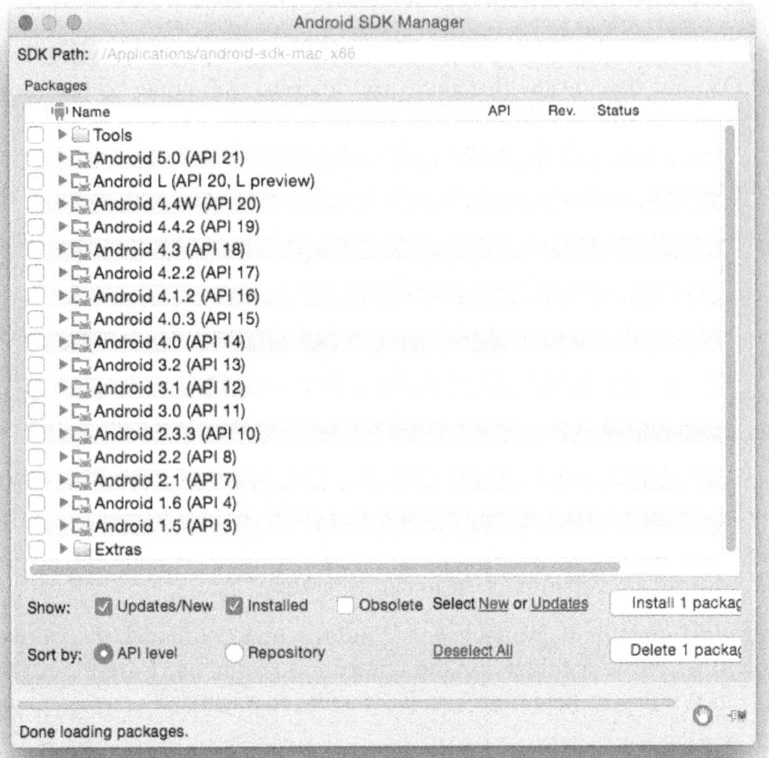

Figure 2-1. The Android SDK manager allows us to download different versions of Android OS to emulate

You can download as many packages as you want, one per operating system version; you can even download vendor-specific emulators, such as for the Galaxy devices or Amazon Fire Phone. Try to download different releases of Android versions up to 4.3, which was the last version with Android Browser, and beyond, such as Android 4.1, Android 4.4, Android 5.0, and Android 7.0. After you download the packages you want to use, you need to create an Android Virtual Device (AVD), as seen in Figure 2-2, specifying a combination of hardware features and OS image to emulate.

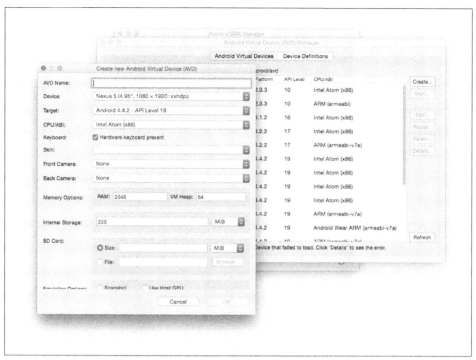

Figure 2-2. Once you have the image of the OS version you want to emulate, you need to create an Android Virtual Device (AVD), an instance of an emulator

Another solution for emulating Android Browser is to install Genymotion (*http://www.genymotion.com*). Genymotion (Figure 2-3) is a an alternate Android emulator based on VirtualBox and the AOSP. It's roughly 10 times faster than the original Android SDK before Android Studio 2.0, and it includes the same version of Android Browser.

As of 2016, a new, faster Android Emulator (2.0) is included as part of Android Studio 2.0. This emulator simulates some of the features of Genymotion (such as window resize) and includes some of the features of Google Play Services.

Figure 2-3. Genymotion is a faster Android emulator; it can be used to emulate Android Browser (you can also install Firefox or Opera, but not Google Chrome)

Google Chrome

Unfortunately, Google Chrome for Android requires Play Services, a set of tools that are outside of the AOSP. That means that we won't find Google Chrome on AOSP images that run in the Android emulator, and we can't install it.

We can emulate Chrome for Android using the Device Mode & Mobile Emulation (*https://developer.chrome.com/devtools/docs/device-mode*) tools available in Chrome for desktop, on macOS, Linux, Windows, and Chrome OS. If you open Developer Tools, you will see a small device icon at the top-left corner, as you can see in Figure 2-4.

Figure 2-4. With Google Chrome, you can emulate Chrome on Android devices and you can simulate other mobile phones or tablets

The Google Chrome emulator can be considered an emulator for Chrome on Android and a simulator when you choose other non-Android devices, as in those cases you'll still be working in Chrome even if it looks like you're in a different browser (such as Safari on iOS or IE on Windows).

To enable device mode, press the Toggle Device Mode button (it looks like a mobile phone or tablet). When device mode is enabled, this icon will turn blue. You can simulate different mobile scenarios, but remember the engine will be the desktop one; it won't change to match the specific engine of the device you are simulating. When simulating Chrome on Android devices, the engine is mostly the same.

Figure 2-5. Once enabled, you can set different properties to match the simulation you want while having access to the full Chrome Developer Tools

When working with the Device Mode & Mobile Emulation tools in Chrome, a good idea is to dock the Developer Tools window to the right.

Samsung Browser

The Chromium-based Samsung Browser available on most Android devices, such as the Galaxy series, can't be emulated. Samsung doesn't provide the code, even if you download its SDK add-ons.

Because it's Chromium-based we can assume that most stuff will work similar to Chrome on the same version, but we are never sure.

The best approach for this browser is using a real device.

Amazon Silk, LG, and other custom browsers

Following Samsung, Amazon doesn't provide any way to test the Silk browser—the one available on Kindle Fire and Fire Phone devices. The same is true of LG and the browser available on some of its devices, such as the G3, as well as some other manufacturers.

Safari on iOS

Available only for macOS, the iOS Simulator (shown in Figure 2-6) offers a free simulation environment for the iPhone and iPad, including the mobile browser Safari. It is not an emulator, so it does not really provide a hardware emulation experience and is not a true performance indicator. However, the Safari code that is being executed in this simulated environment is the real MobileSafari.app, so we can think of it as a Safari emulator running over an iOS simulator.

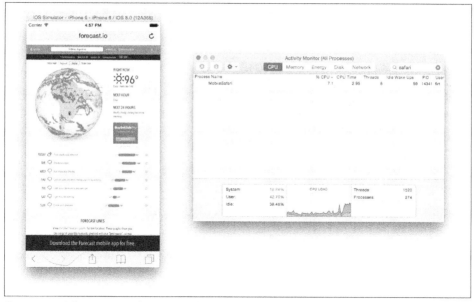

Figure 2-6. The iOS Simulator runs the real Safari and web app code on your Mac with an iOS skin. While it runs as a simulation, the real Safari on iOS and WebCore are running your code.

The iOS Simulator is included with the SDK for native development and available for free at the Mac App Store (search for Xcode) or from Apple's website (*https://developer.apple.com/xcode*). The SDK may take a while to download, because it's about 4 GB. You will always download the latest version of the operating system and can then add previous versions (such as 8.x), in which case you can switch between versions using the Hardware→Version menu option (Figure 2-7).

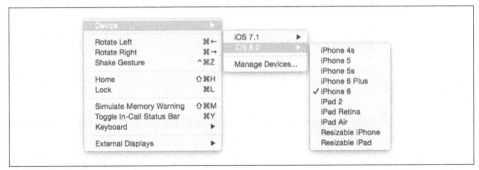

Figure 2-7. In the Hardware menu, you can select which iPad or iPhone you want to simulate

The iOS Simulator can also be used to measure performance for web apps and web view–based solutions.

To download a previous version of the operating system to the Simulator, you need to open the Xcode app, open Preferences, and select Downloads, as seen in Figure 2-8.

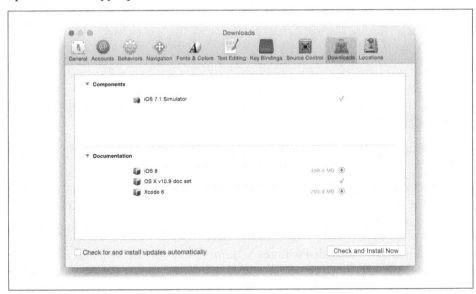

Figure 2-8. You can download previous versions of iOS simulator from the Preferences menu

You can only use the iOS Simulator with Safari on macOS. If you are using another operating system, you can use the cloud-based service BrowserStack (*http://browserstack.com*). It includes emulation of Safari on iOS, Android Browser, and Opera through different device profiles without the need of any local installation.

Internet Explorer

If you want to test your applications on Windows Phone, you can download the free Windows Phone SDK, buy a license for Visual Studio, or download Visual Studio Community Edition. The Windows Phone Emulator (Figure 2-9) comes with the SDK and includes the current version of Internet Explorer to test web content.

Figure 2-9. The Windows Phone Emulator includes the Internet Explorer mobile runtime and can be used for testing

The Windows Phone Emulator from version 8 is compatible with only Windows 8 Pro and requires a graphics driver with WDDM 1.1 support. You can check your hardware specifications to verify whether your graphics driver is compatible. If not, you will see the emulator, but you will see only a white page when trying to load Internet Explorer.

If you want to emulate Windows 8 for tablets, use the Windows Simulator included with Visual Studio for Windows 8 (even with Express, a free version of the IDE). The Windows Simulator works only on Windows 8 desktop machines; it emulates a tablet touch environment and allows you to test touch gestures, geolocation, and different screen sizes and orientations (Figure 2-10).

Figure 2-10. The Windows Simulator allows us to test on Windows tablets, but it's not emulating the real hardware as in the Phone version

Microsoft Edge

The new browser from Microsoft is available only on Windows 10. At the time of this writing, only a preview emulator (*https://www.microsoft.com/en-us/download/details.aspx?id=46893*) is available to test Edge on Windows 10 Mobile edition. You will need Windows 8 or 10 Pro and Visual Studio 2015 at least to make it work.

You can also use the developer tools in Edge on your desktop to simulate a mobile viewport, including Windows 10 for Mobile and older IE versions on Windows Phone, as we can see in Figure 2-11.

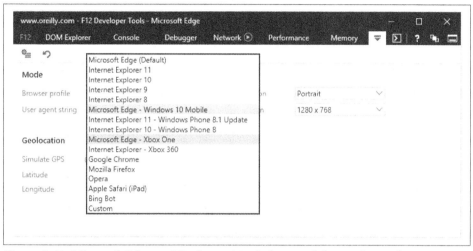

Figure 2-11. Microsoft Edge on Windows 10 includes a mobile simulator when you use F12 developer tools

Other Browsers

BlackBerry, Firefox OS, Tizen, and other operating systems also have emulators or simulators available. Check *http://emulato.rs* for more links.

Real Devices

There is nothing like real devices when measuring mobile websites. You will find differences not only in performance but also in behavior, like when you use your fingers to navigate and not a precise mouse pointer.

While creating your own testing lab is ideal, it's also expensive and needs to be updated frequently. At the time of this writing, I currently have around 45 devices for testing. Figure 2-12 shows a selection of them.

If you have a limited budget, you should try to buy one key device per platform (and if you are targeting tablets, you should get one). When you are building or adding to your collection, don't buy just expensive phones, but a mix. For example, you can buy:

- An old Android phone (it can be 4.0)
- A very cheap new Android phone

- An average Android phone
- A high-end Android phone
- An old iPhone (such as a 4S)
- A new iPhone
- A Windows Phone device

One of those Android phones should be a Galaxy S3 or newer, as they have the Chromium-based custom browser.

Also try to get different SIM cards from different providers so you can test in real scenarios.

Figure 2-12. Having several devices is always a good idea when you are doing performance optimization

Open Device Lab

Because we can't purchase every device and keep our labs constantly updated, a great community-based project has appeared in various cities in the world: Open Device Lab (*http://opendevicelab.com*). The idea is simple: to offer a physical place, in different locations around the globe, where developers can go and test on real devices for free.

At the time of this writing, more than 130 Open Device Labs have been established across 32 countries (see Figure 2-13).

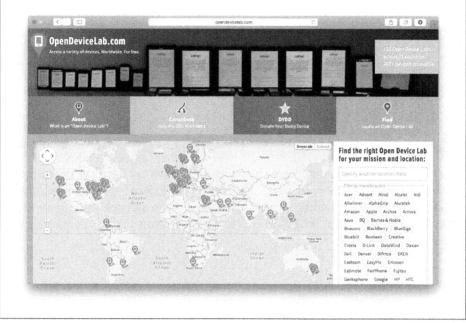

Figure 2-13. When you can't have every device at your home/office, Open Device Lab will help you as a community-based solution to share testing devices

Cloud-Based Services

If you can't afford to buy new devices and you don't have any Open Device Lab in or near your city, you still have another option: remote labs in the cloud.

A *remote lab* is a web service that allows you to use a real device remotely, without being physically in the same place. It is a simple but very powerful solution that gives you access to thousands of real devices, connected to real networks all over the world, with a single click. You can think of it as a remote desktop for mobile phones.

There are three kinds of remote lab solutions for mobile devices:

- Software-based solutions, using a resident application on the device that captures the screen, sends it to the server, and emulates keyboard input or touches on the screen
- Hardware-based solutions, using some technology (magic, I believe) to connect the server to the hardware components of the device (screen, touch-screen, keypad, lights, audio, etc.)

- Mixed solutions, having some hardware connection, some software additions, and maybe a video camera for screen recording

For performance measurement, we need to remember they are real phones over real networks, so they are as accurate as we need.

 Some remote labs connect their phones to WiFi networks automatically. Therefore, we can't test using a cellular network and measure the real latency. Verify if you are able to browse through a cellular connection on these services.

Samsung Remote Test Lab

Samsung offers a free remote lab web service called Remote Test Lab (RTL) (*http://developer.samsung.com/remotetestlab*). RTL, shown in Figure 2-14, includes Android smartphones, Android tablets, smartwatches, and Tizen phones at the time of this writing. The devices don't have SIM cards, though, so you can test only using WiFi connections (not cellular).

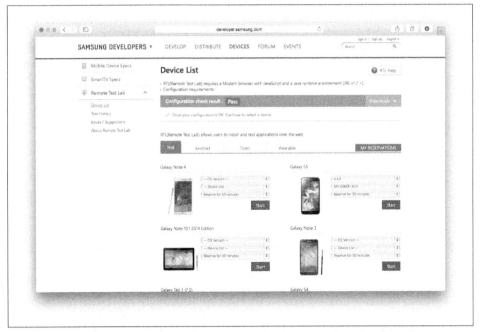

Figure 2-14. Samsung Remote Test Lab allows us to use several Android- and Tizen-based devices through the network for free

RTL offers a great opportunity to test and measure on the Samsung Browser, as this browser can't be emulated. You can also upload APKs (Android native apps) that are using the web view to test on the custom web views on these devices.

 Until mid-2014, Nokia had a cloud-based testing solution for Windows Phone and other devices. This service was discontinued by Microsoft a few months after the acquisition and no replacement was announced.

Keynote Mobile Testing

Formerly known as DeviceAnywhere, Keynote Mobile Testing (*http://www.keynote.com/solutions/testing/mobile-testing*) (Figure 2-15) is one of the leaders in Virtual Labs.

Figure 2-15. With Keynote Mobile Testing, we have the option to use hundreds of different devices on real networks all over the world

The company provides a product called DeviceAnywhere Test Center Developer, with different price models depending on the package. It offers more than 2,000 devices (iOS, Android, Nokia, Motorola, Sony Ericsson, Samsung, BlackBerry, LG, Sanyo, Sharp, HTC, and more) connected to more than 30 live networks all over the world.

There are different commercial plans available, and a free version specially targeting web developers. On the free version, you can use a limited amount of devices (iOS, Android, Windows, and BlackBerry devices are available) for 10-minute sessions only. It's suitable for quick testings of websites, web apps, and hybrid apps.

Perfecto Mobile

Perfecto Mobile (*http://perfectomobile.com*) is a company offering a software/hardware hybrid solution for mobile testing, shown in Figure 2-16. Perfecto Mobile uses a video camera for screen recording on some devices. A good point is that the whole environment is built on top of the Adobe Flash Player, so you don't need to install anything, and it works from any desktop browser. You can try the system by registering for a free trial; it will be activated in minutes.

Figure 2-16. Perfecto Mobile uses an in-browser solution to allow use of several devices on its cloud platform

With this service, you have access to the whole list of devices and carriers from the same pricing policy. The devices are on real networks in Canada, Israel, the United States, the United Kingdom, and France.

AppThwack

AppThwack (*http://appthwack.com*) is a commercial service targeting native apps and web apps.

The service will test your app automatically on 300+ unique, non-rooted phones and tablets and it will give you a performance report. If you want to test a web app, you will provide a URL; if you are testing a hybrid app, you will upload an APK.

When you sign up (*https://appthwack.com/user/register*) for a free account, you will get 100 minutes of usage for free.

AWS Device Farm

Amazon Web Services has released a Device Farm solution where you can use real devices remotely, optimized for native apps, hybrids, and web apps. The price model is more revolutionary, with a per-minute price (US $0.17/minute at the time of this writing) or a fixed monthly price per device slot.

If you want to try it, you can get your first 250 minutes for free at *https://aws.amazon.com/device-farm/*.

 Google also offers a cloud-based service known as Firebase Test Lab (*https://firebase.google.com/docs/test-lab*), but it's more suitable for native apps than for web solutions.

Network Connection

When thinking about where we are going to measure performance, we shouldn't forget about network differences. Having real cellular SIMs on different networks always helps to test everything in different conditions.

We should always measure over 4G, 3G, 2G, and WiFi networks under different conditions to get a more accurate idea of how the experience looks from a user's perspective.

Some performance tools also allow us to measure using a cellular connection from a desktop. We can do this with a laptop with 3G/4G support, by buying a hardware cellular modem for our computer, or using a tethered connection from our phone. The latter is not always accurate, though, as some carriers might change speed when the connection is tethered, and we are also adding more latency from the phone to our computer through the ad hoc WiFi connection.

Besides using real cellular connections, we can also use some tools to throttle our connection to simulate other kinds of networks, adjusting the bandwidth, latency, and packet loss percentage.

With connection simulators, we can slow down our Internet connection and simulate a real 2G, 3G, or 4G connection to get a better idea of performance and how our website is reacting.

Desktop Simulators

These tools run on our desktop computer and they use our current WiFi or LAN connection, throttling it—slowing it down—so we can simulate a mobile connection's bandwidth, latency, and packet loss rate.

We can use it from a simulator, an emulator, or even from a real device if we set up a proxy on it.

Some tools available today are:

- Charles Web Debugging Proxy (*http://charlesproxy.com*)
- Mac Network Link Conditioner (*https://developer.apple.com/downloads/index.action?q=Network%20Link%20Conditioner*)
- Slowyapp (*http://slowyapp.com*)
- Clumsy for Windows (*http://jagt.github.io/clumsy*)
- NetLimiter for Windows (*http://netlimiter.com*)
- Telerik Fiddler for Windows (*http://www.telerik.com/fiddler*)
- Chrome network conditioning settings inside Developer Tools

The Charles Web Debugging Proxy is an HTTP sniffing and proxy tool with a free version available that includes an HTTP throttling mechanism to simulate different bandwidths and latencies (as seen in Figure 2-17). It is available for Windows, Mac, and Linux.

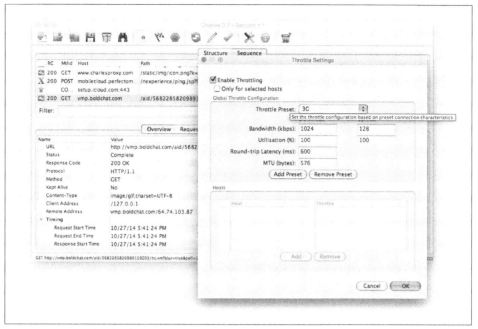

Figure 2-17. With Charles Proxy, we can easily throttle our connection and simulate a real cellular environment for emulators and real devices

Network Link Conditioner is a free tool available as part of the Hardware IO Tools for Xcode (macOS only) that allows us to throttle the connection and emulate different conditions, as you can see in Figure 2-18. Once installed, it will appear in the Mac System Preferences, so we can easily change the settings later.

Slowy is a macOS-only app that will simulate a real-world connection. It includes several presets, including bandwidth, packet loss rate, and packet latency. Slowy is not a proxy, so when using Mac-based simulators and emulators, we don't need to configure a proxy.

 Some of the connection simulators—such as Charles or Network Link Conditioner—allow us to create our own connection profiles, setting the bandwidth, latency, and percentage of packets dropped. We can gather information from the market and then simulate different real scenarios.

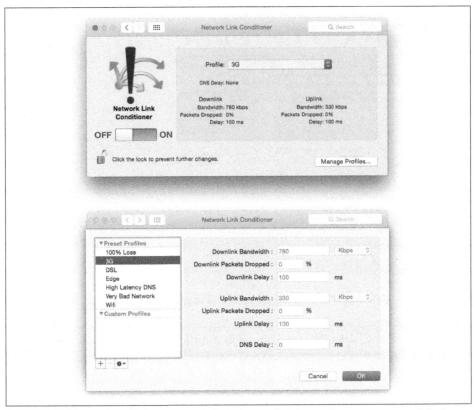

Figure 2-18. Once installed, the Network Link Conditioner will appear in your Mac's System Preferences panel and will let you simulate different real connections

Clumsy is a Windows-only app that will help us with the simulation of different connections, similar to the Mac utilities. NetLimiter is another Windows-only app for the same purpose. A free limited version is available.

Fiddler Connection Simulator is a Fiddler proxy plug-in adding the ability to simulate different network connections on Windows computers. It now also supports other platforms in experimental mode, such as macOS.

For the tools that are creating a proxy, we can then go to our mobile devices and set a proxy while connected to the same network as that proxy, as you can see in Figure 2-19. Then we can see and throttle all the traffic from the mobile browser, web app, or web view.

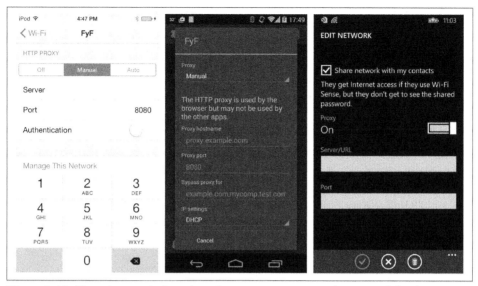

Figure 2-19. If you have a desktop-based proxy, you can set it from a mobile phone so the latter will browse through that throttled connection

Finally, if you're using Chrome, the device mode we covered before to simulate different mobile conditions includes a network conditioning solution that allows bandwidth throttling and latency manipulation, as you can see in Figure 2-20.

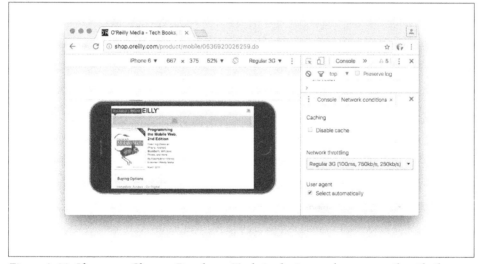

Figure 2-20. If you use Chrome Developer Tools in device mode, you can throttle the connection using the network conditioning feature

Chrome has a CPU throttling mechanism you can use while you are profiling JavaScript to simulate a high-end smartphone or a low-end device.

On-Device Connection Simulators

When we have a real device, we can also simulate a different connection on-device.

iOS has a tool available already on every device from iOS 6. To enable the feature, we need to set up the device for development. We do that from Xcode, by going to Window → Organizer, finding our device (which should be connected to USB), and selecting "Use for development." After that you will find a new Settings options in your device. Open Settings → Developer → Network Link Conditioner to throttle your current connection based on a different profile (see Figure 2-21).

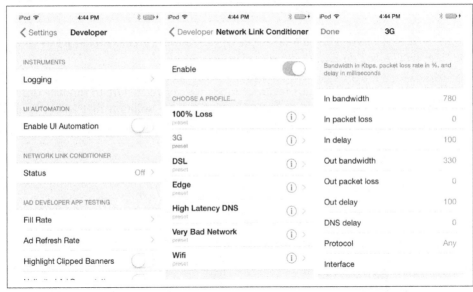

Figure 2-21. After setting your phone in developer mode, you will find the Network Link Conditioner option under Settings. You can use this to emulate a different connection.

Besides throttling the connection on a real phone, you can always force your cellular connection to work in a different mode (such as 3G or 2G mode) from the Settings menu. Just remember to go back to the default value after the testing (or you can keep it and feel the same pain as any user in a remote area).

Unfortunatley, Android doesn't provide a comparable tool for on-device simulation. The only similar tool is available for the Android Emulator. *Android Speed Emulation* is a console-based tool available when we open the emulator. For example, if we want to open an emulator simulating a 2.5G EDGE connection, we can use this command:

```
emulator -netspeed edge
```

By default, it emulates just bandwidth. If we want to also emulate latency on those networks, we need to use:

```
emulator -netspeed edge -netdelay edge
```

Possible accepted values are `gprs`, `edge`, `umts`, or `hsdpa`. You can also define your own customized values following the documentation (*http://developer.android.com/tools/devices/emulator.html#netspeed*).

Selecting Where to Measure Is Important

As we saw in this chapter, several options are available to help us test and measure performance, from real devices, simulators, emulators, and remote labs to tools to help make our measurements accurate. Just remember that testing on a desktop is not enough to make conclusions about the performance of your web solution on a mobile device.

In this chapter, we covered:

- Simulators and emulators and when to trust them
- How to use real devices for performance testing, including cloud-based solutions
- How to simulate real network conditions on real devices or emulators

In Chapter 3, we will cover the basics of web performance measurements, including the metrics that we need to understand before optimizing.

Web Performance Basics

When learning to measure web performance, one of the first goals we need to achieve is understanding the metrics and vocabulary.

Measuring techniques will allow us to get accurate information about our current status, to define goals to achieve, and to measure again to see whether applying a technique improves performance or not.

In this chapter, you will learn about the web performance optimization vocabulary and metrics, so you understand how to analyze your improvements.

We need to remember that measuring is a critical part of improving performance. After all:

> If you can't measure it, you can't improve it.
>
> —Peter Drucker

We will organize performance measurements into two big categories: loading and responsiveness.

Loading Measurement Basics

For years, web performance was defined by two measurements: the window's `onload` event and the time that the server was taking to send the response. Today, we know that these units are not so important in terms of web performance, as they don't focus on the most important factor here: the user's perception.

We'll define loading performance as the measures that define how fast your website or web content appears on the user's screen, including fetching the resources and rendering those resources on the screen. We will see that the "perceived performance"— that is, how fast the user perceives the site to be—is often more important than the

actual total load time. This is determined by the moment when a user can interact with elements on the screen.

We'll start by talking about the waterfall chart, one of the most important charts in the performance world.

The Waterfall Chart

The waterfall chart is a diagram that shows how the resources are being downloaded and parsed by the engine in a timeline that lets us see the sequence and dependencies between resources. Modern waterfall charts also identify where some important events happened during the loading process.

> The performance waterfall chart is similar to project management's Gantt diagram, which let us see a cascade effect over several tasks.

This diagram also lets us see quickly how good or bad the performance of our website is, just by paying attention to some small things such as how many rows we have or how many resources are blocking parallel downloads.

Figure 3-1 shows a typical waterfall chart of a website's loading operation.

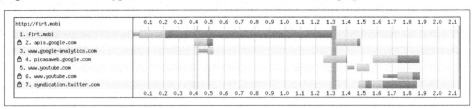

Figure 3-1. A typical waterfall chart shows one row per downloaded resource, with time on the x-axis

The waterfall chart defines time on the x-axis (increasing to the right) and the resources on the y-axis (one row per resource, in the order that they are being managed by the web engine). Additionally, we have vertical lines in different colors crossing the x-axis defining different milestones in the performance measurement.

There are two different kinds of waterfall charts that we can make, based on the user's visit:

Empty cache

We are accessing the website for the first time and have no cached data, including DNS lookups. Typical browser-based tools will empty the cache before making the requests.

Cached

> We are accessing the website for the second time, emulating a second visit from a user's perspective, and have all the files that can be cached in a local storage.

In Figure 3-2, you can see how different the empty cache waterfall chart and the cached version are if you have set up everything correctly.

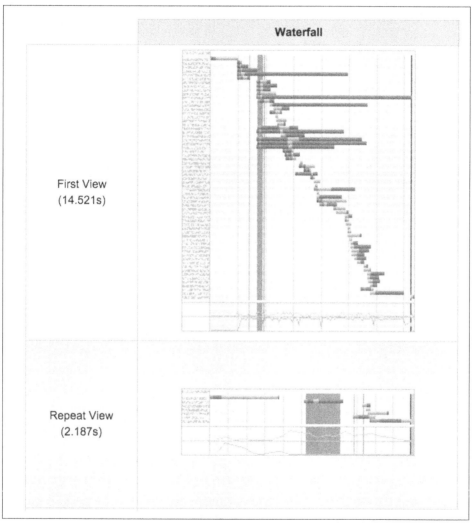

Figure 3-2. WebPageTest.org will give you two waterfall charts: First View (empty cache) and Repeat View (cached mode). You can see how different the charts are if the website is performing well.

Resource timing

Each row will contain one horizontal bar defining the lifecycle of that resource in the timeline. Most performance tools will also divide this bar into several colors for different stages of the resource lifecycle, as seen in Figure 3-3.

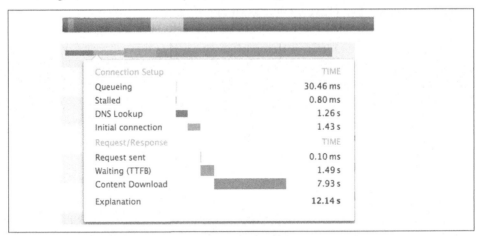

Connection Setup	TIME
Queueing	30.46 ms
Stalled	0.80 ms
DNS Lookup	1.26 s
Initial connection	1.43 s
Request/Response	TIME
Request sent	0.10 ms
Waiting (TTFB)	1.49 s
Content Download	7.93 s
Explanation	12.14 s

Figure 3-3. Color bars define every step of the request processing. The bigger the bar, the more time it took.

The order is fixed, and the stages are usually defined as follows:

1. The *DNS lookup* time is the time that the web engine takes to convert a domain host to an IP address through the DNS system. If you have several resources served from the same domain—and you probably will—you won't see the DNS lookup stage for every resource, as the web engine will cache the result.

2. The *initial connection* stage involves the TCP handshake, which is mandatory in every high-level protocol using TCP (such as HTTP). With HTTP 1.1 and 2.0, in some situations we can serve different resources over the same TCP connection, so it's possible to not see this stage for every resource. If you are browsing through HTTPS, this stage will also include the SSL handshake time.

3. The *Time to First Byte* (TTFB) is basically the time that the server is taking to send the response to the client. The client—the browser or the app—requests something, and the server parses the request and then starts the response. The processing time is what we see here in green. If your server is too busy or if it needs to access several databases or external resources, which may take a long time, you will see bigger green areas in your charts.

4. The last stage is to *download* all the bytes of that resource. The current connection and bandwidth between the client and the server will define the blue area on the screen.

 Most of the performance tools out there have agreed on the colors they use on the resources' bars. However, there are some tools that use other colors, so be careful when making the analysis. The order is always the same, as it's the natural order of the process, so DNS lookup will go always first and content download will always go at the end.

There is one more step involved here: content parsing and/or execution. This stage is not shown explicitly on the chart, but in some situations we will be able to recognize it.

We will have two kind of resources: blocking and non-blocking. *Blocking resources* will not let other resources be downloaded or parsed while they are being parsed. *Non-blocking resources* don't interfere with the downloading of other resources.

When a resource is blocking parallel processing, you will see a gap between the end of the blue area and the start of the next resource's stages. The gap in the timeline is basically the time that the web engine is taking to process that resource (such as executing JavaScript code). Figure 3-4 shows you the gap between the end of one blocking resource and the start time of the next resource.

Figure 3-4. Some resources will block the processing of other resources; in this case, not only can the network operation be detected in the chart but also the rendering time, expressed as the empty space or gap between the end of one resource and the start of the next one

Background colors

When you see yellow or red background colors in a whole row, it means that the resource was not downloaded normally as the HTTP code was not 200 (OK). A yellow background usually means that the resource was moved to a different URL (the server has returned 301 or 302) and the next row will process it. A red background usually means there was a blocking error for that resource, typically a 404 (Not Found) or 500 (Server Error).

Advanced resource timing

Some tools will also show you some other stages from the network, such as stalled/blocking stage (usually in gray), which is the time the request spent on hold in the client waiting before it could be sent; the proxy negotiation time (part of the stalled/blocking stage) for when the user is browsing though a proxy; and the SSL time, which is a substage inside the connection stage (sometimes in orange, sometimes in purple).

The critical path

The *critical path* on a waterfall chart consists of the group of resources that define the minimum load time. The resources in this group are the best candidates to optimize, because if we reduce their bars we will reduce the whole loading time. Google Developers has a great reference on the critical rendering path (*https://developers.google.com/web/fundamentals/performance/critical-rendering-path*), with definitions and ideas to help optimize it.

 A resource that is part of the critical path and is taking longer than usual to complete the stages will delay the processing of all the following resources and increase the final load time.

The first row

The first row with HTTP code 200 of any waterfall chart is always the HTML that the server is sending after an HTTP request. The first resource is always part of the critical path and is a key target for performance improvement. Your first request will be blocking the rest of the resources, as you will see by paying attention to the area below the first row's bar. If it's completely empty, it's because that request is blocking resources.

 If the first request has a 301 or 302 HTTP Redirect code—usually shown with a yellow background on the chart—then we need to analyze the first row with a 200 HTTP response.

In Figure 3-5, you can see that the browser started to download other resources at 0.4 s, before the full HTML was loaded at around 0.7 s on the first row. There are several tips that we will cover later that will allow the browser to start processing other resources before the blue area of the first row is finished.

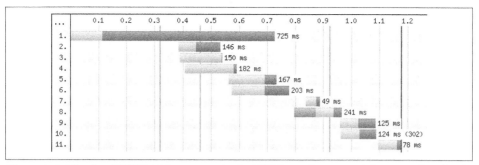

Figure 3-5. The first HTTP 200 response is the HTML and is part of the critical path; if the HTML is blocking the rest of the resources, you won't find any resources starting in the area below the first row's blue bar. If it's optimized, you will see resources starting before the end of the blue bar.

Milestones

The waterfall chart usually gives us one or more vertical colored lines crossing the whole chart, defining different important milestones in the page's lifecycle. The style used for these lines depends on the tools we are using to make the chart, but they are usually marked clearly.

The usual milestones are:

Start Render
> Defines when the rendering has started on the screen; that is, when the user will see something other than blank space or the previous page.

DOMContentLoaded
> Follows the DOM event with the same name that defines when all the DOM elements have been parsed and are ready to be used.

Above the Fold Rendered
> Defines when the initial view of the page has been already rendered on the screen, but content is still being loaded "below the fold" (the first scroll). This milestone is not available yet in every tool and it's viewport-dependent, meaning that the "above the fold" area is different on different screen sizes (the first view is smaller on an iPhone than on iPad with more space to fill).

Load Time
> Defines when the DOM onload event has fired. This event is fired when all the initial resouces have been downloaded, parsed, and executed. It's usually the end of the chart.

The colors of each milestone vary by tool, but they're usually explained in the chart. In Figure 3-6, we can see these milestones in action in charts created by two different tools: WebPageTest.org and Google Chrome Developer Tools.

 Some network-only tools, such as the Charles Web Debugging Proxy or Fiddler, will not add any milestones to the chart because they are not talking to the browser; they are just reading the network layer.

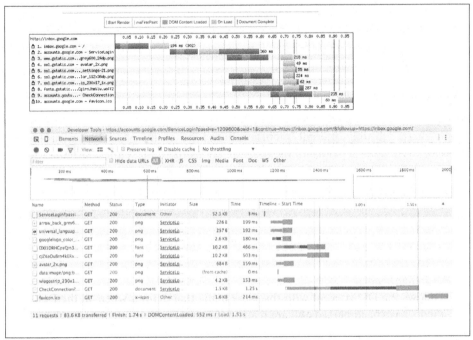

Figure 3-6. Browser-based tools such as WebPageTest.org (top) and Chrome Developer Tools (bottom) will add vertical lines to the waterfall charts defining different milestones in the DOM or UI experience, such as Start Render or Load Time

 When you are measuring a live page, you may see resources that are being downloaded after the Load Time vertical line. These resources can be considered part of the initial loading phase or not; they have usually been deferred by the developer or by third parties to reduce the load time.

Filmstrip

A *filmstrip* is a sequence of screenshots taken on a real mobile device every couple of milliseconds, illustrating how the website renders on the screen over time. It can be used to detect how much time passes before the rendering starts and when the user has enough content on the screen to start reading it or interacting with it.

The filmstrip may be delivered as a sequence of images, as in Figure 3-7, or as a video with a timer always on the screen. The presentation varies per device: a bigger phone will fit more content, so the filmstrip will be different. There are some tools that will let you see the filmstrip connected to the waterfall chart, so you can time travel to any millisecond in the loading process and see what the user was seeing on the screen and what the network operations looked like at that time.

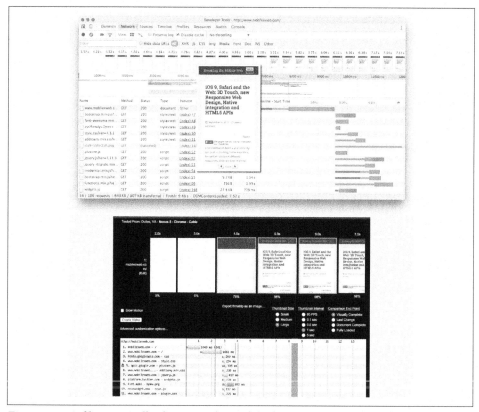

Figure 3-7. A filmstrip will take screenshots of the browser several times per second and let you see what is happening in the UI at every point in time and compare it with the waterfall chart

It often seems that when it's time to sell why performance is important to nontechnical people, they don't see page load times, site speed indexes, or other numeric values as interesting enough. But show them a filmstrip where they can see how much blank space their customers are getting on their phones, and they will probably understand it.

The HAR Format

The HTTP Archive (*http://httparchive.org*) is an online non-profit repository of HTTP requests created by Steve Souders (*http://stevesouders.org*) to monitor performance and gather important stats about how websites are being developed and served over time.

The site has created a JSON-based spec to store, transfer, and manage information about web performance. The spec is known as HAR (HTTP Archive Format), and it's a work in progress in the W3C (*https://dvcs.w3.org/hg/webperf/raw-file/tip/specs/HAR/Overview.html*) for standardization.

 The W3C (*https://www.w3.org*) is the main international organization for web standards. The consortium is made up of a group of member organizations working together on the development of standards for the web.

The format is being used today by browsers, performance tools, and monitoring solutions to export and import collected data useful for analyzing web performance.

The HAR format will store information about:

- The creator and the browser or tool that collected the data
- The pages collected in the file
- Timings of various events for each page, including `onContentLoad` and `onLoad`
- HTTP requests for each page with details about the request and response, including headers, cookies, timings (such as DNS lookup, connect time, etc.), and other useful information

 With a HAR file, you can re-create a performance waterfall chart from an archived website. Keep in mind, though, that the same website on different networks and in different traffic conditions, as well as on different web engines, devices, and browsers, will generate different HAR files and waterfall charts.

Analyzing the details of a HAR file doesn't make too much sense at this point in this book. Usually, we just need to understand that this format is the one being used to analyze traffic between different tools.

Versions

The most common versions of the HAR specification today are 1.1 and 1.2; they basically differ in the number of properties available. Some tools will include the content of each resource (the HTML, CSS, JavaScript, or image) as well as the headers and timing information. Including content makes a much bigger HAR file, however, and it might be ignored by analysis tools.

There is also a nonstandard compressed version of the HAR file, known as ZHAR, that is just a ZIP compressed archive of a HAR file.

Export tools

Several browsers and performance tools will allow us to get a HAR file from a real website interaction with that particular engine, with a real connection at that particular time.

Google Chrome for Android will let us export a HAR file (with content) using the context menu on the Network tab, inside Chrome Developer Tools on a desktop PC (as we can see in Figure 3-8), or using a remote debugger (covered in Chapter 4).

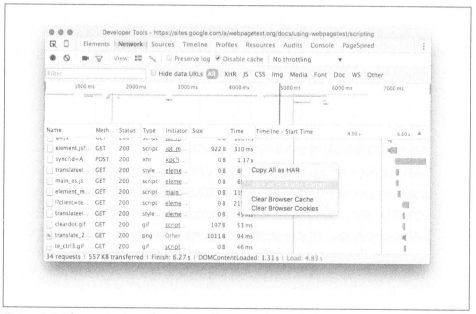

Figure 3-8. If we are using Chrome Developer Tools, we can access a HAR export tool from the context menu in the Network tab

In Safari on iOS, there is no official support for exporting data in HAR format, but we can do it in four ways:

- Using online tools, such as WebPagetest Mobile (*http://www.webpagetest.org/mobile*)
- Using proxy tools, as we will cover in Chapter 4
- Using on-device tools, such as HttpWatch for iOS (*http://www.httpwatch.com/download*) (covered in Chapter 4)
- Using iOS Har Builder (*https://github.com/andydavies/ios-har-builder*), a free tool that uses Node.js with the iOS Simulator to create a basic HAR file

On Windows devices, both Internet Explorer 11 for Windows Phone 8.1 and Microsoft Edge on Windows 10 let us get a HAR file from the F12 developer tools that we are remotely connecting to on the desktop from a phone.

In Firefox and IE, we can also use the plug-in HttpWatch (*http://www.httpwatch.com*) to get a HAR file. Finally, WebPagetest lets us export a HAR file from an HTTP analysis.

 To get a HAR file from low-end devices such as social phones and browsers without any developer tools, such as IE10 or Android Browser, we can use a proxy-based inspection tool or a network sniffer tool. We will cover these in Chapter 4.

Analysis tools

There are several tools that we will cover later that support HAR files for analysis. The quickest way to work with a HAR file is using some online tools that are available for free:

- Chrome HAR Viewer (*http://ericduran.github.io/chromeHAR*)
- HAR Viewer (*http://www.softwareishard.com/har/viewer*)
- Google HAR Analyzer (*https://toolbox.googleapps.com/apps/har_analyzer*) (see Figure 3-9)

These tools will usually do everything locally on your computer using JavaScript so the HAR files are not being uploaded to the server.

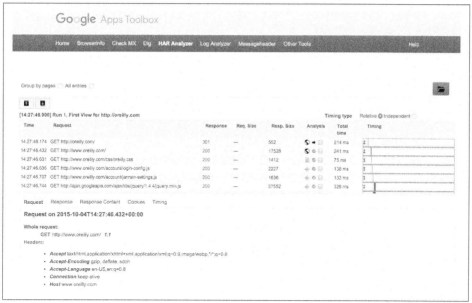

Figure 3-9. If you have a HAR file that you have collected, you can use an online tool such as Google HAR Analyzer to see it in action

More tools supporting the HAR format are listed on Jan Odvarko's "HAR Adopters" page (*http://www.softwareishard.com/blog/har-adopters*).

Speed Index

The Speed Index (*https://sites.google.com/a/webpagetest.org/docs/using-webpagetest/metrics/speed-index*) was created by Patrick Meenan as a new way to see web performance from a user's point of view. It's a metric indicating the average time at which visible parts of the content of a page (above the fold) are displayed.

Imagine your website as a drawing to be filled by the browser; Speed Index will calculate the visual progress of your canvas on a timeline. The Speed Index is a float value that is viewport-dependent, so on different screen sizes (such as an iPhone or iPad) you might get different values.

One way to calculate the Speed Index is through a filmstrip calculating every x milliseconds the percentage of the final page that was rendered at that particular time. When we do this we create a table like Table 3-1.

Table 3-1. Speed Index calculation for a site

Time (ms)	% of visual completeness
100	0
200	0
300	0
400	0
500	0
600	30
700	35
800	50
900	65
1000	80
1100	95
1200	95
1300	100

That table will lead to a curve in a graph, as in Figure 3-10. The area above that curve is what we know as the Speed Index.

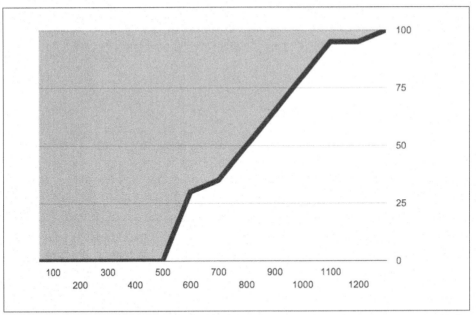

Figure 3-10. The Speed Index measures the area above the line when you measure % of completeness in the canvas (y-axis) over time (x-axis). In this case, we have a bad user experience because the gray area is too big.

Another way I like to define the Speed Index metric is saying that it defines how much blank content the user has seen on the screen during the loading process. If the Speed Index is near zero, it means the user has not seen too much blank space for too much time (which is good from a user's point of view).

If the Speed Index is a bigger value (e.g., more than 1,500) it means the user has seen a lot of "nothing" for too much time, and then the whole content appeared in one shot (which is bad).

A smaller Speed Index value is better, because it means that the user has seen more content in less time. For example, let's compare the previous example with an optimized page that gets to 100% visual completeness in the same time but with a bigger Speed Index. The values are listed in Table 3-2, and the curve is shown in Figure 3-11.

 Sometimes we want to define how fast is fast enough. Paul Irish, Google Chrome Developer Advocate, has defined that a Speed Index below 1,000 will be fast enough to be happy about.

Table 3-2. Speed Index calculation for an optimized site

Time (ms)	% of visual completeness
100	0
200	30
300	80
400	80
500	80
600	85
700	85
800	90
900	90
1000	90
1100	95
1200	95
1300	100

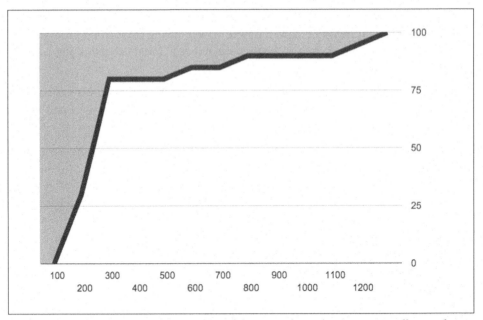

Figure 3-11. We have a good Speed Index if the area above the curve is small enough, meaning that the user has seen more content in less time

The curve for the optimized version has a smaller area over the line, which means the user will perceive the content on the page faster.

In our first example (Figure 3-10), the user sees nothing for 0.5 seconds and then 30% of the page after 0.6 seconds. In the second example (Figure 3-11), the user sees nothing for just 0.1 seconds and the rendering starts sooner (at 0.2 seconds, getting to 85% complete in just 0.6 seconds). The experience for the user is much better in the second case with a smaller Speed Index.

The Speed Index was first introduced in the free WebPagetest (*http://webpaget est.com*) service and is now available on other sites as well. Because it's viewport-dependent we need to use a service that is optimized for mobile devices to get the right Speed Index. Taking screenshots or making a filmstrip video from a mobile device is more complicated than from a desktop, so sometimes it's difficult to find services that use real devices to calculate the Speed Index. Some just use a desktop Google Chrome or Safari with a smaller screen size.

For example, we can use WebPagetest (*http://www.webpagetest.org*) to get the Speed Index for an Android or iOS device (just choose a mirror with support for Android or iOS), or we can use Chrome for desktop as the browser and select the "Emulate Mobile Browser" option on the Chrome tab to enable a mobile viewport and user agent.

What to Measure

We are often tempted to just look at the final loading time, which is usually a red vertical line at the right of the waterfall chart pointing to the final time in seconds (or milliseconds, if we are lucky) on the x-axis.

However, from a user's point of view, it's not the best metric. In the age of Internet Explorer 6, it was a good measure because usually the user wasn't ready to interact with a website before the `onload` event. But that's not the case anymore. We want the user to feel that our website is fast, and unfortunately the best metrics to measure that are still being developed today—and changing over time as we come to better understand the user's perception of speed.

 We need to remember why we are doing this. We are not in a race against the clock. We are in a race against the user's perception. We can be faster in the waterfall but slower in the user's mind, failing in our goals. We want more performance because we know that it will improve conversions and will make our users happier with our product. We should never forget about this.

There are general rules that can usually be applied to most websites and specific rules that will work only for your project. In these cases, we are defining our own "user's perception ready event." For example, Netflix has created its own metrics to define how performant its website is, because its developers felt that the standard metrics weren't good enough to measure how quickly users were ready to interact with Netflix (and be happy about it).

As an example, on Twitter we could define that a ready event is when the Post textbox is ready to use, or on a news site when there are two articles on the screen that might get the user engaged with them for a couple of milliseconds.

As general rules, we will want:

- A low Speed Index (< 1,500)
- To show content as soon as possible (less than a second after the request is sent)
- To remove blocking resources from the waterfall chart
- To have small waiting (TTFB) areas on the resources
- To reduce the final `onload` time and, more importantly, to start rendering as soon as possible
- To find the critical path and rearrange things to keep it under control

Custom Metrics

Sometimes, finding a custom metric that has a meaning for you is important. For example, Twitter (*https://blog.twitter.com/2012/improving-performance-on-twittercom*) has created the metric "time to first tweet," defined as "the amount of time it takes from navigation (clicking the link) to viewing the first tweet on each page's timeline."

Think about what makes sense for your content and find a way to measure. You can do this using the techniques and APIs we will cover in Chapter 5.

Steve Souders has also described how to measure "time to hero image" (*http://www.stevesouders.com/blog/2015/05/12/hero-image-custom-metrics*) on websites where there's a big image in the front that makes the content (so, if no image is present, the content that does appear is useless or totally imcomplete).

 The Chrome team has coined the term, "Time to First Meaningful Interaction," which defines a timing that is more difficult to measure and that requires you to think more deeply about what interaction means for your content. If you want to read more about it, check out the article "Stop Painting and Have a Meaningful Interaction with Me!" (*https://medium.com/ben-and-dion/stop-painting-and-have-a-meaningful-interaction-with-me-86ef8eb4f5b3#.d0neit29i*).

The RAIL Approach

Google has released a methodology for web performance with a fancy new name to remember: *RAIL* (*http://bit.ly/chrome-devtools-rail*). RAIL stands for Response-Animation-Idle-Load and it defines a series of goals to achieve in terms of measurement of our web performance. These goals are:

- Response: 100 ms (immediate feedback)
- Animation: 16 ms to achieve 60 fps
- Idle: 50 ms (every noncritical operation that you are doing should take no more than 50 ms to keep a good perception)
- Load: 1 s to load the initial contents of the page

The RAIL approach defines maximum goals. Achieving all of them all the time is not always possible and might be challenging on some devices, so it's a matter of setting what we want and trying to get as close as possible.

Also, priorities in RAIL might not be equal between each goal. For example, for a typical website, the L (load) and R (response) might be the first priority, before I (idle) and A (animation). When talking about native web apps or progressive web apps, R (response) and A (animation) might be your first priorities, as loading is done from a local cache or package.

Responsiveness Measurement Basics

Performance is not just about the initial loading; keeping the user engaged with the content while he's interacting with it is also important. In this section, we will talk about responsiveness measurement.

Measuring responsiveness is not as simple as measuring loading times because it usually involves user interaction and it will differ on different hardware, web engines, and screen sizes. However, there are some bottlenecks we can identify that will affect most users.

Responsiveness metrics usually involve measurements of:

- Feedback lag time after some interaction (such as a touch)
- Frame rate, expressed in frames per second (FPS) while scrolling and animating elements
- Network time (waterfall chart) for on-demand resources, such as XHR requests

Automating feedback lag is not an easy task. Mozilla has worked on a project called Eideticker (*https://wiki.mozilla.org/Project_Eideticker*) that measures user-perceived performance of web browsers by video-capturing them in action and subsequently running image analysis on the raw result. It currently works on Firefox on Android and Firefox OS.

There are several things that can affect the responsiveness of your website that are out of your control, including:

- Video acceleration and GPU memory
- CPUs: cores and clock
- JavaScript runtime (JIT availability)
- RAM

However, bearing in mind that we have those limitations, we can use a few tricks to improve responsiveness.

To find problems with responsiveness, we need to test on real devices and measure feedback lag, frame rate, and network times.

Frames per Second

Some mobile browsers will allow us to enter a developer mode that enables an FPS counter on the screen. We can then scroll, start animations, and interact with the content and see how the counter changes.

60 fps is a goal we have in terms of animations for the user's brain to not perceive any lag in the animation or scrolling. It's difficult to get the same values on every device, though.

There are also some researchers who have found that having a high FPS value is not the only important metric. Sometimes keeping the frame rate consistent is what matters the most. That is, if sometimes your frame rate is 60 fps and sometimes 30 fps, the user will perceive your website as slower than the other website that keeps the frame rate constant at 30 fps.

In Chrome for Android, you can enable the FPS counter when using the Remote Inspector.

JavaScript Performance Monitor (*https://github.com/mrdoob/stats.js*) is a free JS-based tool that will work in any browser compatible with `requestAnimationFrame` support. It lets us monitor the frame rate and also lag time in some interactions that are defined by code.

Profiling Charts

If you find a feedback lag or a problem with the frame rate in some situation—for example, if you touch on a button and the reaction appears 500 ms after you remove your finger or if the frame rate goes down from 60 to 10 fps while you're scrolling—you should profile the memory and CPU usage to find the problem.

According to Wikipedia (*https://en.wikipedia.org/wiki/Profiling_(computer_program ming)*), profiling is "a form of dynamic program analysis that measures, for example, the space (memory) or time complexity of a program, the usage of particular instructions, or the frequency and duration of function calls. Most commonly, profiling information serves to aid program optimization."

In our case, we will typically want to profile CPU usage and memory. Additionally, we can profile the paint process on the device's video card and network operations. Memory is important because of the JavaScript garbage collector. The garbage collector takes CPU time to free unused objects from memory and it can be activated at inconvenient times, such as when we are scrolling or doing an animation, reducing the frame rate.

Typical profiling tools will have a record button that will start recording internals from the system and a stop button that will generate a report and a chart over a timeline.

To profile web content on mobile devices, we will need support from the web engine natively (therefore, it can't be emulated). On mobile engines, we have profiling support in:

- Chrome for Android, through Chrome Remote Developer Tools on a desktop
- Safari on iOS, through Safari Developer Tools on a Mac
- Firefox on Android and Firefox OS through Firefox on desktop
- Internet Explorer 11 on Windows Phone 8.1 and Edge on Windows 10 through Visual Studio
- BlackBerry 10 Browser, through Remote Tools

CPU Profiling

Profiling CPU usage will give us a usage chart that we can usually drill down into. We can select a region and see which part of our code was being executed at that time, as you can see in Figure 3-12.

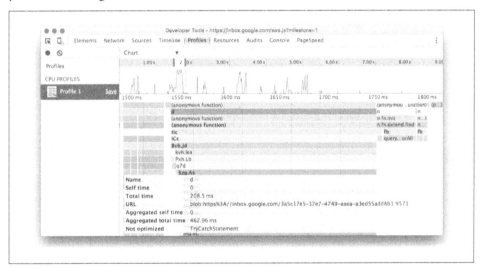

Figure 3-12. With CPU profiling, you can find peaks in CPU usage and then drill down to see what part of your code was actually using the CPU at that time

Memory Profiling

To find memory leaks and the garbage collector's performance problems, we can profile memory allocation over time. The diagram (as seen in Figure 3-13) will show a line chart and a list of object types with a count and the amount of memory that is being occupied by those objects.

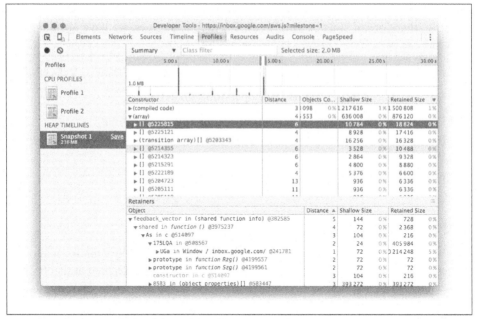

Figure 3-13. Most tools for debugging will let you profile your memory usage over time

Some web engines will let you take a snapshot of the heap memory at one point instead of looking at a timeline-based chart.

Mixed Profiling

Some newer web engines will give you more insights over a timeline of what is happening in different layers, so you can find the problem once a bottleneck in the responsiveness has been found.

These tools, such as the Timeline in Chrome Developer Tools and Performance in Firefox Developer Tools, will tell you what the engine was doing at a particular time, as we can see in Figure 3-14.

They will also add screenshots of the viewport so we can understand what the user was seeing on the screen at the time we are analyzing. In some situations, such as the small red triangle markers we see in the lower screenshot in Figure 3-14, the chart can indicate FPS issues as well that we should check.

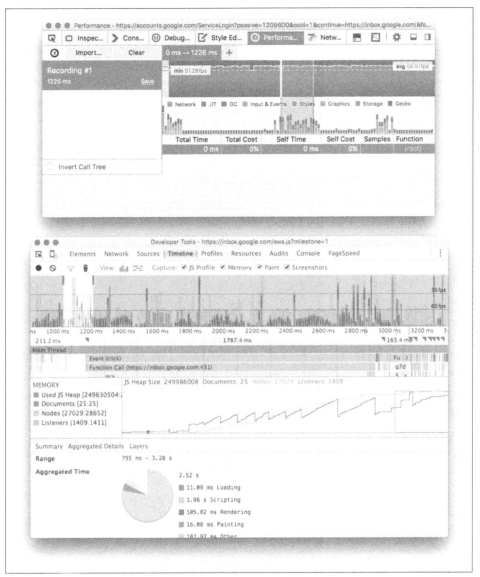

Figure 3-14. Some browsers will show you a mixed profiling report where you can see CPU, memory, network and paint operations all in the same timeline

When you are profiling, part of the CPU and memory will be used by the profiler. Therefore, profiling has a slight impact on the real performance. If we enable video or screencast generation, the impact will be stronger.

You Can't Improve Something If You Don't Measure It

Understanding the fundamentals of performance measurement is a must before seeing the actual tools and how to use them. In this chapter, we've covered the basics of the waterfall chart (including how to read it), the Speed Index, and the basics of profiling charts.

As a review, the most important diagrams for measuring web performance are:

- Waterfall charts
- Visual Progress Curve

The most important metrics we need to measure for the loading process are:

- Page load time
- Time to First Byte (TTFB)
- First render
- Speed Index
- Your own custom metric

The goals to achieve based on RAIL are a response time of 100 ms, an animation speed of 16 ms (60 fps), an idle time of 50 ms, and a load time of 1 second.

And finally, the primary metric for responsiveness is frames per second. To achieve 60 fps, you will probably use different profiling charts.

In Chapter 4, we will analyze the tools available that can get actual data from mobile browsers to help us measure and make decisions about performance.

Measurement Tools

We already know what to measure when we are talking about web performance. The next step is to understand which tools available on the market will help us with measurements on mobile web engines.

Remote Inspectors

One of the most useful tools for us are *remote debuggers* or *remote inspectors*. They allow us to connect a desktop browser's tools with a mobile counterpart to do analysis and profiling and get reports from a mobile device. This is particularly useful when measuring things that will be different from the desktop's viewport or that are network-dependent (and therefore using a real phone to test the user experience makes a difference).

 The RemoteDebug project (*http://remotedebug.org*) is an open initiative to bring interoperability between different browser vendors and different developer tools. It's still in the early stages, so in the meantime we will have to use the developer tools available on each platform.

Safari on iOS

If you have a MacBook or a Mac desktop computer and an iOS device, you can remotely debug websites, home screen web apps, and hybrid applications on the iOS Simulator and on actual devices.

Unfortunately, at the time of this writing, there is no way to open the iOS web debugger from a Windows or Linux desktop computer. We must rely on other nonnative solutions if we need to debug from a non-Mac desktop computer.

To use the Web Inspector on iOS, you must first enable it from the iOS device (it's enabled by default on the Simulator), by going to Settings→Safari→Advanced and turning on the Web Inspector feature, as seen on the right in Figure 4-1. Then, you need to connect your device through USB to your desktop computer.

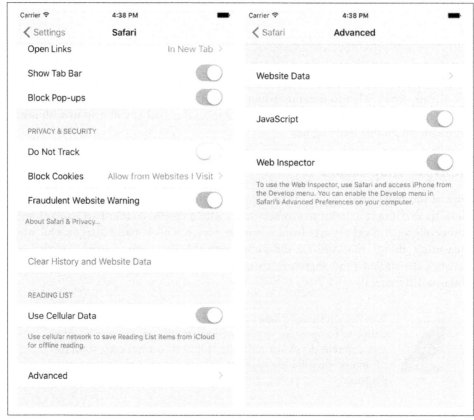

Figure 4-1. On iPhones, iPod touches, or iPads you can enable the Remote Web Inspector from Settings to start measuring performance on your actual device

The next step is to enable the developer tools in Safari for Mac, via Preferences→Advanced→"Show Develop menu in menu bar." When you've done all this and the session you want to debug is open on the device or in the Simulator, you can access the Develop menu in Safari for Mac; in that menu, you'll see the name of your device as a submenu with all the available web sessions to connect to on it, as seen on the right in Figure 4-2.

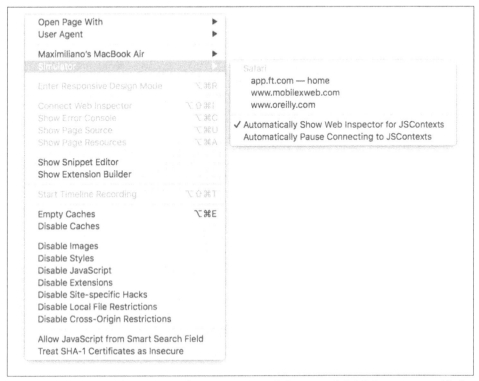

Figure 4-2. Once you have a Simulator or an actual device with Web Inspector enabled, you can see all the available sessions ready to inspect, from Safari, a web view, or a home screen web app

When you're connected, Safari for Mac will open a window with your debug session user interface (as seen in Figure 4-3).

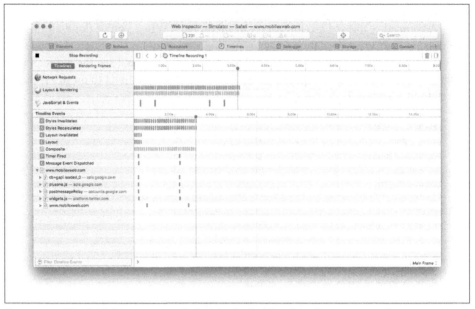

Figure 4-3. The Web Inspector on Safari 9+ looks like this when connected to a remote session from an actual device or the iOS Simulator

In the debug session, you will be able to:

- Inspect the HTML, CSS, and JavaScript
- Browse storage, inspecting cookies, local storage, SQL databases, and more
- Record and measure timelines, including network requests, layout and rendering, and JavaScript execution and events
- See network requests
- See warnings and errors
- See web workers (threads)
- See and manage JavaScript breakpoints, including watch expressions

 We can connect a Remote Web Inspector to a web view running inside a native app only when the app was installed in debug mode —that is, it's our app and we are installing it from Xcode. Therefore, if you have an app that was installed from the App Store and it's using a web view, you won't be able to connect the Inspector to it.

Timelines

The Safari Web Inspector has different options available depending on the desktop's Safari version, such as Safari 8 on macOS 10.10 (Yosemite) and from Safari 9 on macOS 10.11 (El Capitan).

The section of the Web Inspector that matters to web performance is the Timelines tab, though we can also get useful information from the Network tab. There is a record button at the top left of the screen that we can use to start profiling a website or web app.

 It's better to stop the recording after you have collected the information you're looking for, such as after the page has loaded. It'll help the analysis of the results if the timeline is static (not changing, and not adding more items while recording).

There are three timelines available, providing information about different areas:

Network requests
All the network communication, including initial loading, lazy resources, and other calls after the onload event.

Layout & Rendering
All the paint, layout, and CSS operations

JavaScript & Events
JavaScript code being executed by the runtime, as well as events being fired by the DOM

 While we can make do with only using the analysis from the iOS Simulator, it's always a good idea to check real performance on actual devices. Some features, such as real cellular network conditions or touch feedback, can only be experienced with actual phones or tablets.

Once you have a recording dump on the screen, you will find several colored bars over the timeline. If you scroll up or down (using the mouse wheel or a touchpad gesture) over the timeline, you will be able to zoom in or out in the timeline.

If you select a region in the timeline, you will see a detail view in the lower section of the screen. Each row will represent one entry (e.g., one downloaded resource or one paint operation).

You can filter the list of entries from the selected region by using the search box in the bottom-left section and/or clicking on one of the timeline names, such as "Network

Requests" or "Layout & Rendering." To remove a timeline filter, just click on the "X" at the right of the timeline's name.

Starting with Safari 9 on macOS El Capitan, the timeline can be replaced with a different mode: Rendering Frames. Instead of seeing events in the timeline, you will see a representation like that in Figure 4-4: a frame-based, task-specific view of existing profiler/instrumentation data. The data is displayed in three sections: an overview graph (top left), a records table (main), and a summary chart (top center and right). If you have a performance issue, you can see frame by frame what the engine is doing and find the bottleneck. You can read more about the new Rendering Frames mode in the WebKit Blog (*https://www.webkit.org/blog/3996/introducing-the-rendering-frames-timeline*).

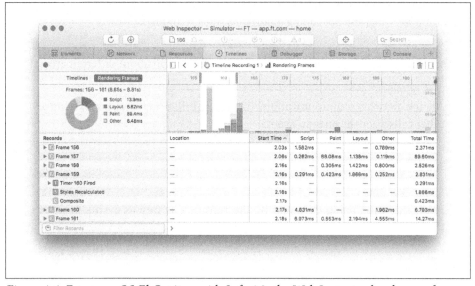

Figure 4-4. From macOS El Capitan with Safari 9, the Web Inspector has been redesigned, including a new Rendering Frames view that allows us to detect frame drops or problems keeping the frame rate consistent

Network tab

From macOS El Capitan, Safari offers a redesigned Network tab where we can see all the resources in list mode, as shown in Figure 4-5. We can't see them in a waterfall chart. You can filter by name, by resource type, or by document (main document or iframes available).

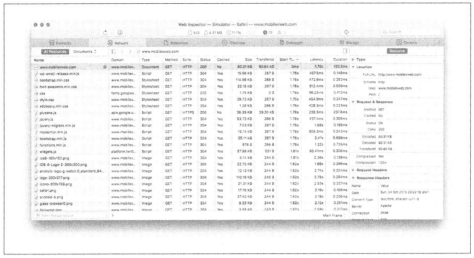

Figure 4-5. The Network tab will list the resources and the details of each one, including timing information. When you open the tab for the first time, you might need to refresh the page. To do so, you don't need to go to your device; you can use the reload button on the desktop interface.

The iOS WebKit Debug Proxy (*https://github.com/google/ios-webkit-debug-proxy*) allows you to connect an iOS device or simulator to the Google Chrome Developer Tools on macOS or Linux. It acts as an experimental proxy translating Apple WebKit's debugging protocol to the one that is used by Chrome. A Windows version (*https://github.com/artygus/ios-webkit-debug-proxy-win32*) has been ported, and Firefox also has its own solution based on these proxies that enables you to use Firefox Developer Tools with iOS, known as Valence (*https://developer.mozilla.org/es/docs/Tools/Valence*).

Chrome for Android

Google Chrome for Android supports remote debugging through a USB connection using the Developer Tools available in Chrome for desktop.

To use the Remote Inspector, follow these steps:

1. Enable USB debugging on your Android device (see the instructions in the sidebar that follows).

2. Connect your mobile device to your desktop using USB. If your host is a Windows-based computer, you will need debug USB drivers from the manufac-

turer; see Android Studio's list of OEM Drivers (*http://developer.android.com/tools/extras/oem-usb.html*).

3. Accept the RSA key fingerprint on your phone (it gives the right permission to your desktop computer).

4. Open Chrome on your desktop and type "chrome://inspect" in the address bar, or select More Tools→Inspect devices from the Chrome menu in Developer Tools.

5. Select the "inspect" link that matches your device's name and web session from the list (see Figure 4-6).

Figure 4-6. When connected with USB debugging enabled, you will be able to see and inspect websites and home screen web apps using Chrome for Android, as well as Chromium-based web views in apps in debug mode

 In Google Chrome for Android, Web Inspection is automatically available after you enable USB Debugging mode on your phone. Enabling USB debugging mode and accepting the host computer allows anyone connecting your phone with a desktop computer to access most of the stuff on your device.

Enabling USB Debugging on Your Android Device

To enable USB debugging on your Android phone or tablet, you need to open the Settings app, go to "Developer options," and enable the "USB debugging" option. It's an easy task, right? Well, it is if you have an Android 4.1 or older device. But if you are doing this for the first time on an Android 4.2+ device, you won't find the "Developer options" menu inside Settings.

So, you first need to put your device in developer mode. To do so, you need to do something a little weird. Go to Settings→"About phone" (or Settings→"About tablet") and find the "Build number" entry (the last item in the list on most devices). You will need to tap on that Build item seven times. It's not a mistake—it's like an Easter egg. To enable developer mode in Android 4.2+, you need to tap seven times on the build number. After you do that, your phone will show you a toast message saying that "You are now a Developer!" The developer options will now be available in the main Settings window.

When connected, you can use the Chrome Developer Tools as usual to do all of the following:

- Inspect elements
- Access the resources list, including local storage, and SQL and IDB databases
- Access network information
- Add JavaScript breakpoints and use debugging tools
- See useful timelines, such as rendering information
- Profile JavaScript code
- See the console and execute JavaScript code on it

 Google Chrome for desktop has an emulation mode that you can use without a phone connected through USB. You can use this mode to get information from Developer Tools, but for performance issues you need to remember you are using your desktop browser and not the Android version of it.

LIVERPOOL JOHN MOORES UNIVERSITY
LEARNING SERVICES

Screencasting

When you connect your Android device's Chrome or Chromium-based web view, Chrome on the desktop allows you to do a *screencast*. With screencasting enabled, you can see and interact with your mobile web content from the desktop (see Figure 4-7). Therefore, you can leave your phone on the table and work on the desktop while executing everything on the phone.

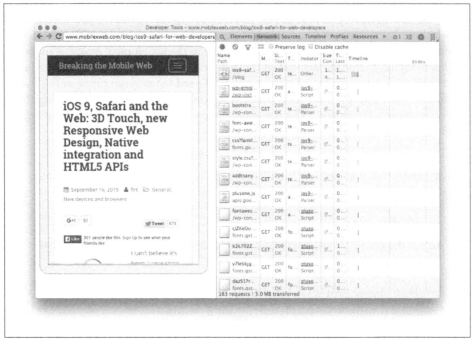

Figure 4-7. When connected to a device using a modern version of Chrome or Chromium-based web view, you can enable the Screencast feature (the phone icon at the top right position of the inspector). The screencast is also interactive, so you can click, scroll, and type on your desktop and it will be translated to the device.

Rendering settings

Chrome Developer Tools has several not-so-visible rendering options that will help you a lot when measuring performance and understanding bottlenecks under Rendering Settings (*https://developer.chrome.com/devtools/docs/rendering-settings*).

To define advanced rendering settings, you need to open the drawer in the Developer Tools pane (using the Escape key or the console icon in the DevTools pane). The drawer has several tabs; the last one is Rendering, as we can see in Figure 4-8. The first important option here is "Show FPS meter." This will add a layer in your actual device (not in the screencast) with live information about the current frame rate, CPU, and memory usage so you can touch, scroll, and interact with your web content and see when it's dropping frames (see the right side of Figure 4-8).

Figure 4-8. "Show FPS meter" lets you see a frame rate graph on your device to find responsiveness problems

"Continuous painting mode" will force a repaint on each frame. It lets you find rendering issues such as content that is taking too much time to render and might decrease your frame rate or harm the scrolling experience. For example, you can select "Enable continuous page repainting" and start adding or removing CSS properties (such as shadows, transforms, and filters) and see if the graph goes up (it takes more time to render) or down (it's faster). The smaller the rendering time, the greater the frame rate you will get. In Figure 4-9, we can see this in action on a test suite available at *http://ariya.github.io/css/glowingtext*. It creates an animation with glowing text so you can see the peaks in rendering time that the animation takes at some points.

"Show paint rectangles" and "Show composited layer borders" will help you understand how the browser is rendering your content on the screen and it will let us find better ways to design it from a video acceleration performance point of view.

Finally, "Show potential scroll bottlenecks" will highlight in your web content which areas will slow down scrolling. More information about this option is available in a GitHub discussion (*https://github.com/GoogleChrome/devtools-docs/issues/65#issuecomment-118373165*).

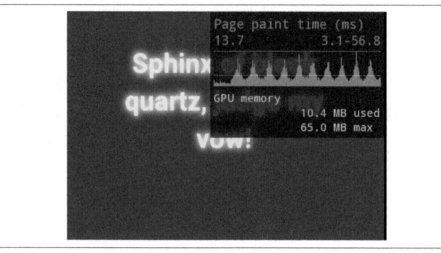

Figure 4-9. With continuous painting mode, we can compare different implementations, styles, and code to see which options take less rendering time. The graph shows page paint time; the bigger the value, the worse from an FPS point of view

The Network tab

The Network tab is where you will find the list of resources and detailed information about each request, including timings, headers, and response bodies.

By default, the requests are not recorded, so after you go to the Network tab for the first time, you will probably need to refresh the page on your mobile device to get all the information. You need to verify that you're recording (the record button is red), and you will probably want to stop the recording after the page has loaded if you are just measuring loading times. You can disable the cache to make a full first page load.

> The Remote Inspector UI will change based on the actual Chrome or Chromium version installed on the device.

If you don't stop the recording, then any Ajax request, advertisement, or script that is updating information after the load will continue modifying the chart while you are analyzing it.

Figure 4-10 shows the UI of the Network tab and the most important sections and buttons on it.

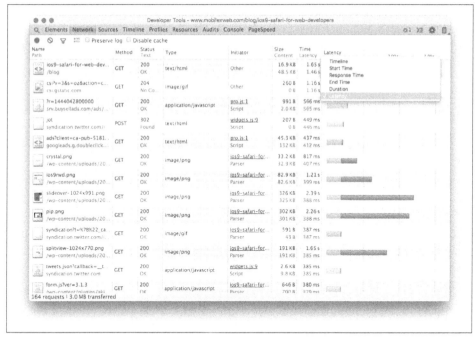

Figure 4-10. The Network tab will show you all the requests being made by the current page. You can order by columns, and if you click on the seventh column, you can select various options, from timeline mode (mini waterfall chart) to latency graph. Also, right-clicking on any column will let you customize that column.

If you click on one of the colored bars in the Timeline column, you will get detailed information about timings for that particular resource, as you can see in Figure 4-11.

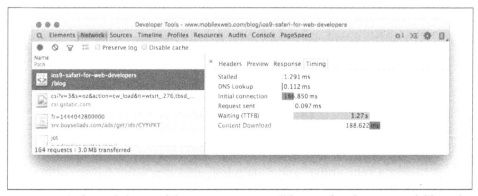

Figure 4-11. If you click one of the resources, you will have a details pane available with headers, a content preview, and timing information

In Figure 4-11, a new measure appears in gray: Stalled. This is the amount of time that the request waited before it could be sent. The delay includes proxy negotiation and the amount of time that the browser waited until a TCP connection was available for reuse.

 If, like me, you have been playing with web performance optimization for a while, you probably have a Page Speed tab in your Chrome Developer Tools pane. That tool is now deprecated and has been replaced by the online tool Speed Insights (*https://develop ers.google.com/speed/pagespeed/insights/Page*). If you want to remove it, you can do so from *chrome://extensions*.

The Timeline tab

The Timeline tab is a mixed profiling window where you can see, all at the same time, what is happening in JavaScript (Events mode), memory (Memory mode), and paint operations (Frames mode) and what the user is seeing at that point through screenshots.

It's one of the most complete and complex profiling tools available today in the web world. For more information, consult the documentation (*https://devel oper.chrome.com/devtools/docs/timeline*).

 If you right-click on the Timeline, you can save the data for future analysis in JSON format.

The Profiles tab

The Profiles tab lets you record and profile:

- JavaScript and CPU usage
- Heap snapshots (lets you see the memory's content at one particular point)
- Heap allocations (lets you see the memory's evolution over time)

You start by selecting which report you want to create and start recording. When you are done, you stop it and the report will be generated. You can get a summary, specific reports based on your profile, and a statistical chart if you use the top drop-down menu (Figure 4-12). You can save each data collection for future analysis.

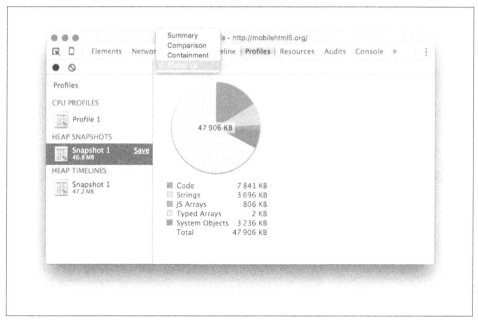

Figure 4-12. If you want to profile memory or CPU usage, the Profiles tab will make the reports for you

The Audits tab

Audits is a basic tool for performance analysis. It will make an analysis of your network usage and it will give you a report and suggestions to improve performance. This tool has been superseded over time by other solutions that we will cover later. Therefore, it's not too important today.

Internet Explorer and Edge

Both Internet Explorer and Edge come with the F12 developer tools (F12 is the key shortcut to open them). These include the Network tool (Ctrl-4), the Performance tool (Ctrl-5), and the Memory tool (Ctrl-6).

The Network and Memory tools work similarly to comparable tool in other browsers, so we'll focus on the features available in the Performance tool (*https://devel oper.microsoft.com/en-us/microsoft-edge/platform/documentation/f12-devtools-guide/ performance*) in Edge.

To start working with the tool, you first need to start a profile recording a performance session. You should do stuff while recording, such as loading the page, scrolling it, or touching UI elements. The report will include a ruler showing performance milestones such as DOMContentLoaded, and if you are using the User Timing API you will see your marks there, as shown in Figure 4-13.

Figure 4-13. In the F12 dev tools in Edge, we can record a profiling session and then see performance milestones in the ruler, including User Timing marks

The timeline will show CPU usage and frame rate over time, and you can get detailed information on what was happening at one particular time or during a range if you select it from the timeline, as we can see in Figure 4-14.

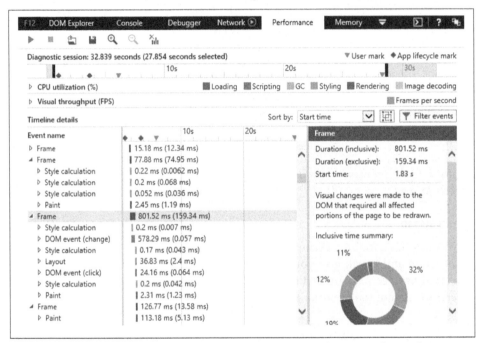

Figure 4-14. The "Timeline details" section has completed information for performance measurement and for finding bottlenecks in Edge on Windows 10

To give you information about responsiveness, Edge will show details about HTML and CSS parsing, HTTP requests, speculative downloads, `requestAnimationFrame` calls, DOM events, script evaluation, timer execution, media query listeners, mutation observers, garbage collector execution, rendering, and image decoding. That level of detail should be enough to find any problems' causes after seeing a suspicious range in the timeline (such as a CPU usage peak or FPS meter drop).

In the Internet Explorer 11 dev tools (connected to a Windows Phone 8.x device), we have a JavaScript profiler tool. In Edge, that tool has been merged with other solutions in the Performance tool.

Vorlon.js

Vorlon.js (*http://vorlonjs.com*) is a remote debugging solution created by Microsoft that helps you remotely load, inspect, test, and debug JavaScript code running on any device with a web browser. You can even connect up to 50 devices and debug all of them at the same time.

It involves a Node server, a script you need to inject, and a desktop tool. Because it's a JS-based solution, its scope for profiling and performance measurement is limited, and it's basically restricted to a Network tab.

Proxies

When a browser does not offer any developer tools, such as Android Browser, Samsung Browser, or Nokia Browser, the only thing we can do is work with the network layer. There are several tools that will let you sniff the network and create waterfall charts from network requests from any device that is using a particular connection or proxy.

With proxies, you can only create waterfall charts and see network details. As there is no connection to the phone or the rendering engine, you can't use these tools for Speed Index calculation, filmstrip generation, or responsiveness measurements.

Setting Up on Android

Because the usage of proxies is more suitable for older or non-Chrome Android browsers, let's see how to set up a proxy on an Android 4.x device.

Go to Settings→Wi-Fi and long-press the WiFi network that has visibility to your desktop computer; then select "Modify network" and enable advanced options. In the proxy settings, you need to select Manual and type in your desktop computer's local network IP address and proxy port, as in Figure 4-15.

When using a proxy to sniff the network, you have to know that these tools are unable to identify the origin of a network request. Therefore, if you have several tabs or apps in the background making requests, they might all get listed in your reports. Some proxies are smarter and will use the HTTP header *Referer* to group the requests by initial response, but it's better to reduce network usage on the phone while recording a session.

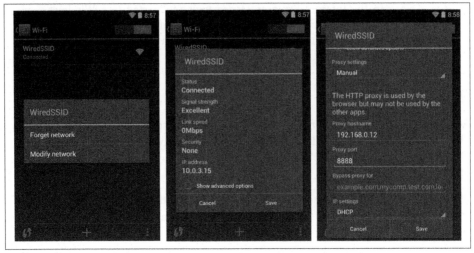

Figure 4-15. On most mobile devices, you can set up the proxy at the OS level. Some browsers allow you to set up the proxy for that browser only.

If you are setting up the Android SDK Emulator for proxy usage, you must use a command-line argument before opening the instance. For details, see the documentation (*http://developer.android.com/intl/es/tools/help/emulator.html*).

Setting Up on iOS

To set up a proxy on iOS, go to Settings→Wi-Fi, expand the details of the WiFi network you want to set up (using the (i) icon), and select HTTP Proxy→Manual. You can then add your proxy's details. All the HTTP communication after that will go through your desktop proxy tool.

Charles Web Debugging Proxy

Charles Proxy[1] is a Java-based tool compatible with Windows, macOS, and Linux and optimized for web debugging that will let us see the network and waterfall charts in a desktop-based interface. To use it with a phone, you must connect the phone to a WiFi network with visibility to your desktop computer and set up the proxy with the IP address and port of Charles.

Once Charles is installed, the first thing you should do is disable the desktop proxy. By default, Charles Proxy will try to sniff your desktop browsing, and that is not something we want at this time. To disable it, go to Proxy→Proxy Settings and disable the Windows or macOS proxy (based on your operating system) and the Mozilla

---

1 There is a 30-day trial version available at *https://www.charlesproxy.com*.

Firefox proxy. Then, on the Proxies tab, set the port number (usually 8888, as we can see in Figure 4-16).

Figure 4-16. With Charles Proxy, you can sniff what your mobile browser is doing if it's connected to the same network

When you are ready to start and you have your phone connected to your proxy, you are ready to record the session. Select Recording from the Proxy menu or use the toolbar icon and start browsing on your mobile phone or emulator. You need to stop the recording as soon as the page is loaded, because Charles Proxy can't separate network requests that are coming from other apps or browser tabs.

Fiddler

Fiddler (*http://www.telerik.com/fiddler*) is a web debugging proxy from Telerik, available for Windows only (it was once a Microsoft product). It lets us debug the network layer in any browser, because it sits between the browser and the network. Fiddler has unique features, such as the ability to debug traffic from any country using a Geoedge service and the ability to create scripts in the proxy itself using a scripting language.

There are also add-ons (*http://www.telerik.com/fiddler/add-ons*) that let you add more power to the tool while sniffing your browsing, such as CertMaker for iOS and Android, which will let you sniff HTTPS traffic on iOS and Android, and Compressibility, which will give you hints on where to improve compression in your requests.

If you want to use Fiddler from a mobile device, you must set up a proxy on your phone.

On-Device Tools

If you are looking for tools that will help you get performance measurements on the device itself, you might be disappointed. That is because, at the time of writing, mobile browsers don't have the ability to add plug-ins or modules that can attach to the browser and get information. Most tools out there providing on-device performance analysis will probably use the web view, not the real web engine inside the browser. While sometimes this can be good enough, in some other situations the results will be different.

Online Tools

There are several tools available in the cloud that will let us measure performance, find bottlenecks, and get help and advice.

WebPagetest

The most prominent solution is WebPagetest (*http://webpagetest.org*), where you can generate charts and get insights browsing from real browsers on real networks all over the world, as seen in Figure 4-17.

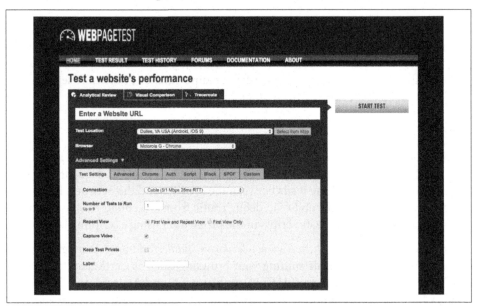

Figure 4-17. Using the free online tool WebPagetest, we can select a mobile device on a real network anywhere in the world and wait just a couple of minutes to get the results

With WebPagetest, we can test our websites on real devices (desktop and mobile) on different real networks all over the world. Several features are available, as we can see in Figure 4-18, including:

- Standard metrics such as Load Time and Start Render on both first view and repeat view
- Speed Index
- HAR file
- Filmstrip view (see Figure 4-19)
- Exporting a video with the filmstrip
- Content breakdown (quantity of files and sizes)

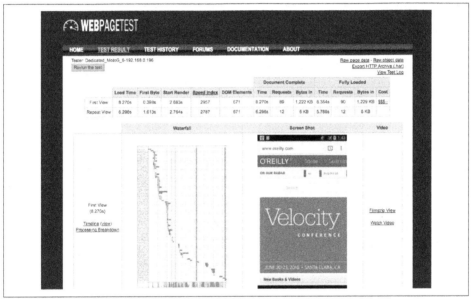

Figure 4-18. With the free WebPagetest service, we can get waterfall charts, CPU and network profiling charts, filmstrip views, page speed, and other metrics

WebPagetest is an open source project and you can run it locally on your own system as a private instance. It also has an API for batch processing, so you can add it to your own testing environment.

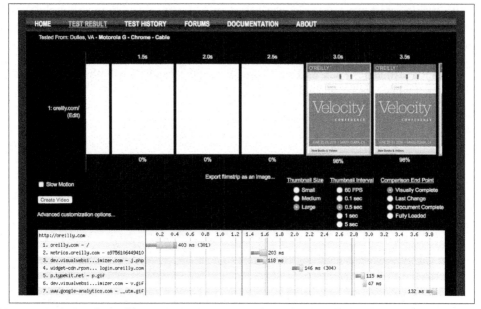

Figure 4-19. With the filmstrip view, we can see how the page looks like at any millisecond matching that timeline with the waterfall chart below

 For advanced settings and tips on using WebPagetest, check out Rick Viscomi, Andy Davies, and Marcel Duran's *Using WebPageTest* (O'Reilly).

PageSpeed Insights

Google has a free service that will give us conclusions—not charts—about web performance, called PageSpeed Insights (*https://developers.google.com/speed/pagespeed/insights*).

The tool will analyze your website in both desktop and mobile viewports, giving you hints on what you should do to get better performance. It also gives you a score from 0 to 100 on how well are you performing on both platforms, as we can see in Figure 4-20.

Figure 4-20. With Google's PageSpeed Insights, we can get quick ideas on how to improve performance and a score indicating how well the website is performing on mobile and desktop

Monitoring Services

Web performance optimization has led over time to a full industry centered on performance. Today, there are hundreds of providers offering performance monitoring services where we can get reports of performance problems from different places in the world. The main providers are:

- New Relic (*http://newrelic.com*)
- Neustar (*http://neustar.com*)
- Keynote (*http://keynote.com*)
- Dynatrace (*http://dynatrace.com*)
- Load Impact (*http://loadimpact.com*)
- Pingdom (*http://pingdom.com*)

Another useful service is Show Slow (*http://www.showslow.com*), an open source tool that monitors public websites over time using several web performance metrics. It keeps data for 90 days, and you can see all the stored data on the website.

The Tools You Need

As with every new job, understanding the tools that will be necessary is must-have knowledge. In this chapter, we've been talking about several desktop-based tools that can remotely connect to your mobile device and some other tools that might be useful, including:

- Remote inspectors for Android-, iOS-, and Windows-based browsers
- Proxies
- On-device tools
- Online tools, such as WebPagetest and PageSpeed Insights

In Chapter 5, we will analyze the JavaScript APIs and new HTTP-based specs that will help us in measuring and improving web performance and user perception.

Performance APIs

The W3C has a Web Performance Working Group (*http://www.w3.org/2010/webperf*) that decides what new APIs browsers might implement to help us measure and improve web performance. In this chapter, we will cover the APIs this group has defined as well as other web APIs that will be useful for us in our performance optimization work.

We will look first at the APIs that are available today on some or all browsers, such as the Navigation Timing and Network Information APIs, and then a list of future specs that will help us with performance optimization in the future, such as Script Timing and Efficient Script Yielding.

Measurement APIs

We will start with APIs that will help us during the measurement phase, so we can gather real data from our users.

Navigation Timing

The Navigation Timing API (*http://www.w3.org/TR/navigation-timing*) was the first browser API with web performance as its focus. It provides a series of timestamps from the initial page loading process through window.performance. It's currently available in most modern mobile browsers, including Google Chrome, IE, Edge, Firefox, and Safari from iOS 9. It's not available in Android Browser or proxy-based browsers.

Some reports claim that Safari has supported the Navigation Timing API since version 8. It was available in that version, but support was quickly removed in release 8.1 a few weeks later due to "performance issues," as Apple stated at the time. It was fully re-enabled in iOS 9 in 2015.

The global `performance` object also acts as the home for other performance-based specs besides Navigation Timing.

Timings

As stated before, the Navigation Timing API offers a list of timestamps that we can use to get real performance measurements for the current page load. You can use this information for analytics or to make live decisions on the fly; for example, if the connection seems to be slow, you may decide to load only low-resolution images and a lighter version of the page.

A Unix timestamp is a long integer measuring the milliseconds that have elapsed between midnight January 1, 1970, and the time we want to measure.

The following timings are available as long integer values in the `performance.timing` object:

navigationStart
: The time immediately after the user agent finishes prompting to unload the previous document

unloadEventStart
: The time immediately before the user agent starts the `unload` event of the previous document (only if both documents have the same origin)

unloadEventEnd
: The time immediately after the user agent finishes the `unload` event of the previous document (only if both documents have the same origin)

redirectStart
: The starting time of the fetch that initiates a redirect from the same origin

redirectEnd
: The time immediately after receiving the last byte of the response of the last redirect, if from the same origin

fetchStart

The time immediately before the browser starts checking any relevant application caches or fetching the resource

domainLookupStart

The time immediately before the user agent starts the DNS lookup

domainLookupEnd

The time immediately after the user agent finishes the DNS lookup (even if the document was in the cache)

connectStart

The time immediately before the user agent starts establishing the connection to the server to retrieve the document

connectEnd

The time immediately after the user agent finishes establishing the connection to the server

secureConnectionStart

For HTTPS connections only, the time immediately before the user agent starts the handshake process to secure the current connection

requestStart

The time immediately before the browser starts requesting the current document from the server (or from relevant application caches or local resources)

responseStart

The time immediately after the browser receives the first byte of the response from the server (or from relevant application caches or local resources)

responseEnd

The time immediately after the browser receives the last byte of the current document

domLoading

The time immediately before the browser sets the current document readiness to "loading"

domInteractive

The time immediately before the user agent sets the current document readiness to "interactive"

domContentLoadedEventStart

The time immediately before the user agent fires the DOMContentLoaded event

domContentLoadedEventEnd

> The time immediately after the document's `DOMContentLoaded` event completes

domComplete

> The time immediately before the user agent sets the current document readiness to "complete"

loadEventStart

> The time immediately before the `load` event of the current document is fired (0 if it wasn't fired yet)

loadEventEnd

> The time when the `load` event of the current document is completed

Figure 5-1 shows these timings in the timeline chart.

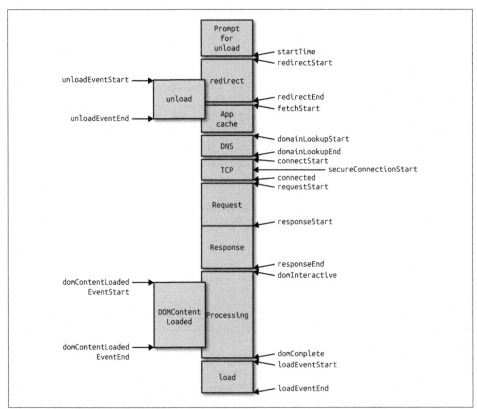

Figure 5-1. The Navigation Timing API gives us lots of useful timing information from the browser that can't be calculated in any other way

Internet Explorer added `timing.msFirstPaint` as a nonstandard timing measuring when the page has started to draw on the screen. Chrome also has a nonstandard list of timing and navigation information available through `chrome.loadTimes()`, including `first PaintTime`.

Timestamps alone are not really so useful. What make timings interesting are the combinations of timings that will tell us how long certain things take, expressed in milliseconds. For example:

`domainLookupEnd-domainLookupStart`
DNS query duration

`connectEnd-connectStart`
TCP connection duration

`responseEnd-fetchStart`
Network latency

`redirectEnd-redirectStart`
Time spent during redirection

`loadEventEnd-responseEnd`
Processing time to load the page after network fetch

`loadEventEnd-navigationStart`
Duration of whole process of navigation and page load

`responseEnd-fetchStart`
Network fetch time

`domainLookupStart-fetchStart`
Application cache duration

For example, we can do something like:

```
var dnsQuery = performance.timing.domainLookupEnd-
               performance.timing.domainLookupStart;
```

Breaking Down onLoad (*http://kaaes.github.io/timing*) is an open source bookmarklet we can use to break down the Navigation Timing API's information into a chart, as we can see in Figure 5-2.

Because of lack of navigation, the Navigation Timing API is not available from web workers—including service workers. From Chrome 45, workers will have access to the Resource Timing and User Timing APIs covered later in this chapter.

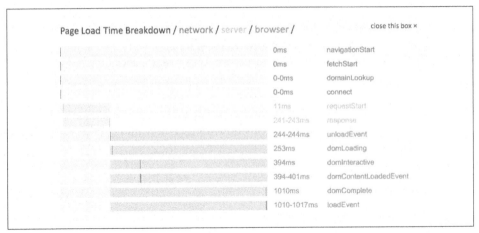

Figure 5-2. Breaking Down onLoad is a bookmarklet that we can use to see timings in a useful chart

Timing.js

Timing.js (*https://github.com/addyosmani/timing.js*) is a small open source library (1.45 KB gzipped) offering us useful information drawn from the Navigation Timing API and custom timing APIs in some browsers— for example, for getting paint timings not available in the Navigation Timing API.

After installing the script in your page, you can access a `timing` global object with several useful timings; you can also use `timing.printSimpleTable()` to get all the information in the console as a table, as we can see in Figure 5-3.

Q 🗋   Elements Network Sources Timeline Profiles Resources Audits Console » ≥ ⚙ ▣ ×

| ⊘ ▽ <top frame> | ▼ ☐ Preserve log |

> `timing.printSimpleTable()`

(index)	label	ms	s
0	"appcacheTime"	70	0.07
1	"connectTime"	182	0.18
2	"domReadyTime"	440	0.44
3	"firstPaintTime"	751.567138671875	0.75
4	"initDomTreeTime"	418	0.42
5	"loadEventTime"	4	0
6	"loadTime"	1541	1.54
7	"lookupDomainTime"	0	0
8	"readyStart"	183	0.18
9	"redirectTime"	0	0
10	"requestTime"	244	0.24
11	"unloadEventTime"	0	0

VM103:103

Figure 5-3. If we include the open source Timing.js framework in our script, we can get useful data from the Navigation Timing API as well as from other non-standard specs

Navigation Timing Level 2 (*http://www.w3.org/TR/navigation-timing-2*) will change how the API delivers timings, including the change from a long integer timestamp to a double `DOMHighResTimeStamp` value that will express milliseconds in the integer part and be accurate to 5 microseconds, if the browser supports it, in the decimal part of the value.

Navigation metadata

The Performance interface also provides a `navigation` object with information about the current page load process. This object has two properties:

- `redirectCount`, with the amount of HTTP redirects (301 or 302) processed before the current page load (0 means no redirects)
- `type`, with the type of navigation as an integer that matches a constant from Table 5-1

Table 5-1. Navigation types

Numeric value	Type	Matches constant
0	Normal load (URL typed or link clicked)	`performance.navigation.TYPE_NAVIGATE`
1	Reload	`performance.navigation.TYPE_RELOAD`
2	Load after Back or Forward in history	`performance.navigation.TYPE_BACK_FORWARD`
255	Other	`performance.navigation.TYPE_RESERVED`

High Resolution Time

The High Resolution Time API (*http://www.w3.org/TR/hr-time*) is a different spec from the W3C available in most of the browsers supporting the Navigation Timing API. It will let us take our own measures without incurring JavaScript delays.

Before this API, the way to measure JavaScript code execution time was using `Date.now()`, as in:

```
var startTime = Date.now();
domeSomeHeavyTask();
var duration = Date.now() - startTime;
```

The previous approach is not accurate enough for several reasons, including the time that it takes to talk to the Calendar to get the time and inaccuracies of the Calendar itself when it comes to highly precise times.

The only browser supporting the Navigation Timing API but not High Resolution Time is Internet Explorer 9; in the mobile world, it's only used on the old Windows Phone 7.x. Windows Phone 8, 8.1, and Windows 10 support both with IE or Edge.

The High Resolution Time API adds a now method to the performance global object from the Navigation Timing API. Therefore, the previous code can be replaced by:

```
var startTime = performance.now();
domeSomeHeavyTask();
var duration = performance.now() - startTime;
```

While Date.now() gives us a timestamp from 1970, performance.now() gives us the number of milliseconds from the performance.timing.navigationStart attribute.

Although it is still in draft at the time of this writing, the next version of the spec (*http://www.w3.org/TR/hr-time-2*) will increase the accuracy of performance.now() from 1 millisecond to up to 5 microseconds, and it will allow web workers—including service workers—to use it.

Resource Timing

The Resource Timing API (*https://www.w3.org/TR/resource-timing*) is useful to retrieve network timing information from each web resource that was loaded into the document, not just the main HTML page, as with Navigation Timing. It will help us in getting the same timings as the Navigation Timing API but for each image, CSS file, JavaScript file, or XHR call, using high-resolution timestamps.

The API exposes a getEntriesByType method to the performance global object where we can query for resources. Each resource will have timing and other information available, using code such as the following:

```
var resourceList = window.performance.getEntriesByType("resource");

for (i = 0; i < resourceList.length; i++) {
    var resourceInfo = resourceList[i];
    {
        var totalTime = resourceInfo.responseEnd - resourceInfo.startTime;
    }
}
```

The list of properties available per `PerformanceResourceTiming` object in that collection is as follows:

`initiatorType`
A string (from one of the following values: `img`, `css`, `link`, `script`, `subdocument`, `svg`, `xmlhttprequest`, or `other`)

`workerStart`
The time immediately before the `fetch` event when a service worker is present

`redirectStart` *and* `redirectEnd`
Timings available if a redirection was set for the resource

`fetchStart`
When the browser starts checking if the resource is in an application cache or if it should start a request

`domainLookupStart` *and* `domainLookupEnd`
Timings for DNS query resolution, if necessary

`connectStart` *and* `connectEnd`
Timings for the TCP connection phase

`secureConnectionStart`
If TLS is used, the timing for the negotiation phase

`requestStart`
When the request starts from the browser to the server

`responseStart` *and* `responseEnd`
When the response from the server starts and ends

`transferSize`
The total transfer size in bytes for the resource, including all HTTP headers

`encodedBodySize`
The total transfer size in bytes for the compressed body of the resource

`decodedBodySize`
The total size in bytes for the body of the resource after it was decompressed

The recommended minimum number of `PerformanceResourceTiming` objects is 150, though this may be changed by calling `setResourceTimingBufferSize`.

At the time of this writing, Resource Timing is available in most browsers, but not Safari.

Network APIs

It's time now to review events and APIs that will help us in the detection of the current network status.

Network Status Events

Thanks to the HTML specification, browsers expose two events—`online` and `offline`—on the `window` object that we can use to detect changes in connection status, as well as the `navigator.onLine` Boolean property:

```
window.addEventListener("offline", function(e) {
        console.log("offline");
});
window.addEventListener("online", function(e) {
        console.log("online");
});
window.addEventListener("load", function(e) {
        console.log(navigator.onLine ? "online" : "offline");
});
```

When the browser provides a value of `true` for the `onLine` property or fires the `online` event, it usually means that the mobile operating system is exposing a data connection to us (a WiFi or cellular data connection), but there is no guarantee that it's really working properly. When the property is `false`, we know for sure that the offline situation is guaranteed.

 If you want to detect whether you are really online or not, you must use an XHR request to your server and verify that a response comes, and with the type you are expecting. Offline.js (*http://github.hubspot.com/offline/docs/welcome*) is a JavaScript library that will help you in these situations.

Also, when we are online on mobile devices there are several other situations that might occur, such as when we need to log in or activate our accounts when using a captive portal from a WiFi or cellular network. In these cases, requests might get a 404 response or a redirect to the login form. That's why we have to verify that the response we are receiving is the expected one when we are trying to see if we are online.

Network Information

The Network Information API allows us to determine some information about the current connection, such as the type (WiFi, cellular) and estimated available bandwidth.

At the time of this writing, three different implementations of the API are available:

- The first nonstandard spec version, implemented by Android Browser and Apache Cordova/PhoneGap apps
- The first W3C spec (*http://www.w3.org/TR/2012/WD-netinfo-api-20121129*), including bandwidth information, first implemented by the BlackBerry 10 Browser and old Firefox versions for mobile devices
- The latest living spec from the W3C (*https://w3c.github.io/netinfo*), implemented today by Chrome for Android

Safari on iOS is not implementing any version of this API at the time of this writing.

If this API is available, we can decide what kind of experience we are going to deliver, including SD or HD video and different image qualities.

You shouldn't rely exclusively on the Network Information API, especially for good situations. If the API says you are in 2G or offline, you can trust that information. But if it says WiFi or 4G, be aware that the API doesn't really test if the connection is working.

Old specification

The old spec API exposes a `navigator.connection.type` attribute that will match one of the following strings: `unknown`, `ethernet`, `wifi`, `2g`, `3g`, `4g`, or `none`.

This API will give you the connection type of the first node; that doesn't mean that it is working properly, though, or even that it is the ultimate type of connection.

For example, it's common to have WiFi on some buses and trains today, and the WiFi access point may be using a cellular connection.

W3C first spec

Knowing which type of connection the user has may not be enough—she may be on WiFi under a 2G-connection hotspot or have a nonworking 4G connection.

This original W3C spec is based on the same `navigator.connection` object, but instead of exposing a `type` attribute it exposes `bandwidth` and `metered` attributes.

The bandwidth can be 0 (offline), infinite (unknown), or any estimation in MB/s (megabytes per second); metered is a Boolean attribute indicating that the current connection may be limited by the Internet provider and that we should be careful about bandwidth usage.

Besides the online and offline events, this spec also delivers a new change event over navigator.connection that will trigger a call every time the connection changes.

W3C latest spec

The latest spec, available as a Living Document (*http://w3c.github.io/netinfo*), has changed with time and is the one that is currently supported by Chrome for Android and Firefox.

The spec goes back to the original idea of exposing a connection type within the following options as string values: bluetooth, cellular, ethernet, none, wifi, wimax, mixed, other, and unknown. The spec doesn't differentiate between 2G-, 3G-, or 4G-based connections.

Besides the type, a big change in the latest spec is the ability to detect changes in the connection type, such as changing from WiFi to cellular or vice versa through the typechange event. We can use it as in the following sample:

```
var initialType = 'none';
if ('connection' in navigator) {
    initialType = navigator.connection.type;
    navigator.connection.addEventListener('typechange', function() {
        var newType = navigator.connection.type
    })
}
```

The API has also added a downlinkMax attribute that Chrome supports from version 48. It will tell us in Megabits/second as a double value the upper bound on the downlink speed of the first network hop, so it will give us information about the connection speed, such as LTE, HDSPA, or EDGE.

The value is kind of useless when we have a WiFi or Ethernet connection, as, for example, it will simply tell us if the user is on an 802.11b (11 Mbps) or 802.11n (600 Mbps) network. The data becomes useful when talking about cellular connections, as we can detect which network the user is on.

Some older Firefox or Android Browser versions expose the API through prefixes, such as navigator.mozConnection or navigator.webkitConnection.

Beacon

There are some situations where we want to store stats and information about the current navigation of the user on the server side. Typically, these situations are handled using `XMLHttpRequest`—aka Ajax requests-to guarantee that the server has received the data. The problem appears when we want to track information when browsing out of the current web scope, such as tracking a link to a third-party server.

Typically we track operations after the `unload` event using HTTP redirects or synchronous `XMLHttpRequests` to ensure that the browser will send the request. Both solutions harm performance, spending precious milliseconds just for tracking purposes.

The W3C has been working on a new spec to solve this problem: the Beacon API (*http://www.w3.org/TR/beacon*) will guarantee the developer that the request will be made to the server from the original web page while the browser is working on a different page. The browser will make a POST request as soon as possible without harming performance or delaying the load process of the new resources.

The API exposes a `sendBeacon` method to the `navigator` object receiving the URL and an optional second argument with the data you want to post.

Therefore, typical code will look like:

```
var data; // Optional data

window.addEventListener('unload', function(e) {
    navigator.sendBeacon("track.script", data);
}, false);
```

This code will send a beacon to the server even if the user has closed the tab.

HTTP Client Hints

HTTP Client Hints (*http://httpwg.org/http-extensions/client-hints.html*) is not a browser-based JavaScript API but an extension to the HTTP headers to enable content negotiation between client and server based on hints sent by the browser.

It reduces the usage of the `User-Agent` header with a server-side device library (such as WURFL) for dynamic serving, for example, to decide which image to serve.

Client Hints is available in Chrome from version 46. It defines a list of HTTP headers that the client will send, including:

DPR

The device pixel ratio (i.e., the ratio between CSS and physical pixels)

Width
> The expected resource width in physical pixels

Viewport-Width
> The current layout width in CSS pixels

Downlink
> The client's maximum downlink speed in Mbps, defined by the latest Network Information API as downlinkMax

Save-Data="on"
> A flag asking for reduced data usage due to high costs, slow connections, roaming, or other reasons

The Save-Data flag is available from Chrome 49.

In Chrome, Client Hints is disabled by default. If we want to enable it, we can use the Accept-CH meta tag with the list of attributes we'd like to send to the server:

```
<meta http-equiv="Accept-CH" content="DPR, Viewport-Width, Width">
```

Using these client hints with the addition of the currently standard Accept header, the server can decide which image to return to the client based on image format, image size, DPR, and data saving.

UI APIs

We've been talking about several APIs that will help us improve performance and perception from the network layer. In this section, we will cover APIs available from the user interface layer.

Page Visibility

The Page Visibility API (*http://www.w3.org/TR/page-visibility*) allows us to capture events indicating when our website is being activated or deactivated. With this API, we can check the document.hidden property to see whether the document is actually hidden (true) or visible (false) based on the status of the tab or window.

It also exposes a new event, visibilitychange, that we can use to detect changes in visibility.

The Page Visibility API is currently available in most mobile browsers, including Chrome for Android, Safari on iOS, IE 10+, and Edge. UC Browser for Android and some other Android browsers (not Chrome) make this API available with a prefix. The document.hidden property can be accessed through document.webkitHidden and the event name is webkitvisibilitychange.

When we detect that our website is not active anymore, we can:

- Store state to be restored on the next load, if the browser or website is deleted from memory, improving the experience and performance when the user comes back
- Stop timers and animations
- Pause a game
- Release big resources that could potentially get our website kicked out of memory
- Stop server calls
- Log out the user from the server
- Close sockets or other server connections

Remember that when we detect that the website is not on the screen anymore, we should not update the UI, such as showing a dialog. We can send Ajax requests to the server without any problem that can keep the UI updated.

The following code snippet illustrates use of the Page Visibility API:

```
var eventName = "visibilitychange";
if (document.webkitHidden!=undefined) {
    // webkit prefix detected
    eventName = "webkitvisibilitychange";
}

function visibilityChanged() {
    if (document.hidden || document.webkitHidden) {
        // Our website has just hidden
    } else {
        // Our website is back in the foreground
        // In some situations, the website will load from scratch
    }
}
document.addEventListener(eventName, visibilityChanged, false);
```

With the Page Visibility API, we can stop scripts, timers, and animations that are not visible on the screen. This is particularly useful in older browsers without support for automatic pausing of animations and scripts in the background.

requestAnimationFrame

Timing control for script-based animations (*http://www.w3.org/TR/animation-timing*), also known as animation timing or as the function named requestAnima tionFrame, is a W3C draft specification that allows us to use an animation-optimized timer instead of setInterval or setTimeout.

When using this technique, we don't specify the frequency interval; instead, the browser will determine the best time to update the animation with regard to the current scenario.

That is, the browser specifies the frame rate, and it will pause the animation if it believes the animation should be paused (such as in a background operation). The standard API is simple: we have a global `window.requestAnimationFrame()` function that receives only the function to execute and returns an ID that we can store, to use with `cancelAnimationFrame` as we would with `clearTimeout`. If we want the animation to continue to the next frame, we must call `requestAnimationFrame` in the animation function; therefore, there is no easy way to use this technique with anonymous inline functions.

Figure 5-4 shows what happens in the browser when doing animations in the continuous event loop: we run some tasks in each frame, then the browser renders the UI changes for that frame, and finally there might be an idle time before the next frame.

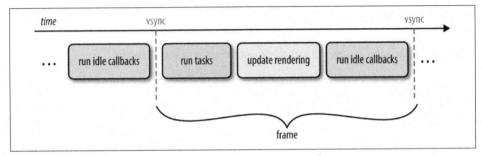

Figure 5-4. Diagram of a frame within a continuous event loop

 `requestAnimationFrame` works in a similar manner as `setTimeout`, not `setInterval`, as it doesn't execute many times automatically.

To start an animation frame, we can use code like this:

```
var animationId = requestAnimationFrame(animate);
function animate() {
    // animate
    if (!endAnimation) {
        requestAnimationFrame(animate);
    }
}
```

And to stop the animation:

```
cancelAnimationFrame(animationId);
```

Fortunately, this API is currently available in most mobile browsers. In terms of performance, using this API is the preferred way to create animations to keep a consistent frame rate.

 Using `requestAnimationFrame` increases our chances of reaching the target of 60 frames per second in animations, one of our performance goals.

The API is sometimes also used to track the first paint event when the browser doesn't support the Navigation Timing API, as the first execution of the `requestAnimationFrame` function will be fired when the rendering time has begun, while `setTimeout` can be fired before that.

requestIdleCallback

Sometimes a web page, web app, or game wants to do something in the middle of an animation or scroll operation. If we use `setTimeout`, `scroll` event handlers, or code in `requestAnimationFrame` to do that, we might be spending precious milliseconds at the wrong time, such as when the browser needs to paint the next frame.

Cooperative Scheduling of Background Task (*https://w3c.github.io/requestidlecallback*), also known as `requestIdleCallback`, is a draft spec that will allow us to execute some time-consuming, non-critical task when the browser has some idle time for it to reduce the probability of dropping frames.

 Operations being executed in an idle callback should not take more than 50 ms to avoid the user detecting a lag. If your code takes more than 50 ms, you should split the task and request an additional idle callback after finishing the first subtask.

The API is pretty simple. We have a window's `requestIdleCallback` function receiving the callback as the argument. The callback will receive an argument that we can use to query on time remaining in the idle loop before the next frame paint:

```
requestIdleCallback(doNonCriticalJob);

function doNonCriticalJob(deadline) {
        var remainingTime = deadline.timeRemaining();

        // If remainingTime==0 we don't have more time,
        // we must schedule a new requestIdleCallback
}
```

Usually you split the task into pending subtasks and you query `dead line.timeRemaining()` on each loop after executing any subtasks. If the remaining time is zero and you still have pending subtasks, then you schedule a new idle callback that will be fired after the next frame is rendered.

This API is still experimental at the time of this writing, and it's available only in Chrome from version 47. The API is something that must be supported by the browser's internals, so it can't be added to a browser without support. However, we do have a shim available (*https://gist.github.com/paullewis/55efe5d6f05434a96c36*) that will emulate the API using `setTimeout`.

When you want to force the browser to execute your callback within a time limit, you can use a second optional argument, setting the deadline in milliseconds for your code to be executed (even if that means that some frames will be dropped):

```
requestIdleCallback(doNonCriticalJob, { timeout: 3000 });
```

 The browser will try to reach 60 fps, executing your `requestAnimationFrame` callback every 16 ms. Afterward, if there is still enough idle time before the next frame, it will execute any pending `requestIdleCallback`.

User Timing

The User Timing API (*http://www.w3.org/TR/user-timing*) defines a way to measure performance of our own code by adding marks before a JavaScript operation on top of the `window.performance` object. To add a mark to the timeline, we should use the `mark` method, which will receive a name as the argument:

```
performance.mark('operation-name');
// Do something here
```

After setting several marks, we can store the duration between two operations using the `measure` function, which receives two names: the name of the first operation and the name of the second operation. As names, we can use a mark's name and any name from the Navigation Timing API, such as `domComplete`, so we can measure time between custom operations and between our operations and the browser's milestones.

Once you have added marks and measures, you can retrieve them by type using `getEntriesByType(mark)` or `getEntriesByType(measure)`. It's also possible to use `getEntriesByName`. These functions return a collection of entries that we can query and get an item's attributes, such as `name` and `duration`:

```
var list = window.performance.getEntriesByType('measure');
for (var i=0; i < list.length(); i++) {
```

```
        console.log(list[i].name + ' took ' + list[i].duration + 'ms.');
    }
```

 The User Timing API can be polyfilled for browsers not supporting it. One polyfill is available at *https://gist.github.com/pmeenan/ 5902672.*

The User Timing API is available in Chrome or Android, Firefox, IE 10+, and Edge. It's not available on Safari up to iOS 9.

Future APIs

Some new APIs that will help us with performance measurement, problem detection, and optimization are coming in the next months and years. These APIs are in early drafts at the time of this writing and they are not implemented yet. However, it's important to review them to get an idea of what abilities we will have in the near future.

Frame Timing

The Frame Timing API (*http://w3c.github.io/frame-timing*) will allow us to measure when the browser is not reaching a target frame rate (such as 60 fps) so we can identify such cases and tweak them to improve the perception of responsiveness.

The API will look like the following code:

```
// subscribe to Frame Timing notifications for slow frames
var observer = new PerformanceObserver(function(list) {
    var perfEntries = list.getEntries();
    for (var i = 0; i < perfEntries.length; i++) {
        console.log("Slow frame: ", perfEntries[i]);
    }
});
observer.observe({entryTypes: ['frame']});
```

With this script, we will be able to log when we don't achieve our FPS goal and then act in consequence, probably profiling what's happening there and hopefully finding a solution to the bottleneck.

Script Timing API

The Script Timing API (*https://w3c.github.io/server-timing*) allows the server to send metadata on performance metrics about the HTTP request/response cycle through HTTP headers.

These metrics will be collected by the compatible browser and exposed through the JavaScript Performance Timeline API.

Performance Timeline

The Performance Timeline API (*http://www.w3.org/TR/performance-timeline*) is a unified specification to retrieve performance information from different APIs. A second version (*https://www.w3.org/TR/performance-timeline-2*) of the API is also a work in progress: it adds a performance observer interface that we can use to get performance metrics as they are available.

Through `getEntries` or `getEntriesByType`, we can get performance measurement entries available from different types, such as:

mark
> Marks coming from the User Timing API

measure
> Measures coming from the User Timing API

navigation
> Browser milestones coming from the Navigation Timing API

frame
> Animation frame measures coming from the Frame Timing API

resource
> Information coming from the Resource Timing API

server
> Measures coming from the Server Timing API

At the time of this writing, support for this API is based on which other APIs are supported, such as the User Timing API.

> The W3C Web Performance Working Group has published a document for a Network Error Logging Spec (*http://www.w3.org/TR/network-error-logging*) that will allow an origin to capture network errors and customize the user experience after that.

Efficient Script Yielding

Efficient Script Yielding (*https://dvcs.w3.org/hg/webperf/raw-file/tip/specs/setImmediate/Overview.html*), also known as `setImmediate`, is an API proposed by Microsoft that allows scripts to be executed immediately after the browser has finished doing rendering operations in a more efficient way than `setTimeout(func, 0)`. The API is available only on Microsoft IE 10+ and Edge, but there are several polyfills available, including the one at *https://github.com/YuzuJS/setImmediate*.

`setImmediate` usage is similar to `setTimeout`, including the ability to clear a pending execution using `clearImmediate(id)`, as in:

```
var idImm = setImmediate(function() {
        // Code to execute ASAP after the browser has finished some UI tasks
});

clearImmediate(idImm);
```

Using Specs and APIs in Your Favor

Modern browsers include several new APIs that will let us measure performance to make decisions on the fly, and/or solve critical performance issues interfering with the browser's rendering flow.

We have covered:

- APIs to measure performance, such as Navigation Timing and Resource Timing
- Events and APIs for the network layer, such as the Network Information and Beacon APIs
- The new HTTP Client Hints spec
- APIs that can help with the user experience, such as Page Visibility and `requestAnimationFrame`
- Future APIs that will appear in the next few years

We always need to verify whether the API is available before using it, and see if it can be polyfilled somehow if not.

In Chapter 6, we will start analyzing how we can optimize the performance of our website during the first load, using the most common techniques.

Optimizing for the First Visit

The first visit to our website is one of most important ones in terms of performance and the conversion impact of it. The user has just typed a URL, clicked on a search result at Google, or seen an interesting tweet with a related link and she is expecting our content as soon as possible.

Failing in delivering the fastest experience at the first visit can lead to fewer conversions and more people just leaving our websites forever. We know we don't want that, and that's why we are now going to cover the basics of optimizing web content for the first visit.

In this chapter, we'll focus on the main techniques that will increase performance—and the perception of it—with normal effort, such as setting up our server and understanding how the CSS and JavaScript load and block rendering.

I'm saying this because in Chapter 10 we will enter into the extreme side of web performance optimization, leading to faster websites and more conversions but with bigger efforts in terms of implementation—techniques such as using new compression algorithms or separating out the above-the-fold content while inlining everything to fit in one TCP packet.

The HTTP Side

HTTP—and HTTPS, its secure counterpart—is the protocol we are going to use by default for the initial load process when working with websites and web apps. This section is useless when talking about hybrid apps, as the initial loading of these will be based on a local filesystem, as we will cover later in the book.

In this section, we will cover some server configuration tips that we can use to improve performance. You should have some experience working with server configuration (e.g., for Apache or IIS), as well as having permission to do so in your company.

If you don't have access, you can always request that the server administrator add these settings, or in the case of shared hosting services, ask the support staff or check in the web configuration panels.

We will cover some basic configuration steps for Apache, IIS, and Express.js for Node.js. If you are using a different web server, you will find instructions in the documentation.

HTTP Version

As a review, here are the HTTP versions that we have available today:

- HTTP/1.0, published in 1996 and still compatible with all the web browsers out there on mobile devices.
- HTTP/1.1, published in 1999. This is the most-used version on the web today.
- HTTP/2, published in early 2015. Based on SPDY and backward compatible with HTTP/1.1, this is the recommended version to use from now on.

 SPDY was a nonofficial open protocol based on HTTP/1.1 packages created by Google in 2012 and then used by many other providers to improve performance. It was the heart of HTTP/2 and is completely deprecated now.

There is no real reason to still serve websites using HTTP/1.0 by default for a mobile device today. A decade ago, some mobile browsers (in the pre-iPhone era) only supported 1.0, but today your server should support 1.1 if not 2.0 yet.

HTTP/1.0 was much simpler. In this version of the protocol, the body is always plain and uncompressed and the TCP connection is always closed after sending the response, meaning that if the browser then needs to download more files to render the page it will need to start a new TCP connection to the server for that (involving several TCP packets being sent back and forth).

HTTP/1.1 added several features that positively impacted the performance of your initial loading performance including the abilities to compress the response's body and to keep the connection alive while waiting for more requests (usually stylesheets, scripts, or images).

While HTTP/1.1 is probably the most common option and every browser out there will support it, there are some proxies that might downgrade the request to 1.0, so we should always have the option to support it. Optionally serving HTTP/2 today is also starting to be a good idea since most modern browsers support it.

Testing version support

To verify the version of your website, just make a cURL connection from the console to it asking for headers:

```
curl --head www.mobilexweb.com
```

By default, cURL will try to make an HTTP/1.1 connection (in the latest versions). You can check the first line of the server's response to verify that:

```
HTTP/1.1 200 OK
Date: Tue, 16 Dec 2014 21:58:16 GMT
Server: Apache
X-Pingback: http://www.mobilexweb.com/xmlrpc.php
Vary: Accept-Encoding
Content-Type: text/html; charset=UTF-8
```

If the first line says HTTP/1.0, it means you don't have the right configuration or you are browsing through a proxy that is downgrading your connections.

---

cURL: The Quickest Tool to Debug HTTP Connections

cURL is an open source project available for different platforms that helps us make requests using different protocols, including HTTP and HTTPS, from the console.

It's available by default on macOS and Linux. For Windows it can be installed from the official website (*http://curl.haxx.se/dlwiz*), and it's also included in Cygwin and Git PowerShell.

There are also some online solutions available to use it quickly, such as *http://online curl.com*.

If you want to make request in SPDY, there is another project called gURL available at *https://github.com/mtourne/gurl*.

You can also force cURL to use one specific version using the following commands:

```
curl --http1.0 www.mobilexweb.com
curl --http1.1 www.mobilexweb.com
curl --http2 www.mobilexweb.com
```

Configuring HTTP/1.1

If you are running your server through Apache, you probably have support for 1.1. What you can define is the keep-alive timeout, the time that the server will wait for more requests before closing the connection.

You can then set the `KeepAlive` and `KeepAliveTimeout` properties in Apache's configuration both at the server's level (*httpd.conf* file) and at the virtual host's level.

For example:

```
KeepAlive On
KeepAliveTimeout 150
```

On Internet Information Server, you can define these properties from the IIS Manager, as you can see in Figure 6-1.

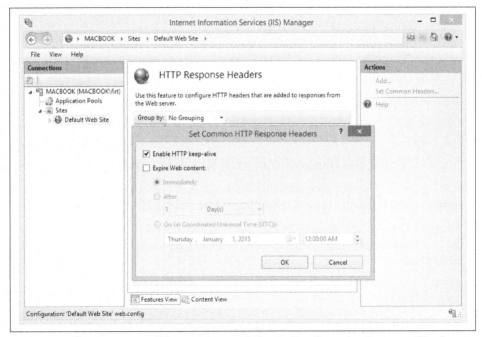

Figure 6-1. If you are using IIS, you can enable keep-alive from the Common Headers dialog inside HTTP Response Headers. The timeout can be specified in web.config or in Advanced Settings.

If you are using Node.js and Express for your server, then keep-alive will be enabled by default.

Adding support for HTTP/2

HTTP/2 is the current major release and it includes several improvements for performance, such as:

- Multiplexed support (one single TCP connection for all requests)
- Header compression
- Server push (the responses—which usually go to the cache—to the client without waiting for an explicit request)

There's a wiki that tracks HTTP/2 server implementations (*https://github.com/http2/http2-spec/wiki/Implementations*); these include IIS on Windows 10/Server 2016 and Apache from version 2.4.12 through the `mod_h2` module.

A Node.js implementation of HTTP/2 is available at *https://github.com/molnarg/node-http2*, following the standard Node HTTPS API with the addition of server push. Nginx also has support for HTTP/2 since version 1.9.5, and some cloud-based solutions (such as Google App Engine) and CDNs (such as Akamai and CloudFare) are now offering HTTP/2 support.

> Every browser supporting HTTP/2 does it only over TLS (a secure connection). Therefore, adding support for HTTP/2 on your website involves the decision of moving the content to HTTPS, which is a good idea anyway.

Compression

HTTP/1.1 supports data compression, meaning that the browser will compress the file before sending it and the client must decompress it before rendering it. That means that for text-based files we can save up to 70% of the data transferred, and we know that cellular connections are not reliable or fast, so saving data is a must.

Today, every mobile browser out there supports the compression method, so make sure to leave it enabled. Fortunately, with current devices—even social phones—there are no great drawbacks to decompressing a file on the client side.

> While there are some proxies and routers that might disable the compression method, most web servers will manage this automatically for us. Therefore, it's safe to enable compression on text-based files.

The two common compression methods available are *deflate* and *gzip*. The *gzip* method includes a checksum for error checking that requires more CPU power both server- and client-side. However, *gzip* is the recommended method on today's servers and clients. Servers can be smart enough to precompress and cache hundreds of static files without the need of doing it per request. Dynamically generated files will need a compression operation after the server finishes the response.

 Google has open sourced Zopfli (*https://code.google.com/p/zopfli*), a compression library that can replace the compression algorithm while still using *deflate*, *zlib*, or *gzip*. It has better compression results (around 3%–8%) but is much slower (up to 80x), so it's preferred for static content that can be precompressed before serving. The decompression time is not altered and all browsers will be compatible with it.

HTTP/2 also adds a compression algorithm to the headers that is always on, so there is nothing to set up there.

Brotli compression algorithm

In 2015, Google open sourced a new compression algorithm that can achieve a compression rate up to 25% greater than *gzip* for text-based files, such as HTML, CSS, or JavaScript. It was cowritten by Jyrki Alakuijala (also the inventor of Zopfli) and named Brotli.

From Chrome 50 and Firefox 44, Brotli is supported as an additional compression algorithm to *gzip* and *deflate* using the name `br`. Therefore, if the `Accept-Encoding` HTTP request's header includes `br`, we can safely answer from the server with a Brotli-compressed body, saving up to 25% of the data transferred to the client.

For example, this is the header Firefox is using in HTTP requests today:

```
Accept-Encoding: gzip, deflate, br
```

Facebook has done reseach on Brotli and found it saves about 17% of CSS bytes and 20% of JavaScript bytes compared with *gzip* using Zopfli.

At the time of this writing, no Apache modules or plug-ins for other web servers are available to automate Brotli compression.

 Chrome supports Brotli-compressed responses only when served over HTTPS. This is due to old proxies that are online on the Internet that will not understand the new compression method and will mess with your response. Using a secure tunnel with TLS, those proxies won't see what's inside.

SDCH compression algorithm

Google supports Shared Dictionary Compression for HTTP (SDCH) in Chrome for Android based on VCDIFF (*https://tools.ietf.org/html/rfc3284*). SDCH achieves compression based on a dictionary that is negotiated before the data is sent that "warms up" the internal state before decoding. The algorithm's efficiency relies on having a lot of content that can take advantage of a shared dictionary after a traffic analysis. Its implementation is not simple, but some companies, including Google and LinkedIn, are using it when the encoding is present.

Files to compress

While always compressing files server-side may seem like a good idea, this might not be the case for every kind of file. All the text-based files involved in a website or web app should be compressed, including HTML, CSS, JavaScript, JSON, SVG, and XML. In term of images, only icons (*.ico* files) and the old *.bmp* format that nobody uses on the web any more are worth compressing.

Some mobile browsers today use the website's icon (usually known as a favicon) for the window's icon or for other UI purposes. Most websites use the old *.ico* format for it. Based on HTTP Archive (*http://httparchive.org*) data, an *.ico* file has an average size of 5 KB uncompressed, and compressing it cuts that size in half.

However, have you ever zipped a ZIP file? Once the file is already compressed, you will probably not save any space by doing this. The same is true of binary files that are already using some compression algorithms, including image files, PDFs, and audio files.

In the case of font files (*.ttf, .eot, .otf*), while being mostly binary files they can usually take advantage of a *gzip* on top, so you can compress them. The only exception is Web Open Font Format (*.woff* files), which are already compressed.

Compressing very small files (let's say smaller than 800 bytes) won't make too much difference, and in some cases (smaller than 150 bytes) will lead to a bigger transfer with the compression/decompression time. And when talking about small files that fit into a TCP packet, there is not much difference in having these compressed.

Table 6-1 shows you the file formats that should be compressed.

Table 6-1. File formats for compression in HTTP/1.1 and HTTP/2

File format	Extensions	MIME types
HTML	*.html, .htm*	`text/html`
XML	*.xml*	`text/xml`
Text	*.txt*	`text/plain, text/text`
CSS	*.css*	`text/css`
JavaScript	*.js*	`text/javascript, application/javascript, application/x-javascript`
JSON	*.json, .js*	`application/json`
EOT (uncompressed)	*.eot*	`application/vnd.ms-fontobject, font/eot`
Open Font	*.otf*	`application/x-font-opentype, font/opentype, font/otf`
True Type Font	*.ttf*	`application/x-font-truetype, application/x-font-ttf`
SVG	*.svg*	`image/svg+xml`
Icon file	*.ico*	`image/vnd.microsoft.icon`

Enabling compression

On Apache 2.x, you can set the compression through the `mod_deflate` extension. While the name says "deflate," it's actually using *gzip*; you can set the compression enabled based on the MIME type (the file format) using the following configuration declaration at the server level (*httpd.conf*) or at a folder level (*.htaccess* file):

```
AddOutputFilterByType DEFLATE text/html text/plain text/xml text/css text/java-
script application/javascript application/json image/svg+xml
```

 Setting compression by MIME type (using the `Content-Type` header used in the response) is better than by file extension (such as *.html*, *.css*) because when working with dynamic scripts (such as Python, PHP, or .NET) the response is being generated by a script and not by a static file. The MIME type will always be there, both when a static file is being served and when a dynamic script is generating it.

There are also other independent extensions available for Apache that you can install and use.

On IIS, you can use the user interface of the IIS Manager to get into the Features View, where you will find the Compression option. There, you will be able to set up the content compression for both static files and dynamic content, as you can see in Figure 6-2.

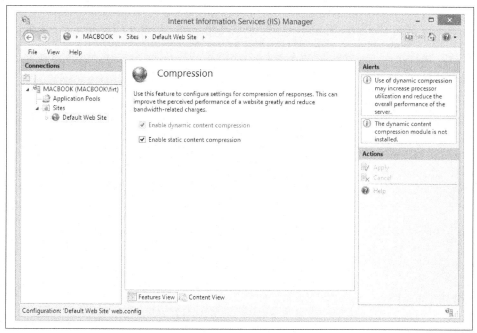

Figure 6-2. On Windows, you can use IIS Manager to enable compression

If you are using Node.js and Express for your web server, you can use the compression module as described at *https://github.com/expressjs/compression*.

While not always useful, you can enable compression at the application level instead of the server level. For example, on PHP you can manage compression for the output with the `ob_gzhandler` function, for example executing this as the first line:

```
ob_start("ob_gzhandler");
```

Redirections

Let me tell you a short story. Let's say you want to access an airline's website, and you type *megaairlines.com* (a fake URL) into your mobile browser's address bar using your tiny onscreen keyboard. The browser first will need to make a DNS request to get the IP address; when it's done, it opens the TCP connection and sends a GET HTTP request. Then the server says: "Oh, no, it's not here; you need to add *www* as a prefix." So your browser does that. It then makes another DNS request for *www.megaairlines.com* and again opens the TCP connection and sends the first HTTP request. Then your browser says: "Oh, you didn't tell me which page you want to see. Maybe you want to go to the */HomePage.*"

Geting tired at this point, the browser makes a new HTTP request to *www.megaair-lines.com* (thankfully we already have the IP address) asking for the resource */Home-Page*. And then, your worst nightmare happens: the server realizes that you are on a mobile device and not on a desktop and it says, "Oh, I'm sorry you arrived here, because you need to go to *m.megaairlines.com.*"

If you are still there, the browser (thirsty and hungry at this point) will make another DNS request to *m.megaairlines.com* and send the TCP packets and the HTTP request. Finally, the server says, "Oh, you didn't tell me which page you want to see. I guess you might want to go to the */HomePage.*" I'm glad that artificial intelligence hasn't arrived for browsers yet, because at this point it would probably want to kill itself. One more TCP connection and HTTP request and finally, finally, you've received your main HTML file for the airline (without CSS, JavaScript, or images, of course).

Are you tired of reading this? Well, the same happens with the performance of your mobile website when you do this. And believe me, this is based on a real example, and my story was even worse (I won't tell you which major airline is doing it).

The real example

Let's review the case when you access the website from a mobile phone:

```
1- megaairlines.com
2- www.megaairlines.com
3- www.megaairlines.com/HomePage
4- m.megaairlines.com
5- m.megaairlines.com/HomePage
```

So, in this case there were four redirects, or HTTP responses that say to the browser that "the resource is not here" (temporarily or definitely), so it should load it from somewhere else.

Every redirect will take from 100 ms in the best case to 1 full second in the worst case. So, in this example, you might see a white screen for up to 5 whole seconds. This is the worst nightmare for mobile performance, as you can see in Figure 6-3.

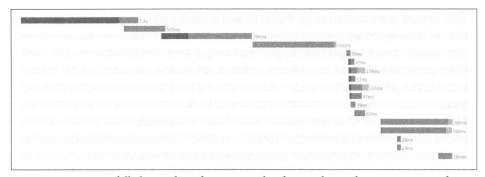

Figure 6-3. A waterfall chart when doing several redirects shows the impact on performance request is delayed with no real advantage for the user. In this example, around 2.5 seconds were wasted on redirects.

Doing too much harm

HTTP redirects will harm your performance, so you need to reduce them to the minimum, zero redirects being the goal.

Sometimes we make redirects because we have different physical servers for the mobile version, sometimes because we didn't realize this was happening, sometimes because of a misconfigured web server. The reality is that today there is no unavoidable reason to have HTTP redirects for the initial view.

Even if you have a weird architecture, you can always add a server-side layer that will make the translation for the user, hiding the real architecture. And you need to count seconds like gold bars here, so avoiding redirects is a must.

I've heard some SEO experts saying that when you have a mobile version you must have a different domain (such as *m.**). That's totally false; there is nothing wrong serving different HTML versions from the same URL based on the user agent (the device) when you are talking about the same basic content. This has been officially confirmed by Google (*http://bit.ly/choose-your-mobile-configuration*).

Even if you still want to have a separate domain, you can reduce the problem for the first load (e.g., the home page or the landing page). That is, the home page can be served from the main domain, and all the links from that point will go to the mobile-specific domain. At least you'll serve the home page (initial view) as fast as possible, and keep your user engaged with your website.

> If you can't avoid having redirects, at least reduce them to just one, having all the logic for getting to the final URL in one place.

To make things more complicated for us, there are now one or two redirects on a big number of requests coming to our websites that we can't manage or reduce: these are due to social networks and URL shorteners.

I'm sure you have seen URLs starting with *g.co*, *t.co*, *bit.ly*, *tinyurl.com*, and the like. These services are basically HTTP redirects that we can't manage, and they will add up to a 1-second delay on a mobile device when used.

When you share a link on Facebook, for example, and the user clicks on it, it will also go through a Facebook redirect for stats purposes.

An HTTP redirect will necessitate at least one HTTP request, in some situations a new TCP connection, and in others a DNS lookup. And we already know that latency on each request on mobile connections can be up to 1 second in the worst scenarios and around 200 ms on average. Therefore, you should avoid HTTP redirects at all costs.

HSTS: Opt-in for HTTPS

When you type a URL for the first time in your browser's address bar, you don't usually add the protocol. That is, you don't type *http://*; you just type *domain.com*. So what happens when a user does this if you are serving your website through HTTPS only (as you should be)? Your server responds with a 301 HTTP response redirecting the browser to the TLS version, wasting time with a redirection. The 301 response can be cached, but it won't be there if the cache is cleared, and that redirect will happen again the next time.

To reduce these redirects, we have HTTP Strict Transport Security (HSTS) (*https://tools.ietf.org/html/rfc6797*). It's a way to say to the browser, "I will never support non-secure connections in this domain, so from now on always go to HTTPS." To do that, our first 301 redirect must return an HTTP header asking the browser to move to HTTPS from now on. The header is `Strict-Transport-Security`, usually defining a `max-age` and two Boolean tokens: `preload` and `includeSubdomains`.

So the response will look like:

```
HTTP/1.1 301 Moved Permanently
Content-Length: 0
Location: https://myhost/
Strict-Transport-Security: max-age: 30000000; includeSubdomains; preload
```

When you define that HTTPS will be your only protocol, some browsers will reject HTTP even when forced by the user, returning a 307 (Internal Redirect) HTTP code.

HSTS is available in Chrome, Android Browser, Safari, Opera, Firefox, IE, and Edge, so it has good support on mobile devices.

But we still have a problem. What happens the first time the user accesses our website? The browser won't have received the HSTS header to know it should try first with HTTPS, so we will still have the redirect, wasting up to 1 second on 2G connections. That's why some browsers allow whitelisting your host in the browser itself if you follow some rules. For example, if you want to be included in a future version of Chrome, you can register your domain at *https://hstspreload.appspot.com*.

App (Spam) Banner

If we think of HTTP redirects as "Slow down" signs, an app banner is a "Stop" sign. An app banner is a splash screen that acts as interstitial HTML before the HTML the user was expecting from your server. These banners usually are promoting native apps from your company, typically saying that the native apps offer a better experience (see Figure 6-4).

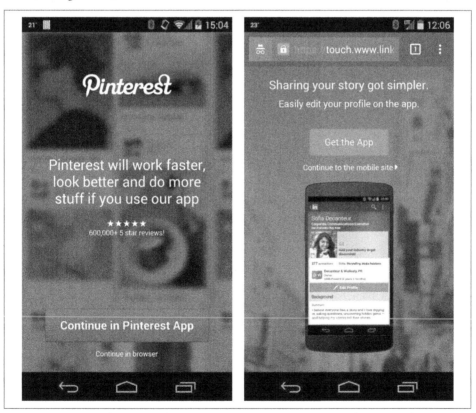

Figure 6-4. An app banner will stop the user from accessing the information she was expecting, adding frustration to the user experience and hindering the site's performance

I like to call them app spam banners; it's spam because the user didn't request it and you are stopping her from seeing the content she wants to see. Many big companies are using this technique without realizing how badly they are harming performance.

Why are we harming performance? We need to remember that from a user's point of view, performance isn't just about the page load time. It's about the perception of the whole loading process. Therefore, if you first load a big image banner and wait for the user to process what you are asking her to do and click the (usually small) link saying "Continue to the website," the final experience in terms of performance is terrible.

When you add an app banner as a full-page first response, you are pushing up the page load time by up to 5 seconds.

The experience is even worse when you are adding this on your home page or the entry point to your website (from a search engine's search results, for example). Think about this: you have just typed a URL for the first time, or clicked on a search result, and the first thing you receive from the website is a banner asking you to install an app. You don't know who the company is, you don't trust them yet, so why are you going to install their app? If you are brave enough, you will find the small "Continue to the website" link. If not, you will probably press the safe Back button and continue with another website.

Google did a case study on app download interstitials (*http://googlewebmastercen tral.blogspot.com.ar/2015/07/google-case-study-on-app-download-interstitials.html*) with strong conclusions: only 9% of the users actually clicked on the "Get the app" button, and 69% of the users abandoned the page at that point. 69%! That only emphasizes what I was saying before.

Google (*http://bit.ly/using-app-banners*) has stated that "After November 1 [2015], mobile web pages that show an app install interstitial that hides a significant amount of content on the transition from the search result page will no longer be considered mobile-friendly."

Promoting your app smartly

There are two ways to promote your app without affecting the first visit performance and, therefore, the first impression: patience and platform tools.

By patience, I mean wait for the user to trust you before promoting your app. A great example today is TripAdvisor.com. TripAdvisor provides thousands of reviews of hotels, restaurants, and tourist sites around the world. Any time you search for a hotel or restaurant review in any city in the world, you will probably end up on a TripAdvisor search result. When you access it from a mobile browser, you won't see any app banner until you've browsed to at least five different pages inside the site. If you've visited several pages, it means that you are finding the website useful and you are starting to trust it, so getting an app banner at this point (see Figure 6-5) won't harm the experience like it might if it were located at the first entry point.

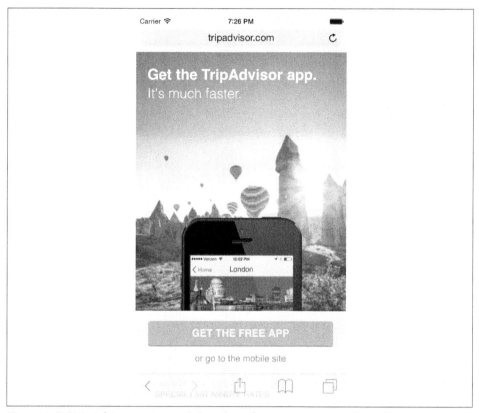

Figure 6-5. TripAdvisor waits until there have been a certain number of page views in the session before giving you an app banner, which improves the general perception of performance. Also, the app banner is not an interstitial page and it's included dynamically on the expected page, so closing it will just hide it, not making another request.

The other solution is to use platform tools. At the time of this writing, Safari on iOS, Chrome for Android, and Internet Explorer for Windows allow you to set some meta tags to promote your native app on your website. Instead of stopping the user from seeing the requested content, you can promote the native app in a nonblocking way (as seen in Figure 6-6).

Figure 6-6. With Safari on iOS, you can use a Smart app banner that will suggest your native app in a nonintrusive way

iOS Smart App Banner

To define a Smart App Banner in an HTML document, you use a meta tag called `apple-itunes-app` with a few declarations, including:

app-id
  The App Store's ID for your app

app-argument
  A string—typically a URL—providing current context to the native app

affiliate-data
  Your publisher ID when you are registered as an affiliate to receive commissions from iTunes and App Store sales

To make it work, the app you want to link to needs to already be approved on the Apple App Store. Then, you can go the iTunes Link Maker (*http://link maker.itunes.apple.com*) to retrieve the application ID you need to use in the meta tag. The ID is a nine-digit numeric value; to find it, search for your app by name in the Link Maker and extract the number from the URL, as seen in Figure 6-7.

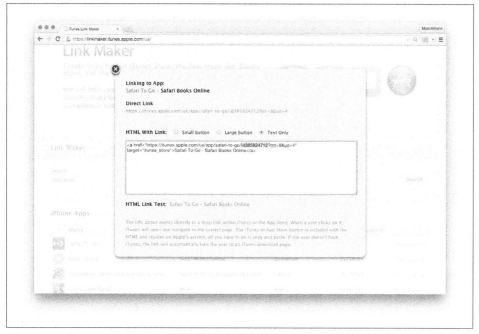

Figure 6-7. To get the app ID for the Smart App Banner, you need to make a search on iTunes Link Maker and copy the ID from the link

For example, to create a Smart App Banner for the app available for the iOS version of another of my books, we would use the following code:

```
<meta name="apple-itunes-app" content="app-id=393555188">
```

We can also send arguments (such as the current article or element) to the native apps through an `app-argument` inside the content.

Advanced tips for connecting your website to your native app are out of the scope of this book. You can learn more from the official docs of every browser or from my other book, *Programming the Mobile Web* (*http://firt.mobi/pmw*).

Windows Store apps

If you have a Windows Store app (from Windows 8 and Windows Phone 8.1), you can connect your website to it with some meta tags too without harming the initial loading performance.

The two basics meta tags you need to define are msApplication-id, with the identifier defined in the app's manifest file, and msApplication-PackageFamilyName, with the identifier created by Visual Studio to identify the app.

To get more detailed information, visit the official documentation (*http://msdn.micro soft.com/en-us/library/ie/hh781489%28v=vs.85%29.aspx*).

 You can also link your Windows app to Bing's search results, following the App Linking (*http://www.bing.com/dev/applink*) guide.

Android solutions

A similar solution known as Native App install banners (*https://develop ers.google.com/web/updates/2015/03/increasing-engagement-with-app-install-banners-in-chrome-for-android#native*) is available from Chrome 44 for Android. It works only over HTTPS with a manifest JSON file attached. With this manifest file defined, if a user accesses your website twice in the course of two weeks, he will see the invitation to install the app.

You can also use App Indexing for Google's search results (*https://develop ers.google.com/app-indexing*). If you apply this, when the user is making a search and your website has a companion app, Google will promote it directly in the search engine, as you can see in Figure 6-8.

Figure 6-8. If you have an Android native app, you can use App Indexing for Google's search results. In this case, for Wikipedia, you can open the native app directly.

App Links

Finally, if you have a native app and you prefer your users to go there instead of to the website, you can follow the open protocol App Links (*http://applinks.org*) promoted by Facebook and used by other apps as well. If you set some meta tags on your website, compatible native apps (such as Facebook and Pinterest) will use them when your users share your content. Therefore, if a user is sharing a URL from your website, and another user is seeing it from a mobile device, these apps will try to honor your native link instead of the web link, opening your native app instead of the website or inviting the user to download your app.

You can find all the meta tags in the App Links documentation (*http://applinks.org/ documentation*), but if you have your native app's IDs from the stores, this is what your meta tags will look like:

```
<meta property="al:ios:url" content="myapp://">
<meta property="al:ios:app_store_id" content="1234567">
<meta property="al:ios:app_name" content="My native app">
<meta property="al:android:url" content="myapp://">
<meta property="al:android:app_name" content="My native app">
```

```
<meta property="al:android:package" content="com.mobilexweb.myapp">
<meta property="al:windows_phone:url" content="myapp://">
<meta property="al:windows_phone:app_id" content="appid-from-store">
<meta property="al:windows_phone:app_name" content="My native app">
```

 For App Links to work, you need to set custom URI handlers (intent filters on Android) that will allow any app to open your app using a custom URI, such as *myapp://*.

Reducing Requests

As we saw in Chapter 3, every request on a mobile website has a cost, involving optional DNS lookups, TCP packets, and HTTP headers being sent over unreliable and high-latency connections. Also bear in mind that browsers will have a maximum number of parallel requests that can be made—usually six per host on HTTP/1.1-, delaying the loading of other resources until some network channels are freed up.

Therefore, we should reduce requests as much as we can, with one request being the best solution, but as you might expect, this is not always possible. We will get into extreme cases in the following chapters, so for now, let's just try to reduce requests to the minimum and use some tricks to reduce their impact.

 When using HTTP/2 to serve web content, the cost of every request is not so high, as they are being multiplexed on the same TCP connection and their headers will be transferred compressed. Therefore, the tips in this section might not be so useful on HTTP/2, but they are really important while serving over HTTP/ 1.1.

While in the following pages we'll cover techniques for reducing requests for CSS, JavaScript, and images, let's first focus on reducing the impact of requests on the final loading experience.

Domain Sharding

I've already mentioned that most mobile browsers will download up to six resources at the same time from the same host. Therefore, if your website needs 18 external resources, the download will be done in steps.

What happens if you split the resources across two or three different hosts? The browser's limits are per-host, not per-IP address or per-server; therefore, it will be able to download 12 or 18 resources at the same time.

This trick is known as *domain sharding*, and it has the ability to positively impact the final web performance when you're working with more than 15 resources and using two or three different domains in HTTP/1.1. Using more than three domains usually harms performance, and domain sharding isn't necessary (and, in fact, can be harmful) when your website uses just a few external resources.

You are still using the same network and in some situations the same server to get the files from, so there is a limit to the effectiveness of this trick.

The impact of domain sharding will depend on the website, but as a general rule, let's say that if you have more than 20 resources currently being downloaded from the same host and you are using HTTP/1.x, domain sharding will improve your final performance.

The easiest way to implement domain sharding is to determine after measuring performance which resources are being queued because of the parallel download limit and move them to a different host. The new host can be a real new server or just a DNS alias (CNAME in DNS) to the same web server; for example, *mydomain.com* can have an alias such as *resources.mydomain.com* or *r1.mydomain.com* and *r2.mydomain.com*.

As an example, if you have the following resources on *mydomain.com*:

```
<img src="images/img1.png">
<img src="images/img2.png">
<img src="images/img3.png">
<img src="images/img4.png">
<img src="images/img5.png">
<img src="images/img6.png">
<img src="images/img7.png">
<img src="images/img8.png">
<img src="images/img9.png">
<img src="images/img10.png">
<img src="images/img11.png">
<img src="images/img12.png">
```

You can optimize fetching them using:

```
<img src="images/img1.png">
<img src="images/img2.png">
<img src="images/img3.png">
<img src="images/img4.png">
<img src="images/img5.png">
<img src="images/img6.png">
<img src="http://r1.mydomain.com/images/img7.png">
<img src="http://r1.mydomain.com/images/img8.png">
<img src="http://r1.mydomain.com/images/img9.png">
<img src="http://r1.mydomain.com/images/img10.png">
<img src="http://r1.mydomain.com/images/img11.png">
<img src="http://r1.mydomain.com/images/img12.png">
```

In Figure 6-9, you can see the differences in performance based on the waterfall charts.

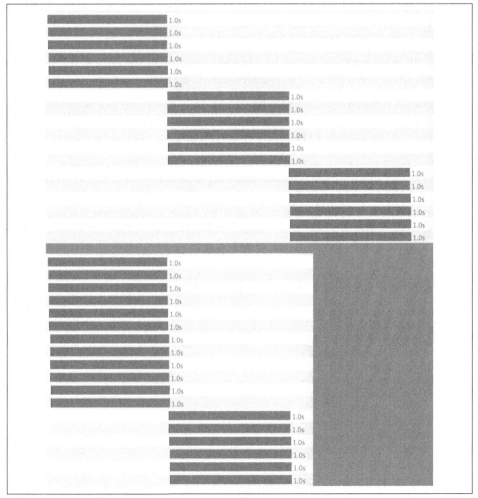

Figure 6-9. In this case, we see a waterfall chart without domain sharding (top) and the same website with domain sharding (bottom)

It's easy to think that we can shard resources across *n* domains then. However, tests show that sharding resources in just two domains will bring the best performance. Remember that the browser doesn't care about the final IP address, so if the two domains are being resolved to the same IP address, the trick will work anyway.

You may say that our new solution has bigger HTML, but remember we are compressing our HTML with *gzip*, and the compression algorithm will take care of the repetitions. Therefore, the bigger HTML is likely to have a very low impact on the size of the final compressed response through HTTP.

 The domain sharding technique might be an antipattern (bad practice) when moving to HTTP/2, because you will be reusing the same TCP connection there for every request. However, you can still use it if two conditions are met: (a) the domain names must resolve to the same IP address; and (b) your SSL certificate must have a wildcard for all the domains used, or you must be using a multidomain certificate. In these cases, HTTP/2 will still reuse the same connection even on different domains, and you will have the advantages of sharding on HTTP/1.1.

Cookieless Domains

When you set a cookie from the client or the server, every request in the future to the same domain will send the cookie's data again. *Every request.* Therefore, if you have 30 external requests, you will duplicate in the cookie's data in the upload streaming over the cellular connection 30 times, in some cases.

Cookies can have a size of 50 to 4,093 bytes based on what you are storing. A few years ago, the Yahoo! team did some research on cookie sizes and response times (over a desktop DSL connection) and found that, for example, a 1 KB cookie can have an impact of around 100 ms (per request with the cookie) and a 3 KB cookie can impact 150 ms. Bandwidth on mobile networks might differ, but on average the impact will be greater than this.

Therefore, reducing cookies is a good idea, mostly because they are being transferred on each request to the same server, even if we are not really using them (such as when requesting images).

To solve the problem, we can:

- Reduce and/or compress cookies to the minimum
- Store the data server-side and use cookies to identify the record only
- Use cookie-less domains

Let's get deeper into the last option. If your additional resources are being served from a different domain than your HTML, then the browser won't send the cookies. Therefore, a *cookieless domain* is another host—it can be an CNAME DNS alias to the same server—that will be used for linking external files.

Let's see a small example from *mydomain.com* with cookies:

```
<link rel="stylesheet" href="styles.css">
<script src="script.js"></script>
<img src="logo.png">
```

If our domain is setting a 1 KB cookie from the server, then the browser will upload that cookie three times to the server per request (with a potential time penalty of more than 300 ms). More importantly, we are not going to use that cookie server-side when requesting CSS, JavaScript, or images.

Therefore, we can separate our resources onto another host (let's say *r.mydomain.com*, with *r* for *resources*):

```
<link rel="stylesheet" href="http://r.mydomain.com/styles.css">
<script src="http://r.mydomain.com/script.js"></script>
<img src="http://r.mydomain.com/logo.png">
```

The host *r.mydomain.com* can be the same server or a different one, but we set it up to not use any cookies at all.

When using a cookieless domain, we can also take advantage of domain sharding, as we are using a separate host from the one serving the main HTML document.

Freeing Up Our Server

In some situations, we can also use a different server for serving static files to free up our main server, which may be responsible for database access and scripting.

Using this technique can also help us when working with cookieless domains and domain sharding.

We can do this in two ways:

- Using a light server for static files
- Using a CDN

A light server is usually a simple HTTP server, such as lighttpd (*http://www.lighttpd.net*).

A CDN, or content delivery network, is a service provided by a company that will serve static files for us.

The advantages of using a CDN are:

- Great infrastructure and bandwidth
- High availability
- Mirrors located near the user, reducing latency (although this is not as useful on mobile network as on desktop connections)
- Automatic HTTP performant features with some providers, such as compression and caching
- HTTP/2 support from the CDN to the client while still using HTTP/1.1 on your server

CDNs are typically commercial, with providers including companies such as Akamai, Amazon, and CloudFare, but they often also offer free plans with limited capabilities.

HTML

We've already optimized the server to serve the initial HTML as fast as possible, compressed and with a keep-alive HTTP/1.1 connection.

Now let's see what can we do from the HTML side and the delivery of it to improve the initial loading performance.

Semantic Web

The first thing I have to say here is: try to create simple, semantic, easy-to-read HTML code. I'm sure at this point I don't need to even remind you that you shouldn't lay out your HTML using tables, but the new `<table>` is the abuse of +<div>+s and containers.

If you keep your HTML clean and semantic, using the new HTML5 elements available when possible, it will be fast in transmission through the network, fast in parsing, and fast in rendering—not to mention easier to understand when you are writing the CSS and JavaScript side.

Remember you are targeting a mobile device. Do you really need all that CSS code for the first load? Don't get me wrong, I'm not saying that a mobile website should be a reduced or simple version—but think about how important the first load experience is for conversion and reducing the number of users abandoning your website without even seeing it.

In Chapter 9, we will discuss how to deal with responsive websites; that is, websites that are serving the same HTML for desktop browsers, tablets, and phones.

Flush the HTML Early

We want the browser to start some processes as early as possible, but by default, most web servers send the HTML response as one piece when it's all been processed on the server.

Let's say we have an HTML template that includes a header section, as you are probably accustomed to, and the body needs to make some queries to a database that might take a while (let's say 200 ms). Why can't we start sending some content to the browser before making those database queries? For example, we can send to the server what we already know it will need, such as the URL of the CSS style to load or some information for DNS resolution.

We can do that by flushing the response early through the HTTP channel. By default, most server-side script platforms such as PHP or ASP.NET, are writing to a buffer, not to the real output, when we use writing functions such as `echo`, `print`, or `Response.Write`.

Most server-side scripts have flush methods, including PHP, Python, Ruby, and ASP.

When sending partial responses using a flush mechanism, a new HTTP header, `Transfer-Encoding: chunked`, will be sent to the client so the client will know that the response will be sent in chunks.

However, if you have *gzip* enabled (and you know you should), some server-side scripts might buffer the output anyway before sending it to the client for compression. So, you should test the responses before applying this in production.

For example, in a simple PHP script, we can flush the header section of the HTML early, before any database connection, following this example:

```
<!doctype html>
<head>
 <meta charset=utf-8>
 <title>My super website</title>
 <link rel=stylesheet href=styles.css>
</head>
<body>
<img src="logo.png">
<?php flush(); ?>
```

```
<?php
    // Database access
?>
</body>
```

In this example, we will send the response to the browser in at least two chunks: we send the head with the metadata information, the CSS file, and the logo while the server will continue working on the database query to fill the rest of the HTML.

The browser will anticipate the download of the external CSS and image files and will probably render the logo faster compared to not flushing the document earlier.

DNS Prefetching

You already know that every time your website uses a new domain or host the user's browser needs to make a DNS lookup, which on a cellular connection might take up to 200 ms. This means every time you add a script or style from an external host (such as a Facebook Like button, Google Analytics script, etc.), the browser will need to make a DNS lookup.

Earlier in this chapter, I also mentioned some optimization techniques that will require the use of other domains, such as domain sharding or cookieless domains. If we can ask the browser to start a DNS lookup as soon as possible, we can gain some time. But this is only useful for the most important hosts that will affect initial loading.

Fortunately, some browsers support *DNS prefetching*, a way to start DNS lookups in advance that is really important on mobile websites. To do it, we just need to set a `<link>` HTML element with a `rel="dns-prefetch"` attribute and the domain as the `href` attribute.

Because the DNS resolution has nothing to do with the HTTP protocol, you can also set the `href` without it, using just `//<domain>`. For example:

```
<link rel="dns-prefetch" href="//google-analytics.com">
```

If we insert this at the top of the HTML and we flush it as soon as possible from the server, our sites will perform better.

 Some browsers also have a feature to prefetch DNS records for links (besides resources) that you can disable or enable based on your needs for next pages; we'll cover this feature in Chapter 7.

DNS prefetching works in Firefox, Chrome for Android, IE since Windows Phone 8, and Safari on iOS. If a browser doesn't support DNS prefetching, it will just ignore the HTML declaration, so its usage won't do any harm.

Other hints are also available in the Resource Hints spec (*https://www.w3.org/TR/resource-hints/#resource-hints*) that will get more support with time.

HTML Compression

There are some techniques in HTML5 that might reduce the size of your final HTML file, such as:

- Removing spaces, tabs, and newline characters
- Removing quotes on simple values—for example, `<section id=news>` instead of `<section id="news">`
- Removing optional elements in HTML5, such as `<html>`, `<body>`, and `<head>`
- Removing optional closing tags, such as `</body>`, `</p>`, and `</li>`

 As a general rule, HTML compression is considered an antipattern. It won't cause any harm to do a quick test to see what you gain, but if it's not considerable, it's probably better to keep it out of your solution.

While it's true that the final HTML size will be smaller, we are not considering the HTTP compression that will be applied on the server. Once the file is compressed, you might find that taking out the spaces, newlines, tabs, and optional elements doesn't really make any difference, so you need to analyze how useful the technique will be for your project.

These tricks will make no big difference in performance. However, when you compress or minify your HTML and then apply HTTP compression, you may see a small improvement. If you are using a publishing process—doing a set of things before publishing your website—minifying the HTML won't do any harm, and you might gain some milliseconds.

The compression tools that might have a bigger impact on performance are the ones that are doing a complex job with the HTML, CSS, and JavaScript at the same time, such as changing the names of IDs and classes to shorter versions.

While compressing the HTML might not have a performance impact, you should remove HTML comments as a general rule, as they don't have any usage and they increase the final size, even compressed.

CSS

HTML5 doesn't work alone, and it's very common to have a companion piece of CSS code for styling and layout. Several questions arise when working with CSS and performance that we will answer in this section.

Internal Versus External

There are three ways to work with CSS: inline, using internal stylesheets, and using external stylesheets.

Inline CSS involves the use of the `style` attribute on one HTML element, such as:

```
<section style="background: blue">
    Some content
</section>
```

Internal stylesheets are the ones that use the `<style>` element with selectors, such as:

```
<style>
section { background: blue }
</style>
<section>
    Some content
</section>
```

And finally, external stylesheets use external files:

```
<link rel="stylesheet" href="styles.css">
<section>
    Some content
</section>
```

Apart from in some specific and rare situations, you won't want to use inline styling, and compared to internal stylesheets it doesn't have any performance difference.

The question arises when discussing external versus internal stylesheets. Before answering that question, let's remember two things:

- Each HTTP request has a cost in terms of TCP connections, HTTP headers, and the high latency we have on mobile connections
- The browser will not start the rendering process until all the known CSS stylesheets are loaded

Based on the previous sentences, we can argue that internal stylesheets are better: they don't create a new HTTP request (they travel within the HTML), and the browser doesn't need to wait more time to start rendering.

Well, for the initial view, internal CSS is the best. However, I know what you might be thinking: what happens with caching and the rest of the HTML files that may use the same CSS file? Here comes the part when you have to decide and find your own balance between performance for the initial view and performance for next visits.

What is clear is that for both internal and external stylesheets you need to avoid the inclusion of "future CSS," meaning CSS selectors that you are not using in the first visit. It was common a couple of years ago to just create one big CSS stylesheet that was linked to from every web page. This is fine from a cache point of view, but it will harm your user's perception of first-visit performance—the most important visit. Only use the CSS that you really need for that first view to reduce the rendering latency.

Only One External File

If you are going with an external stylesheet, be sure you use just one file, so there's only one HTTP request. You can join multiple CSS stylesheets manually into one file or you can use server-side scripts, tools, or modules that will do it for you.

Over HTTP/2, this advice is no longer valid, as using the same TCP connection or using server push may load things faster while sending small files that can be cached separately.

Loading External CSS

There are two ways to load external CSS files—through a `<link>` element (the HTML way) or through an `@import` declaration inside a stylesheet (the CSS way):

```
<!-- The HTML way -->
<link rel="stylesheet" href="styles.css">

<!-- The CSS way -->
<style>
@import url('styles.css')
</style>
```

In terms of performance, the HTML way is the preferred one because the browser will realize it has to download a CSS file while parsing the HTML code. With the CSS way, the browser will realize it has to download the file only after parsing the CSS; that happens after the HTML parsing, so we are delaying by couple of milliseconds the request for the CSS file.

In terms of where to use the `<link>` element, the quick answer is as soon as possible, and that is always at the top of your HTML, while in the `<head>` context. Although technically you can insert references to external CSS files anywhere in the HTML page, doing it at the top will guarantee that the browser will download the file and start the first render as early as possible.

In Microsoft Edge, when you have a `<link>` inside the `<body>` context, the browser renders everything above that link without waiting for that CSS, but it will wait for the CSS to render what is below. This behavior will also be implemented in Chrome in late 2016. See Jake Archibald's article "The Future of Loading CSS" (*https://jakearch ibald.com/2016/link-in-body*) for more information about this technique.

Remember to flush all your CSS declarations from your server early so the browser can start the download process as soon as possible. That will lead to a faster rendering initial process and a better speed index.

Nonblocking CSS

As I've already mentioned, the browser will block the rendering until all the known stylesheets are downloaded and parsed. Therefore, every CSS declaration you have—internal or external—is a potential performance issue that will affect initial rendering.

If you have a media query that is false at the time of the loading (e.g., `orientation: landscape` when the browser is in portrait mode), the browser will download that file anyway, but in some browsers at least it won't block the rendering process.

Even if you put your CSS `<link>` element at the bottom of the page or with a false media query, the browser will prioritize it and download it before starting to render the page.

If you have some CSS stylesheets that you know for sure will not affect the initial rendering, you can use an asynchronous loading operation that won't defer initial rendering.

A library that can help you is loadCSS (*https://github.com/filamentgroup/loadCSS*).

To inject CSS through JavaScript, we can use different JavaScript events, such as `DOM ContentLoaded`, or `load`, or even a trick to detect the first paint operation (after the first rendering) using the Animation Timing API (known as `requestAnimation Frame`) on supported browsers.

LIVERPOOL JOHN MOORES UNIVERSITY
LEARNING SERVICES

For example:

```
// Multiplatform support
window.requestAnimationFrame = requestAnimationFrame ||
  mozRequestAnimationFrame || webkitRequestAnimationFrame ||
  msRequestAnimationFrame;

if (window.requestAnimationFrame) {
      window.requestAnimationFrame(loadCSS);
} else {
      // API not available, we use the load
      window.addEventListener('load', loadCSS);
}

function loadCSS() {
      var link = document.createElement('link');
      link.rel = 'stylesheet';
      link.href = 'nonblocking.css';
      var head = document.getElementsByTagName('head')[0];
      head.appendChild(link)
}
```

Here, we are injecting an external stylesheet after the first paint operation is done on the screen.

Link in body pattern

Firefox and Chrome are changing the behavior of how a <link> in the <body> context blocks rendering.

In late 2016, CSS stylesheets will be treated as partially nonblocking—i.e., they won't block rendering of the content above the <link>—if they are defined inside the <body> element and not inside the <head>, to match Microsoft Edge behavior.

That is, content above the <link> element will be rendered without being blocked while content below the <link> element will wait for that CSS. For details, see "The Future of Loading CSS" (*https://jakearchibald.com/2016/link-in-body*).

That will probably lead to a new recommendation for CSS loading starting in 2017:

- Use a <link> in the <head> context for ATF content and basic CSS that is needed ASAP
- Use one <link> element for each section of the page that will be loaded and parsed separately after the first rendering has happened
- The first CSS files should also be pushed from the server

Here we have an example of this pattern:

```
<head>
  <!-- Blocking stylesheet, it can also be inlined -->
  <link rel="stylesheet" href="/main.css">
</head>

<body>
  <link rel="stylesheet" href="/header.css">
  <header>(content)</header>

  <link rel="stylesheet" href="/main.css">
  <main>(main section)</main>

  <link rel="stylesheet" href="/comments.css">
  <section id="comments">(content)</section>

  <link rel="stylesheet" href="/footer.css">
  <footer>(content)</footer>
</body>
```

Minifying

Even when doing HTTP compression, compressing or minifying the CSS will help in a smaller transfer and a faster rendering. There are plenty of tools available for the job, including some online solutions, such as CSS Minifier (*http://cssminifier.com*) or CSS Compressor (*http://csscompressor.com*). You can use these tools from Grunt or Gulp, or just as manual tools that you can run from the console.

For console tools, the YUI Compressor (*http://yui.github.io/yuicompressor*) is a great option; the YUI browser plug-in will also do the work for you.

Web Fonts

Web fonts give us the ability in CSS3 to load custom fonts to render on the screen. While it's a very nice feature, it has a big impact on performance.

Text by default is a nonblocking resource; that means that when we have text in our HTML, the browser will render it as soon as the render starts. However, when we apply a custom font, we convert nonblocking text into blocking. As you can see in Figure 6-10, it's common to see empty boxes with no text in these situations while the font is being loaded.

Because of this problem, some mobile browsers (such as Chrome and Firefox) have started to define a request timeout in the latest versions after enabling a default font family on the text. If after 3 seconds the font file hasn't been loaded, they will default to the fallback font. Safari, on the other, hand will hold off on the text rendering until the font file is complete, while IE renders the text in the fallback font and then re-renders everything when the font is downloaded.

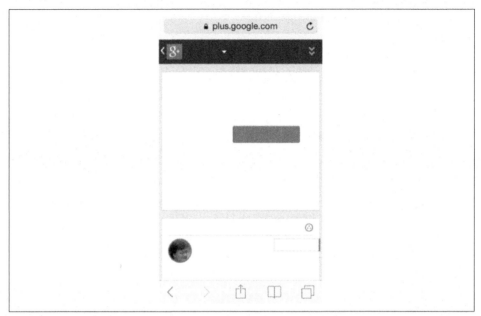

Figure 6-10. While a custom font is being loaded, some browsers will not render any text at all

Every variant of the font (including italics, bold, and bold+italics) will use a separate font file, so try to keep their usage to a minimum.

As mentioned earlier, apart from the *.woff* format (which is already compressed), you should compress all the other font file formats; this will give us an additional 15% savings in data transferred.

Selecting web fonts

The browser needs to download the font before rendering the text; therefore, the font file size should be as small as possible. Smaller files can be found with simpler glyphs. Some font files are optimized for printing and therefore have glyphs with more information than is needed for a mobile screen. That means that there is room for optimization, removing complexity from some glyphs in the font file when you have the right to do it.

Also, sometimes you can remove glyphs that you are not going to use at all, such as Greek characters on a website primarily in English.

A free online tool available for font manipulation is Webfont Generator (*http://www.fontsquirrel.com/tools/webfont-generator*).

Web font CDNs

Google has a free tool with more than 600 open source fonts available at Google Fonts (*http://www.google.com/fonts*). There you can pick one font, select the styles and character set you want, and see the impact on the page load time for the selection, as shown in Figure 6-11.

Figure 6-11. At Google Fonts, we can get a preview of how much impact a particular font will have on our website's performance

Adobe also has a selection of more than 500 web fonts available to use at Adobe Edge Web Fonts (*https://edgewebfonts.adobe.com*), as well as Adobe Typekit (*https://type kit.com*) for commercial fonts.

 The advantage to using a font CDN such as Adobe Edge Web Fonts or Google Fonts instead of serving the files ourselves is that the user might have already the font cached from another website using the same provider.

Loading web fonts

Web fonts are declared in an `@font-face` declaration inside a stylesheet. Therefore, if we want the loading process to be as fast as possible we need to make sure the browser reads that declaration as early as possible. Internal stylesheets are the preferred way, so the browser doesn't need to first download a CSS file to realize it needs to download a font file:

```
<style>
@font-face {
        font-family: MyFont;
        src: url(myfont.woff);
}
</style>
```

An additional requirement for the browser to start a font download operation is to know that the font file will be used, so we also need to have a CSS declaration using that font family at the top. Some browsers (such as Chrome and Safari) will go further and won't download the font file if you apply it with CSS on an empty element with no text.

When using Google Fonts, the fastest way to load the font without any JavaScript code is to use the `<link>` version. For example, to load the Open Sans font, we can use:

```
<link href='https://fonts.googleapis.com/css?family=Open+Sans' rel='stylesheet'>
```

The new CSS Font Loading spec (*http://www.w3.org/TR/css-font-loading*) gives us finer control over font loading, but it's available only in Opera and Chrome for Android at the time of this writing.

Using the API we can request a font loading from JavaScript, detect when a font is ready, and probably make a CSS swap from a fallback font to the newly available font. For example:

```
var myFont = new FontFace("MyFont", "url(myfont.woff)", {});
myFont.ready().then(function() {
    // The font is ready to use
});
myFont.load();
```

While we're waiting for all the browsers to support this API, we can use some frameworks that have fallback mechanisms for font loading, such as fontfaceonload (*https://github.com/zachleat/fontfaceonload*). This framework will use the API when available and will use a different approach on noncompatible browsers.

You can see more updated content on font loading techniques at David Walsh's blog (*https://davidwalsh.name/font-loading*).

JavaScript

JavaScript is typically a big enemy of initial loading performance. The main reason is that JavaScript blocks parsing by default. That means that the browser will stop parsing the HTML when it finds JavaScript code (internal or external) and it won't continue until it's been downloaded and executed.

Internal Versus External

Following the same idea as with CSS, if you have some JavaScript code that must be there for the initial rendering, it will always be better to have it in an internal script compared to an external script, which will need an additional HTTP request.

Remember that with HTTP, it's better and much faster to download one bigger file than several smaller files because of the latency and HTTP overhead.

Therefore, if you have a script that is necessary for the initial rendering, inline it using a `<script>` element.

Minifying

JavaScript can be minified to reduce its size and to obfuscate it. In terms of sizing, even when you are compressing your files on your server thanks to HTTP compression you will gain around 15% when you are also minifying your code.

There are several minification tools available, like the popular JSMin (*http://www.crockford.com/javascript/jsmin.html*), the YUI Compressor (*http://yui.github.io/yuicompressor*), and Google's Closure Compiler (*http://closure-compiler.appspot.com/home*).

The minified code will not have newlines or spaces, and it might change the names of your variables, objects, and functions based on the type of compression you are applying, as you can see in Figure 6-12.

```
!function(a,b,c){"function"==typeof define&&define.amd?define(["jquery"],function(d){return
c(d,a,b),d.mobile}):c(a.jQuery,a,b)}(this,document,function(a,b,c){!function(a){a.mobile={}}(a),function(a,b){function d(b,c)
{var d,f,g,h=b.nodeName.toLowerCase();return"area"===h?(d=b.parentNode,f=d.name,b.href&&f&&"map"===d.nodeName.toLowerCase()?
(g=a("img[usemap=#"+f+"]")[0],!!g&&e(g)):!1):(/input|select|textarea|button|object/.test(h)?!b.disabled:"a"===h?
b.href||c:c)&&e(b)}function e(b){return a.expr.filters.visible(b)&&!a(b).parents().addBack().filter(function()
{return"hidden"===a.css(this,"visibility")}).length}var f=0,g=/^ui-id-\d+$/;a.ui=a.ui||{},a.extend(a.ui,
{version:"c0ab71056b936627e8a7821f03c044aec6280a40",keyCode:
{BACKSPACE:8,COMMA:188,DELETE:46,DOWN:40,END:35,ENTER:13,ESCAPE:27,HOME:36,LEFT:37,PAGE_DOWN:34,PAGE_UP:33,PERIOD:190,RIGHT:39,
SPACE:32,TAB:9,UP:38}},a.fn.extend({focus:function(b){return function(c,d){return"number"==typeof c?this.each(function(){var
b=this;setTimeout(function(){a(b).focus(),d&&d.call(b)},c)}):b.apply(this,arguments)}}(a.fn.focus),scrollParent:function(){var
b;return b=a.ui.ie&&/(static|relative)/.test(this.css("position"))||/absolute/.test(this.css("position"))?
this.parents().filter(function()
{return/(relative|absolute|fixed)/.test(a.css(this,"position"))&&/(auto|scroll)/.test(a.css(this,"overflow")+a.css(this,"overfl
ow-y")+a.css(this,"overflow-x"))}).eq(0):this.parents().filter(function()
{return/(auto|scroll)/.test(a.css(this,"overflow")+a.css(this,"overflow-y")+a.css(this,"overflow-
x"))}).eq(0),/fixed/.test(this.css("position"))||!b.length?a(this[0].ownerDocument||c):b},uniqueId:function(){return
this.each(function(){this.id||(this.id="ui-id-"+ ++f)})},removeUniqueId:function(){return this.each(function()
{g.test(this.id)&&a(this).removeAttr("id")})}}),a.extend(a.expr[":"],{data:a.expr.createPseudo?a.expr.createPseudo(function(b)
{return function(c){return!!a.data(c,b)}}:function(b,c,d){return!!a.data(b,d[3])},focusable:function(b){return
d(b,!isNaN(a.attr(b,"tabindex")))},tabbable:function(b){var c=a.attr(b,"tabindex"),e=isNaN(c);return(e||c>=0)&&d(b,!e)}}),a("
<a>").outerWidth(1).jquery||a.each(["Width","Height"],function(c,d){function e(b,c,d,e){return a.each(f,function(){c-
=parseFloat(a.css(b,"padding"+this))||0,d&&(c-=parseFloat(a.css(b,"border"+this+"Width"))||0),e&&(c-
=parseFloat(a.css(b,"margin"+this))||0)}),c}var f="Width"===d?["Left","Right"]:["Top","Bottom"],g=d.toLowerCase(),h=
{innerWidth:a.fn.innerWidth,innerHeight:a.fn.innerHeight,outerWidth:a.fn.outerWidth,outerHeight:a.fn.outerHeight};a.fn["inner"+
```

Figure 6-12. Typical JavaScript code after being minimized and obfuscated

Loading External JavaScript

To load external JavaScript, we have only one standard way, a `<script>` element with a `src` declaration, as in:

```
<script src='jquery.js'></script>
```

The first question you may have is where to put these declarations: at the top or at the bottom?

If you learned HTML a couple of years (or even decades) ago, the rule was to insert every `<script>` declaration at the top so the browser would download the scripts first. This sounds good, until you realize you are harming performance. So for years we've been seeing millions of websites with hundreds of `<script>` tags in the `<head>`, blocking the parsing and leaving us with a white screen for seconds.

As a general rule, today the recommendation is to insert every standard `<script>` tag at the end, before the `</body>`. This way the browser will download all the CSS and it will have all the content to start rendering the page before blocking the parsing because of the JavaScript download. We are removing the JavaScript code from the critical path.

 When moving the JavaScript code to the bottom on a mobile connection, there is a possibility that the user will engage with the content before the JavaScript is downloaded or executed. We should manage that situation.

defer attribute

If we don't need the JavaScript code to be executed before the page loads, we can now use the new Boolean `defer` attribute. If we include this attribute, the page will download the file but execute it only after the parsing has finished:

```
<script src='jquery.js' defer></script>
```

If you have several scripts with `defer`, it's guaranteed that they will be executed in order.

If you use this approach, your JavaScript code should never contain references to `document.write`, which writes output from JavaScript in the HTML.

async attribute

In newer browsers, we can also specify that a script will not make changes in the HTML and can be loaded asynchronously through the Boolean `async` attribute:

```
<script src='jquery.js' async></script>
```

In this case, the browser will not stop rendering when it finds the script; it will download the file while it's parsing the rest and it will just halt parsing while executing it when it's ready. If we use this technique, we can then define our scripts in the <head> section.

default Versus async Versus defer

Both `async` and `defer` are available in Safari on iOS since version 5.1 (so for every iOS device out there), Android Browser 3+, Chrome for Android, BlackBerry 7+, and IE on Windows Phone 8+. If the browser doesn't support them, it will fall back to the standard behavior.

Figure 6-13 shows the difference between the default script, the `async` script, and the `defer` script in terms of network, parsing, and execution times.

> If your script has a dependency (i.e., it needs other JavaScript), you shouldn't use `async` as there is no guarantee of execution order. You can use `defer` in these cases.

In terms of performance, using `async` or `defer` will improve download speeds and it will reduce the parsing block you have by default with JavaScript code.

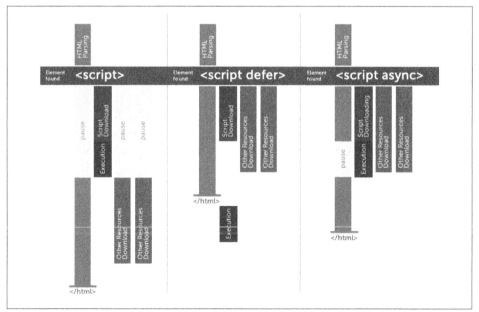

Figure 6-13. How network download, HTML parsing, and JavaScript execution work with the three <script> tag loading options available in HTML5

Script loaders

Another way to load scripts asynchronously is to inject `<script>` tags with JavaScript instead of inserting them in the HTML directly. This idea has led to several loader frameworks becoming available, such as RequireJS (*http://requirejs.org*).

If you have any external widgets in your website, including Facebook Like buttons, Twitter widgets, or Google Analytics scripts, you must use the async versions of those scripts (available on their websites) to reduce the parser blocking.

Browsing Like in Mainland China

In 2014, I traveled to China and I dealt with dozens of websites suffering from something I call the "mainland China effect."

In mainland China some websites, such as YouTube, Facebook, and Twitter, are blocked by the government (this doesn't happen in Hong Kong and Macau, both in China but independent on some matters).

What does this have to do with performance? Well, while visiting from my mobile phone, several Western websites—newspapers, blogs, and other sites—had a very bad performance issue. Most of these websites were blocked for around 30 seconds to 2 minutes while trying to load scripts from Facebook, Twitter, or YouTube. The sites were using standard `<script>` tags, and because those websites were blocked, there were long delays because the browser tried to download the scripts while blocking the parsing of the page.

So, you might not even know that you have this problem; and besides the Chinese people browsing your website, what happens if one day Twitter's or Facebook's servers are down? Your website will take at least 40 seconds to render on users' screens when the timeout happens.

To avoid the "mainland China effect," always use asynchronous scripts when using scripts from third-party servers. To see if you suffer from this problem, you can easily block these websites with a proxy or tamper with your hosts file temporarily.

Using well-known frameworks

When using well-known frameworks such as jQuery, Angular, or Modernizr, you have the option to host the files yourself on your server or to link them from a CDN.

The advantage of linking them from a CDN is that there is a good chance that the user already has the files in the browser's cache thanks to a previous visit to a different website.

Some CDNs available for well-known frameworks include:

- Google Hosted Libraries (*https://developers.google.com/speed/libraries/devguide*)
- Microsoft Ajax Content Delivery Network (*http://www.asp.net/ajax/cdn*)
- BootstrapCDN (*http://bootstrapcdn.com*)
- jQuery CDN (*https://code.jquery.com*)

Only One External File

Following the same rule as for CSS on HTTP/1.1, if you are loading external Java-Script files you should load only one (unless you're using a different asynchronous technique). That will improve the performance, as loading all the JavaScript code necessary in one shot reduces the latency in parsing.

You might be thinking that because of the nature of HTTP/2, bundling several Java-Script files is not necessary anymore as we don't have the overhead of additional requests in this version of the protocol. However, based on an article by Khan Academy (*http://engineering.khanacademy.org/posts/js-packaging-http2.htm*), we can conclude that bundling text-based files is still a good idea in some situations, because we still get advantages from the compression encoding. This is because *gzip* gets more savings if you encode one big file rather than several smaller files separately.

 We need to find a balance between what to bundle and load at the beginning of the navigation and what to defer to be downloaded later.

Load Events

Most JavaScript developers are aware of the `load` event (and its HTML attribute, `onload`). It's the second event you learn about after `click` when learning JavaScript.

The window's `load` event (used in `<body onload="">` in HTML) is executed when the whole page is loaded—which means when the HTML and CSS has been parsed and executed, the JavaScript has been executed, the images have been downloaded, and everything is rendered on the screen.

If you are doing something after the `onload` that doesn't need all this (usually image loading), you can improve the user's perception of loading using a new event that is fired beforehand.

The new event, known as `DOMContentLoaded`, is available in all mobile browsers today. This event will be fired when the DOM is ready (i.e., when the HTML is fully parsed and in memory), while the browser is still downloading resources. You can then bind event handlers, make decisions, and enable features before the onload.

 If you are a jQuery developer, you've probably heard about the `$(document).ready` event. This was a way to emulate `DOMContentLoaded` before it was available.

Therefore, if you are currently using the load event, analyze what you are doing there and think about the possibility of moving it to `DOMContentLoaded` from the document, as in:

```
document.addEventListener('DOMContentLoaded', function() {
        // Do something here
});
```

Images

As mentioned before in this book, images are non-blocking by default. That is, they do not block the parsing (as JavaScript does) or the rendering (as CSS does). The browser will leave a placeholder in the rendering while the image is being downloaded and decoded.

The Q1 2016 Mobile Overview Report (*http://data.wurfl.io/MOVR/pdf/2016_q1/ MOVR_2016_q1.pdf*) has some interesting findings about the extent to which oversized images are slowing down the web, making clear that this is something we need to check:

- Resizing and reformatting images for desktops can reduce the image payload to 0.72 of the original size, or a 28% savings.
- When resizing and reformatting images for mobile smartphones, an image payload that is 0.65 of the original size can be achieved, or a 35% savings.

To improve rendering performance, we should define the image's dimensions from the HTML or CSS side so the browser knows exactly what size of placeholder to use. This will reduce rerendering and repainting operations when the image is ready.

For example, `<img src=logo.png>` can be improved using:

```
<img src="logo.png" width="300" height="100" alt="Logo">
```

If you are using responsive web design techniques, you might want to move dimensions to CSS to apply media queries on them.

305 Bytes That Can Make a Huge Difference

Performance is so important on the mobile web that sometimes we don't fully understand the impact that our changes might have. In 2015, Google changed its logo and published the article "Evolving the Google Identity" (*https://design.google.com/articles/evolving-the-google-identity*).

Besides all the design ideas that led to this new logo, one phrase took my full attention: "It allows us to optimize these assets for size and latency, including building a special variant of our full-color logo that is only 305 bytes, compared to our existing logo at ~14,000 bytes."

That means that the old logo was 14 KB versus the 0.3 KB of the new logo. That's a huge improvement when you want to serve a high-quality web solution to millions of users on very bad connections around the world. Before the new logo, Google had to replace its colorful logo just with plain text for these users, because 14 KB for the logo was not an option.

Responsive Images

One of the first problems with images on a mobile website is not sending the right size for that viewport, and delivering a bigger file that is also serving desktops or tablets. The main problems with doing this are:

- We are transferring more bytes through the network
- We are using more CPU time for decoding the image
- We are wasting CPU time for resizing the image
- We are consuming more RAM, as the image must be decoded into a large bitmap before resizing it

On a mobile device, sizing depends on:

- Viewport width and height
- Device pixel ratio (DPR), or screen density
- Art direction or different versions of the same image for different screen sizes based on what we want to focus on

The screen density is something important that we should understand properly. If we consider iOS and Android devices, we can find today DPR values from 2 to 4. That means that if we specify in our viewport that an img will have a width of 300 CSS pixels, we should have files of 600 pixels (DPR=2), 900 pixels (DPR=3), and 1,200 pixels (DPR=4).

 Even when a device with a DPR of 4—such as a Galaxy S7—is browsing our website, this doesn't mean that we must or even should provide a 4x version of the image, as it will occupy 12x more memory than a bitmap and will mean more data is transferred over the network. We need to find a balance between quality, transfer size, and performance; a 2x or 3x version of the image may look good enough on a 4x device.

Serving different versions of the same image is mandatory for a high-performance mobile or responsive website.

To make it work, we usually have the following options on the client:

- Use CSS media queries
- Use responsive images markup: `srcset` and/or `picture`
- Use a JS-based solution
- Use server-side libraries for resizing images
- Use an image resizing service in the cloud

When we use client-based solutions, we will need to have our images resized in several dimensions manually on our server, or we can combine them with server- or cloud-based solutions that will do the work for us.

Media queries

Using media queries to deliver several images is an antipattern today; if we use them then we need to stop using semantic HTML images (such as `<img>` elements) and replace them with empty containers such as `<div>` elements, and use background images to define different versions of the same images.

Using media queries was necessary a few years ago because no other client-based solutions were possible, but I won't go into much detail here other than mentioning that you usually use the screen's width and DPR, through the `resolution` and `-device-pixel-ratio` conditions.

srcset

The `srcset` attribute (*http://w3c.github.io/html/semantics-embedded-content.html#element-attrdef-img-srcset*) is an addition to the `<img>` tag that defines a list of image URLs that can be used for that image based on device pixel density or viewport width. The browser will pick the best one based on several candidates.

The candidates are defined as a comma-separated list of space-separated pairs of image candidate URL and condition descriptor.

Condition descriptors can be:

- A width descriptor: a value and the lowercase letter *w*
- A pixel density descriptor: a value and the lowercase letter *x*

For example, if we want to just change the file based on DPR, we can use:

```
<img src="lowres.png"
     srcset="midres.png 2x, highres.png 3x,
             superhighres.png 4x"
     width="100" height="50" alt="Description">
```

In this example, the browser will pick from four candidates—including the default one in src—based on the current DPR.

The preceding code is compatible with Safari on iOS since 8.0, Chrome for Android from 34, Edge, Firefox, and Opera.

We can use the srcset attribute safely for every browser as it also involves the usage of the well-known src attribute, which will be used as a fallback for noncompatible browsers.

The srcset attribute also accepts the width descriptor in a newer version of the spec with a sizes attribute. In terms of mobile compatibility, the new complete version is available since iOS 9.2 and Chrome 38.

In this case, we use the width condition descriptor to specify the physical dimensions of the image file, and using sizes, we specify the percentage of the viewport that we want to cover with that image (or a series of possibilities with media queries) using the vw (viewport width) unit. The browser will pick the best one. For example:

```
<img src="lowres.png" alt="Description"
     sizes="80vw"
     srcset="lowres.png 100w,
             midres.png 200w,
             hires.png 300w,
             superhires.png 400w">
```

Here, we define that we want our image to use 80% of the viewport in any situation and we provide four image candidates to fill that space, defining the physical dimensions of each one. The browser will pick the best candidate based on the device's dimensions and pixel density.

picture

The picture element (*http://w3c.github.io/html/semantics-embedded-content.html#the-picture-element*) is a new element now part of HTML5. It's a container that provides multiple sources to its contained <img> element to allow authors to declaratively control or give hints to the user agent about which image resource to use, based on the screen's pixel density, viewport size, image format, and other factors. It represents its children and it will help us with art direction.

At the time of this writing, <picture> is compatibile with Safari on iOS since 9.3, Chrome from version 38, Firefox, Edge, and Opera Mobile.

It defines an <img> element and one or more <source> elements specifying conditions to meet for picking that source, such as:

- A media query using the media attribute
- An image format using the type attribute
- A list of image candidates for the source through the srcset attribute

For example, we can define two image versions for landscape and portrait orientations using:

```
<picture>
    <source media="(orientation: portrait)" srcset="midres.png 2x,
                highres.png 3x, superhighres.png 4x" sizes="80vw">
    <source media="(orientation: landscape)" srcset="lmidres.png 2x,
                lhighres.png 3x, lsuperhighres.png 4x" sizes="40vw">
    <img src="lowres.png" alt="Description">
</picture>
```

We can even have different <source> elements for different image format types, such as SVG, PNG, WebP, or JPEG-XR, using the <type> attribute and MIME types.

JS-based solutions

In the last year, several JS-based solutions have appeared to change an <img> source to a different one, based on the current device pixel ratio and viewport size. However, today (after srcset and <picture>, available in most browsers) the best JS-based solution is to polyfill that markup instead of delivering a custom JS markup.

The best solution for getting <picture>, srcset, and sizes is the Picturefill polyfill (*https://github.com/scottjehl/picturefill*).

Server-side libraries for resizing images

Using device libraries such as WURFL or DeviceAtlas, we can detect the current device's capabilities—such as screen size—and deliver the best image size dynamically.

Also, several libraries are available for server platforms, such as Sharp (*http://sharp.dimens.io/en/stable*) for Node.js or Adaptive Images (*http://adaptive-images.com*) for PHP, that will help you with this task.

 Adaptive Images is a server-side technique that—using Apache or Nginx—will deliver the right image based on the current user agent without the designers' intervention.

Image resizing in the cloud

Some CDNs will offer as a service some optimization and resizing solutions that will compress and resize your images on the fly. Services such as imgix (*https://www.imgix.com*), ImageEngine by ScientiaMobile (*https://web.wurfl.io/#image-engine*), cloudimage.io (*https://cloudimage.io*) and Cloudinary (*http://cloudinary.com*) are available on the market.

Inline Images

Inlining images using data URIs is a way to embed the images in the HTML or CSS instead of requesting additional files.

For example, we can define an `<img>` tag with the image itself inside it, without using an external file. This can be done using a Base64 encoding of the image file—basically, storing the binary file as a set of visible ASCII characters in a string. This is great for small images, icons, backgrounds, separators, and anything else that doesn't merit a new request to the server.

 The size of an image (or any other binary file) will increase by about 30% when it's converted to a Base64 string for a data URI, but its size will be reduced again if we are serving the document using GZIP from the server.

Some examples

The syntax is `data:[MIME-Type][;base64],data`. The data can contain spaces and newlines for readability purposes, but some browsers won't render it properly. It's better to maintain it in one line.

To convert an image file to a Base64 string representation, we can use any online converter or command-line utility. There are free and online alternatives at Web Utils (*http://www.webutils.pl/Base64*) and Base64 (*http://www.motobit.com/util/base64-decoder-encoder.asp*).

For example, the O'Reilly logo (original PNG file 75 pixels wide) attached as a data URI image looks like this:

```
<img width="100" height="17" alt="O'Reilly" src="data:image/
png;base64,iVBORw0KGgoAAAANSUhEUgAAAEYAAAARBAMAAACSi8f4AAAAA3NCSVQICAjb4U/
gAAAAGFBMVEX///////8AAACpqanMzMxmZmaHhoQ/Pz9kt3AEAAAAACHRSTlMA/////////
9XKVDIAAAAJcEhZcwAACxIAAAsSAdLdfvwAAAAcdEVYdFNvZnR3YXJlAEFkb2JlIEZpcmV3b3JrcyB
DUzQGgstOgAAAAFnRFWHRDcmVhdGlvbiBUaW1lADEyLzExLzA5uegApgAAAQNJREFUKJGVkUFT
wyAQhfMXXiH1LA3hDMTeSVDPidW7WnMvkxn/vo+MsamX6s7wgOy3Q29JgetR/
I2Rdy8B8HIcAyhj8PLIr0dsuYlDF8i8KWWC/BRKaVCUTaJmkhcDuNOHLVCaJg6VfJY6JivqGJ
HEjn00q3tpsGcfd0KuuGdx2+fsmSl3m2r2k2gGg30i434xSMlmht0YbR
+EflAU71dMW89zzWcy2W61eF6YssK5j3vlII81Lj0vzOKHaX
CuSz8334ybgC2bkdlUK6ZeMVvTdMM0M0IL3fmQskbD08LA8YHDzGDw9Nyn7Hziuv1hsH/
PltCQi9770MmsXFaGf/z3q/EFatlL/IFsBmgAAAAASUVORK5CYII=" />
```

Performance impact

While it seems like a good idea to reduce external requests, the problem with inlining images is that we are converting our by-default nonblocking images to blocking images.

If we inline an image in HTML, the browser will need to download and parse the image with the HTML, so it will be a bigger download and a larger processing time before rendering.

If we inline the image in CSS, we are pushing the rendering time as CSS blocks rendering by default.

Therefore, I don't recommend using this technique as a general rule. However, there are some exceptions:

- When you are loading a CSS file asynchronously
- When used for really small images (such as bullets)
- When used for images that you really need for the first view, which are important as data and are what the user is expecting
- When there is no need to cache the image for future usage

 As always, the best suggestion for specific cases is to try two or three options and measure them so you can make a decision based on real data.

We are going to use this technique for other purposes as well, such as for a custom cache in Chapter 7.

Image Files

Even with images being nonblocking, that doesn't mean that we shouldn't care about image size. The `load` event will not fire until all the images are loaded, and that means in some browsers that the spinner or animation loader will not stop. And we've already mentioned that perception of speed is sometimes more important than the real speed.

Therefore, image loading should be fast. To achieve that, we need to compress our images and pick the right format per image. There is a lot of discussion around which format to pick, and I will keep that outside of the scope of this book, but I will suggest Smush it (*http://www.imgopt.com*) as a great online tool for optimizing your images without losing quality.

For desktop-based solutions, an option is ImageOptim (*https://imageoptim.com*), a free solution available for Windows, macOS, and Linux.

New optimized formats

Besides the well-known GIF, animated GIF, JPEG, and PNG formats, newer mobile browsers support new formats that will help you in delivering smaller files with the same quality. Unfortunately, support for these formats is still browser-based. so server-side adaptive delivery will be necessary. The new formats include the following:

- JPEG-XR, available only on IE and Edge, is an evolution of the JPEG format that is optimized for high-resolution images, creating better quality with less size compared to JPEG. It supports both lossy and lossless pictures.

- JPEG-2000 (JP2), available only in Safari on iOS, is a wavelet-based format that was created by the Joint Photographic Experts Group committee in 2000 with the intention of superseding the original JPEG standard created in 1992. It offers some advantages in image fidelity over standard JPEG.

- WebP, an open format created by Google, aims to replace both JPEG and PNG files (lossy and lossless formats), getting the same quality with a 25%–40% reduction in file size. It's available in Chrome for Android, Opera, and Android Browser since 4.1.

- Animated PNG (APNG) is a nonstandard animated format based on PNG that can create better and smaller animations compared to animated GIF. It's available only in Firefox and Safari on iOS since 8.0 at the time of this writing.

- Better Portable Graphics (BPG) (*http://bellard.org/bpg*) is a JPEG replacement that can get smaller files with better quality and even animations. Today it's not compatible with any browser, but you can use a JavaScript decoder to test it.

- FLIF (*http://flif.info*), still in the early stages of development, is a lossless image format that outperforms PNG, lossless WebP, lossless BPG, lossless JPEG2000, and lossless JPEG XR in terms of compression ratio. It includes a way to deliver responsive images in different resolutions with the same file.

In Chapter 10, we will analyze the best way to serve content with these new formats while supporting responsive images.

Goodbye, Animated GIF

We live in an era of an animated GIF reborn: emojis, Internet memes, and video-like experiences are all around the web. The problem is that animated GIF is a very old format that is extremely inefficient—and low quality. In some situations, animated GIFs are used because on some mobile platforms a `<video>` element will always render in full-screen mode outside of the context of the page, and there is no autoplay available.

 Compared to a video in MP4, an animated GIF with the same content is extremely inefficient, usually 10x larger.

Therefore, JavaScript solutions appeared for decoding a video using JavaScript and rendering it on a canvas. While it's a working solution, it's still not the best one: JavaScript decoding takes time and battery and it doesn't provide the best experience.

We've seen that other animation formats are available, such as APNG and the forthcoming BPG, but compatibility is not good enough for every browser out there in the mobile space.

Fortunately, starting with Safari on iOS 10 and the version of Chrome for Android due out in late 2016, videos will be played inline and with autoplay if there is no audio, either because they don't have an audio track or because the `muted` Boolean attribute was used. For iOS, the video will have to use a proprietary attribute for this behavior, `webkit-playsinline`, as in:

```
<video width="300" height="150" muted webkit-playsinline>
  <!-- sources -->
</video>
```

Hero Images

Hero images are defined as big images—usually taking up more than 60% of the initial view on a mobile device—that are important because without them the text or content around or above the image is useless or even invisible because of contrast problems.

In these cases, you need to force the download of this image ASAP, as it's a fundamental part of the perception of a page load. Steve Souders has great advice for working with hero images on his blog (*http://www.stevesouders.com/blog/2015/05/12/hero-image-custom-metrics*), including how to get a metric on when the hero image is visible on the screen.

CSS Spriting

CSS Spriting is a web design technique for reducing the number of image server requests on a web page. There are a lot of online resources and books available on this technique. For now, suffice it to say that if you have many images in your site (preferred logos, icons, background images, flags, etc.), you can reduce all of those to one big image with all the originals inside and use a CSS mask to determine which portion of it to show in each container.

This technique has a great impact on web performance. Rather than `<img>` elements, you will instead use any block element (`<div>`) or any block-converted element using `display: block`, such as a span or a tag.

Finally, in some browsers this technique can have an impact on rendering performance, because the big image will be duplicated in memory for each usage. We need to balance the performance gained through the reduction of requests with the performance lost in the rendering engine in some browsers.

 SVG can also be used for spriting. For more information, see "Icon Systems with SVG Sprites" (*https://css-tricks.com/svg-sprites-use-better-icon-fonts*) by Chris Coyier.

So, if you have 10 icons, each one in a different image, instead of 10 different requests (with all the latency involved per request) you can convert it to 1 request only with all 10 icons inside.

CSS Spriting over HTTP/2 might not be necessary, as the impact of every new request is reduced to the minimum.

Don't Forget the Server

When we are doing frontend development, we sometimes think that server-side rendering is something from the past. However, time and performance problems have shown us that server-side rendering is sometimes still necessary. If you need Java-

Script to render content on the first view, your site will probably be 5x more perform-ant if you move that rendering to the server. This is especially important when using client-side UI frameworks, where the user will see nothing (a white page) until the whole framework is loaded and the DOM elements have been created dynamically.

If you are using Node.js, you will find several projects that do server-side rendering for well-known UI frameworks (such as Angular or React) for the initial loading while still using client-side rendering for continuing the interaction after the load.

Also, using server-side device libraries such as WURFL by ScientiaMobile (*https://www.scientiamobile.com*) is still necessary in some medium to big projects.

Optimizing Using Best Practices

In this chapter, we've covered basic best practices to improve the performance of the initial visit to your website or web app without too much effort, such as setting up your server, using non-blocking JavaScript code, and delivering the CSS stylesheets as soon as possible.

As a review, let's make a list of some important things we need to care about to improve performance:

- Server configuration, supporting HTTP/1.1, HTTP/2 and compression
- Reducing requests, making resource loading cookieless and possibly domain sharding
- Optimizing the HTML for early flushing and DNS caching
- Keeping CSS as short as possible, with fast and ASAP loading to reduce render blocking
- Optimizing loading techniques for JavaScript to avoid parser blocking
- Optimizing images to reduce network usage

In the following chapters, we will continue exploring techniques for improving future visits, the experience and perception after the page has been loaded, and also how to apply other techniques that will allow us to get extreme performance on our mobile websites, such as using service workers or separating the above-the-fold code from the rest.

Optimizing After First Load

Optimizing performance for future visits is very important to increase conversions and improve the user's perception of our services and our companies. We can take advantage of previous visits to increase speed of later experiences with the same website. Bad connections and being offline are usual situations on the mobile web; therefore, taking advantage of techniques like caching and prefetching content can enhance the user experience.

In this chapter, we will talk about browser and custom caches, prefetching, and offline experiences to optimize near-future visits (such as what the user is doing in the following few seconds) as well as far-future visits (such as next month's).

The Cache: Your New Friend

I remember the days when every developer was looking for a way to remove the browser's cache at all costs. Googling "no cache in php" was pretty common in the late '90s and early 2000s. We weren't thinking about performance at the time, and the impact of disabling cache abilities was really costly.

Now you are here, reading this book, so you know that performance is a very important feature—and you are now ready to make the cache your new best friend.

The first thing is to understand how browser caching works. Every browser has a database of HTTP resources that have been downloaded before, including the data itself and metadata such as the fetch timestamp and expiration timestamp (provided by the server).

When a browser is loading a website for the first time and it doesn't have any resources cached, it is in the "empty cache" state.

Every time the browser needs a resource from the web, using the URL as the key, it looks in the cache database to see if it already has a version of it. If it has it, then the cache algorithm starts:

1. The browser verifies whether the resource has expired, based on metadata.

   a. If the resource has expired, the browser creates a conditional HTTP GET request with the If-Modified-Since or the If-None-Match header. It's like asking: "Hey, server, I have an expired version of this file downloaded on this date or with this ETag; if you have a newer version, can I get it?"

      i. If the server decides based on the date or ETag that the resource is still valid, it will respond with an HTTP 304 (Not Modified) code.

      ii. If the resource has changed server-side, then the server will deliver the new resource with updated cache headers.

   b. If the resource has not expired, then it will use the local version and it won't generate any HTTP request (the best scenario for performance.)

2. The browser moves to the next resource.

Cache Policy

Defining a cache policy usually has to do with futurology, and that's why most developers didn't want it years ago. How long will this CSS live without any update? The company's logo seems to be static, but what happens if we want to decorate it for any reason in the near future? Defining the cache policy usually involves a fight between performance and the risk of not delivering updated content.

 Usually you cache GET requests only. Caching POST, DELETE, or PUT requests might end in weird behaviors in dynamic activities.

While the cache policy will vary per resource type, we can group them into:

1. Resources that can't be cached, because they are probably different for every request (such as a JSON response with the latest stock values).

2. Resources that can be cached for just a small period of time, such as weather information that can be stored for a couple of minutes without too many risks

3. Resources that won't change for a while (from an hour to a year) but we don't know when they are going to change, such as a CSS file, a logo, or a user's avatar

4. Resources that will never change, such as historical data

The simplest cache policies are for groups 1 and 4: we are going to define a no-cache policy and a future expiration (year 2036 maybe?), respectively. For group 2, the best idea is to define a `max-age` of whatever value minimizes the risk.

The most common scenario is in fact group 3: static resources that may change in the future, but we don't know exactly when. While we can think of different policies, the best one is to use a far-future expiration date, as for group 4. Wait a minute; we've said that these resources may change! Well, this is a two-step policy:

1. Set a far-future expiration date, so the browser will always use a cached version.

2. Add a version or hash to the URL, so if you change the resource you change the URL and the browser will treat it as a new resource.

For the second step, let's say we have a *styles.css* file with a far-future cache policy. If we change the file, we then should also change the name of it (physically or virtually). Approaches to renaming the URL usually include:

- Adding a version number, such as *styles-v2.css*, *styles.v2.css*, or *styles.css?v2*

- Adding a timestamp, such as *styles.20160103.css* or *styles?20160103*

- Adding a hash, such as *styles-AB24FG11.css*

For example, Google's home page includes an *https://www.google.com/images/ nav_logo242.png* URL at the time of this writing. If you pay attention, the filename, *nav_logo242.png*, seems to have a version number in it. The headers are:

```
Cache-Control: private, max-age=31536000
Date: Fri, 06 Nov 2015 17:10:25 GMT
Expires: Fri, 06 Nov 2015 17:10:25 GMT
Last-Modified: Thu, 22 Oct 2015 17:33:49 GMT
```

When both `Cache-Control: max-age` and `Expires` are defined, the latest takes priority, even if `Expires` has a more restrictive rule. You only define both to support HTTP/1.0-only situations.

Expiration Headers

The cache policy is defined by the server through HTTP headers in the response and usually honored by the browser. The browser might delete the cache for different reasons, such as lack of space, user action, or the use of private or incognito mode.

Nevertheless, defining a cache policy is a very important part of delivering websites that perform well.

Expires header

The older method (from HTTP/1.0) to define a resource's expiration is through `Expires`, which receives an absolute date as an argument. For example:

```
Expires: Thu, 15 Apr 2020 20:00:00 GMT
```

The browser then will use this value as the expiration metadata. The problem with using `Expires` is that we need to manually or dynamically shift the date as time passes; also, it assumes that the client and server are synchronized.

`Expires` was usually used as a way to disable the cache really quickly on a website; we just defined it as a date in the past.

Cache-Control

The recommended method that was incorporated in HTTP/1.1 defined a new header, `Cache-Control`, that takes several comma-separated attributes. The most useful one is a relative lifespan for the resource, expressed in seconds as the `max-age` attribute. The browser will calculate the expiration timestamp based on the current time at the time of receiving the resource and the value of `max-age`.

The header for a 1-hour lifespan looks like:

```
Cache-Control: max-age=3600
```

Usual values for `max-age` are 3600 (1 hour), 86400 (1 day), 604800 (1 week), 2592000 (1 month), and 31536000 (1 year).

`Cache-Control` includes several other attributes besides `max-age`, such as:

`public`
> Usually not necessary when `max-age` is defined; sets the resource as cachable by anyone (the browser or intermediate proxies)

private

> Indicates that the response is private to the current user, so it can be cached by the browser but not by intermediate proxies as the response will be different to that received by other users

no-cache

> Specifies that the resource must not be used for a future request; if ETag was set, then a conditional request can be used in the future

no-store

> Defines that we don't want this response to be cached in any way

For example, if we want to set a 1-minute cache only for the browser and not for proxies, we should define:

```
Cache-Control: private, max-age=60
```

Setting up servers

Every server has its way to define expiration headers. They usually are defined by file extension or MIME type, but can also be defined per resource.

On Apache, for example, we can use the *.htdocs* file and define something like:

```
<FilesMatch "\.(gif|jpg|js|css)$">
ExpiresDefault "access plus 2 months"
</FilesMatch>
```

On IIS, you need to find the node you want to configure and then use Features View. Double-click HTTP Response Headers and then, in the Actions pane, click Set Common Headers. You can select "Immediately" to disable the cache, "After" to use a relative max-age policy (setting the amount of time to use), or "On (in Coordinate Universal Time)" to set an absolute expiration. If you are doing ASP.NET websites, you can also manage your policies through the *web.config* file.

 The cache can be flushed by the browser or the user at any time, so don't assume that if a resource was cached, it will be honored for its lifespan.

If you are using a cloud-based hosting solution such as Amazon AWS or Firebase Hosting, you need to check its documentation to find out how to properly set expiration headers.

ETag Header

An *entity tag* (ETag) is a hash identifier assigned by the server to one particular instance of a resource at a URL. We can think of it as a fingerprint. If the resource changes server-side, so does the ETag.

The ETag was an optional addition to HTTP/1.1. It's a header in the HTTP response with the ETag key, as in:

```
ETag: "12093809QRRP23"
```

The ETag can then be used by the browser for a conditional request later, asking for a resource if the ETag is different and therefore the resource has changed from the cached version:

```
If-None-Match: "12093809QRRP23"
```

If the current version of the resource server-side has the same ETag, it means the resource hasn't changed, so an HTTP 304 (Not Modified) response will be returned.

> If you only use ETags as a cache policy, the browser will always need to make a request to the server to see if it has changed. Therefore, Expires or max-age is preferred, as they don't generate any HTTP requests while within the non-expiration range.

Most web browsers have ETags enabled by default, as do Apache and IIS. Apache, for example, creates the ETag based on the file's inode number, last-modified date, and size. The inode has to do with the local filesystem on the server, so if different servers are serving the same file, the ETag might be different. In that case, we should change the ETag algorithm being used, or just disable ETags and rely on expiration dates only.

The Vary Specification

Caching may happen not only on the client side, but also on intermediates, such as proxies. They might have some internal memory for caching HTTP requests, and therefore the request will never get to the final server if another client is requesting it within the non-expired zone.

There are some special cases where caching can lead to problems with intermediates, usually when talking about server-side dynamic serving. Let's say, for example, that you are serving three different HTML files to the client on the same URL based on the User-Agent (e.g., a mobile phone, a tablet or desktop, and a smart TV). The URL is the same but the response is not, and if a proxy is caching the phone response, other devices will inadvertently get the response.

To avoid these situations, we must define the Vary HTTP header in our response, listing the HTTP headers that will vary the response, such as User-Agent. The proxy will then cache different versions of the URL, based on different values for those headers. We need to be very careful, though, because there are literally thousands of different values for User-Agent. If you want to get more insights on the Vary header, you can read "Best Practices for Using the Vary Header" (*https://www.fastly.com/blog/best-practices-for-using-the-vary-header*) by Rogier Mulhuijzen.

Custom Client Cache

There are some situations where you will want to have more control over caching without relying on the browser's cache. In these cases, you will need to implement a custom client cache using any of the available APIs for offline storage and caching, such as:

- Local storage
- IndexedDB (WebSQL on older platforms)

While using these techniques involves more work, it also keeps content client-side even when the user flushes the browser's cache. The user can delete the data anyway through "Website Data," but it's more hidden than the browser's cache. We will have available roughly 5 MB in local storage and 5 MB on IDB or WebSQL, without the user's intervention or permission.

In Chrome and Safari on iOS, local storage will use 2 bytes per character, so we will need to compress Latin-based files to take advantage of the 5 MB container. The best solution to do this is FTDataSquasher (*https://github.com/ftlabs/ftdatasquasher*) from the Financial Times team.

Client-Side

A local client cache framework will involve the use of JavaScript to download files using XHR or the Fetch API and store those files in local storage, IDB, or WebSQL. Text-based resources are preferred for compatibility, and images can be converted to Base64 server-side for this purpose.

The framework has to have a way to know if a resource was updated on the server side and download it again, while injecting those files into the DOM when needed locally.

Server-Side

For a custom client cache, we just need a way to deliver files based on version numbers. For example, we can have a script that will serve files that are needed, such as:

```
http://myserver/fetch/styles.css-v2/logo.png-v4/script.js-v1
```

The client generates an XHR request with this URL specifying that it has *styles.css* version 2, *logo.png* version 4, and *script.js* version 1. Then the server can verify whether any of these resources have changed and deliver the result in a JSON response, such as:

```
[
    "styles.css": false,
    "logo.png": "data:image/png;base64,...",
    "script.js": "// I'm an updated string"
]
```

Some implementations of custom caches use cookies stored on the client side, so at the next visit the server will know which versions of each resource the client already has and can avoid embedding or linking to them.

Prefetching

Optimizing the next visit through caching is a good idea, but it's also important to optimize the user's current visit by accelerating the next content the user is about to access through *prefetching*. Prefetching means loading a resource before it's actually needed.

Offering immediate feedback when the user is interacting with our content is one of the most important aspects of perception. To do this, we should prefetch the content before the user wants it, so it's immediately available. The usual questions are when to do it, how we know what to prefetch, and what the cost is to the user.

We can prefetch resources (images, JSON data, CSS, JavaScript code) or HTML pages, based on what we think the user's next move is going to be.

Deciding What to Prefetch

Deciding what to prefetch is the key for a successful performance experience. The first answer to the question of what to prefetch is that there is no single answer: every project is different, and you must analyze your situation and content to make the final decision. Prefetching has to do with probabilities.

There are a couple of instances where it's perfectly clear what to prefetch. For example, if the user is in a photo gallery looking at the first picture, it's common in that situation to load the next picture. Therefore, we can prepare that and prefetch the next image (we can also take advantage of the request and prefetch more than one).

You can be as smart as you want; for example, if you are displaying search results spread across 10 pages, is it common enough for users to go to the second page to prefetch it? Well, it depends on the case. Instead of prefetching the second page after the first one is loaded, we can wait for some trigger. For example, if the user scrolls to the end of the page, presumably looking at every result until the end, we might start loading the next page.

Using context

Using context to prefetch content is a great way to surprise the user with performance. Context can be anything from the user's country or language to the current time (morning, afternoon, night). While a web server and a web browser are both limited in the amount of data they can get from the user's context without permission, it's important to keep your eyes open and to use all the clues available to increase the user's perception of your site's performance.

Let me give you an example that doesn't have to do with a website but illustrates the idea. I bought a new iPhone and Apple Watch while in the United States, and I didn't open them until I was in Amsterdam for the Velocity conference (*http://velocity conf.com*). When I turned both devices on, the displays were in Dutch by default. Now think about it. I didn't buy these devices in the Netherlands, I hadn't set them up yet, I hadn't added any SIM card or WiFi network—but both devices knew I was in Amsterdam, so it was probable I would want Dutch as my primary language. That wasn't the case, by the way, but I recognized the value of preselecting the language based on the context. You can do the same thing to add value and improve the user's perception of your website.

 Prefetching means using more data than the user requested. We need to balance the offer of a better experience with being a good citizen and avoiding high costs to the user. Finding the right balance will be the key to success, such as not prefetching if the user is on a cellular network or a bad WiFi connection.

Collective data versus user's history

We've been looking at very clear examples where prefetching can be used. But in most generic scenarios, what to prefetch might not be so clear. Let's think about a newspaper's home page. What will the next link followed be for that user? Will she click on the first main headline? Will she go to the sports section?

We have two ways to answer this question: collective data versus the user's history.

We can use accumulated data in our server's logs or analytics to decide which is the user's most probable next move (collective data). In this case, we will look at our stats and decide manually or automatically which resource is best to prefetch next. Another example is a pair of country/state drop-down elements; when the user selects a country, we make a request to load the states/provinces for that country. If, based on stats, we know that 80% of our users come from the United States, we might prefetch that API call.

A harder to develop but more efficient way to decide what to prefetch is to collect the user's history. For example, if one particular user accessed our newspaper website 5 times in the last month and he always clicked on "Sports" in the first 10 seconds, we can prefetch that section for his next visit. To do this, we need to find a way to detect the user's navigation patterns and store them on the server or client side. Then, we can use that data per-user to decide what to prefetch.

 Tracking user data and navigation history, even anonymously, is always a privacy and legal issue. In this book, we are just talking about technical solutions, but always think about legal considerations when tracking user data.

When to Start a Prefetch

In trying to determine when to start a prefetch, the answer is clear: after the current page has loaded. We don't want to interfere with the initial load by prefetching resources that we are not 100% sure we'll need later.

The next question is *when* after the page has loaded. And here several approaches appear based on the fight between performance and cost. While prefetching as soon as possible after the initial page has loaded seems like a good idea, we are also minimizing the advantage of it. Several users will probably just abandon the page at that point, so prefetching a lot of stuff is a waste of resources.

Also, we need to remember that if the user is on a cellular network, she might be paying for the data traffic, so we need to be very careful about using that bandwidth for useless data.

Therefore, the usual approaches are:

- Use the Network Information API or HTTP Client Hints when available to enable prefetching only over WiFi or to decrease its usage while on cellular networks.
- Wait a couple of seconds before starting to prefetch, to reduce the risk of the user abandoning the website.

- Wait for a trigger, such as scrolling to some point on the document.

Wait for a `touchdown` event instead of a `click` or `touchup`. When the user taps on a link, the first event being triggered is `touchdown`, then `touchup` and finally `click`. We can gain between 100 and 400 ms by starting a prefetch request on `touchdown` instead of `click` or `touchup`. We also need to handle cancellations (if the user moves her finger out of the element before releasing it).

How to Prefetch

Prefetching can be done in three ways: by the browser, by the server, or by our code. When the browser or server is in charge of the prefetching we don't change our implementation, but when our code is in charge we must create our own prefetching JavaScript framework to avoid request duplication.

The whole idea of prefetching is to leave a resource in the browser's cache so it's ready when we need it without an HTTP request at that time. The problem appears when our code or the browser wants that resource and the prefetching process hasn't finished: is the browser smart enough to realize that it's already downloading that resource or not? It will depend on the manner in which we are prefetching.

Browser prefetching

Browser prefetching involves the definition of the URLs that the browser needs to prefetch and leave ready in the cache for future usage.

The older way to do it is with images and JavaScript:

```
// Prefetching an image
new Image().src = "http://myserver.com/myimage.png"
```

The previous example will trigger an HTTP request from the server to download that image, even though it's not used yet. If the server is returning the right expiration HTTP headers, then that image will be stored in the cache and therefore it will be ready to be used later. For non-image content, we should use XHR or the Fetch API because if we inject scripts or `<link>` elements with CSS they will be downloaded but also executed.

The great advantage of using browser prefetching is that if a browser is not compatible with it, the prefetching code will be ignored—the content won't be prefetched, but the current page will work as normal.

Resource Hints

Modern browsers support other ways to do prefetching through `<link>` tags, defined by the W3C's Resource Hints spec (*http://www.w3.org/TR/resource-hints*).

The spec defines several "link relation types" that we can use to give the browser more information about what's coming next. The browser is in charge of how and when that data will be used.

The possible hints that we can send to the browser are:

- DNS prefetch: `dns-prefetch`
- TCP preconnect (including DNS lookup, TCP handshake, and TLS negotiation if applicable): `preconnect`
- HTTP prefetch: `prefetch`
- HTTP prerender: `prerender`

Google has suggested a new `preload` Resource Hint (*https://w3c.github.io/preload*) that is not for prefetching but for preloading. The difference has to do with the guarantee of download. With `prefetch`, the browser will decide whether to download it or not, and when. With `preload`, the browser *must* download that resource, but we will use it later. It's here to replace using XHR to load assets that are not API calls.

Each hint will be defined as the `rel` attribute of a `<link>` element, and they may include an optional `pr` attribute for probability (from 0 to 1, with 1 being a hint to say that we will need that resource for sure).

For example:

```
<link rel="prefetch" href="http://mynewdomain.com/next.html" pr="0.6">
<link rel="prefetch" href="http://mynewdomain.com/prev.html" pr="0.3">
```

Because Resource Hints are just speculative requests, the browser may decide to delay them based on activity, so the current navigation context is not affected.

We've already seen in previous chapters how to use DNS prefetching so the browser can start a DNS query as soon as possible:

```
<link rel="dns-prefetch" href="http://mynewdomain.com">
```

Besides DNS prefetching, we can ask the browser to prefetch a whole document using:

```
<link rel="prefetch" href="http://mynewdomain.com/next.html">
```

In the case of `prefetch`, the resource will be downloaded but not parsed at all—meaning that in an HTML file, no CSS or JavaScript will be executed, downloaded, or parsed. The `prefetch` link also supports an `as` attribute that accepts values such as `audio`, `image`, `font`, `script`, `style`, and `video`, which will help the browser know what type of content we are expecting to set the right headers.

A `prerender` will download the resource and execute it, meaning that the CSS or JavaScript in an HTML file will also be parsed and executed. It's like opening that resource on a hidden tab ready for when we need it.

 For content loading, Chrome for Android, IE 11 for Windows Phone, and Edge for Windows support `prefetch` and `prerender` at the time of this writing. Firefox supports `prefetch` only, and Safari on iOS does not support either. Only Chrome and Firefox support the `preconnect` hint. Keep track of compatibility at Can I Use (*http://caniuse.com*).

If you want to get more information, check out Ilya Grigorik's article "Eliminating Roundtrips with Preconnect" (*https://www.igvita.com/2015/08/17/eliminating-roundtrips-with-preconnect*).

Prefetching from the server

The Resource Hints spec that we covered in the previous section also supports declarations in HTTP headers, so the server can make the decisions. While I can't see a good reason to do this, the option is there. It's done through the `Link` HTTP header, with the following syntax:

```
Link: </styles/styles.css>; rel=prefetch
```

This case can be defined as an extension to client prefetching.

If we are serving files through HTTP/2, we have the option to push resources to the client's cache through the TCP channel from the server. In this case, we will move the decision to the server and we must have logic server-side indicating which resources were delivered to know when the page is ready client-side. The difference from browser prefetching is that in this case the server will send the file without any browser request. The browser is always in charge of rejecting the file, but it will usually store it in the cache.

Firefox will add an X-moz: prefetch header in the request so we can differentiate normal requests from the ones that were triggered by a prefetch mechanism.

Custom prefetching

Prefetching by our code is usually useful with single-page applications (SPAs) or resources that are loaded dynamically on the same page, such as progressive web apps. It involves the usage of JavaScript, XHR, or the Fetch API to download resources and store them in the browser's cache or in a custom cache. We must provide logic to avoid duplications and to wait for the resource to be ready before using it.

If you are using XHR or the Fetch API over HTTP/1.1 with a custom client cache, you can reuse the same HTTP network request to download and cache several resources at a time in a JSON format.

The Offline Experience

The last thing we can do to improve the performance of the next visit is to cache locally all the files, including the initial HTML. Therefore, the next time the user accesses our website, all the files will already be stored locally. Of course, the website will appear as it did on the last visit, so if we update the UI frequently, this might not be a good idea; if we update the data frequently, we should show in the UI somehow that the data is old and we should use XHR to load new data and replace it.

This is how native mobile apps work: all the logic and the main UI are already stored on the phone so when we open the app everything is there immediately; then, we just download new data only. You can also do this on the mobile web when a user accesses your website: you can download locally all the necessary files, so next time the files are already there waiting.

There are currently two APIs available for supporting this behavior: Application Cache and service workers. Application Cache is the older and more compatible API (covering most of the mobile browsers out there); the service workers API is more experimental at the time of this writing (Chrome and Firefox only) but it has more freedom and advantages than the Application Cache API.

For years, the Google home page for mobile devices was served using the application cache for offline access. Therefore, every time you typed *google.com* or opened the browser in Android, the logo and the search form were already there. The perception was that Google was too fast.

We can use these techniques for:

- Improving perception of performance, predownloading the HTML, CSS, and JavaScript for the initial loading for next access, but not for the data
- Total offline usage, for web apps where everything will be downloaded
- An alternate offline website, offering alternative content and services when the user doesn't have a connection

For example, the *Guardian* (*http://guardian.co.uk*) has created alternate content for when you are offline and you've previously accessed the website on HTTPS with a crossword game and custom error information, as we can see in Figure 7-1. The code is available on GitHub (*https://github.com/guardian/frontend*).

Figure 7-1. The Guardian uses a service worker to provide an offline custom experience when the user doesn't have a connection

Table 7-1 compares using the application cache with using the Cache Storage API with service workers.

Table 7-1. Application cache versus service workers and Cache Storage API

Feature	Application cache	Service workers
Offline installation	Yes	Yes
Cache installation events	Yes	Yes
Cache Status Query API	No	Yes
Third-party resources	Yes	Yes
HTML must be cached	Yes	No
Use it only as a fallback	No	Yes
Served over HTTP	Yes	No
Served over HTTPS	Yes	Yes
Partial updates	No	Yes
Automatic version control	Yes	No
Mock responses on the fly	No	Yes
Compatibility	Excellent	Regular

Application Cache

HTML5 allows us to create offline-capable web apps using a mechanism known as the application cache. The concept is very simple. The user first opens the website in normal online mode, and it provides the browser with a package declaration text file called the manifest file, which lists all the resources (images, stylesheets, JavaScript, etc.) we want to be stored for offline navigation in the future. The next time the user visits the page, the HTML document is loaded from the cache, as well as all the resources in the manifest.

Our first step is to define what we want. Do we want a full offline application? Do we want some pages or data to be updated from the server every time the application tries to access them? Do we want to have a local data cache and update it whenever online access is available?

The second step is to define the manifest, or the list of files for the browser to download the first time the user accesses our website. This list must include every JavaScript script, stylesheet, image, or other resource that we want to access offline.

The Manifest File

The package list is delivered through a text file known as a cache manifest. This file must have as its first line the literal text CACHE MANIFEST. This line is followed by a list of all the URLs—relative or absolute—of the resources to download to the device.

The manifest file must be served as `text/cache-manifest` and needs to be defined as the `manifest` attribute of the `<html>` element:

```
<html manifest="appcache.manifest">
```

The HTML file that is pointing to the manifest, as well as the manifest itself, will be stored locally in the application cache implicitly; we don't need to declare them inside.

 If any file listed in the manifest fails to download while the package is being installed, the entire package is invalidated. That means that if we are defining resources on third-party servers, we will rely on these servers for our apps to be installed.

The initial `CACHE MANIFEST` line can be followed by a series of relative or absolute URLs that we want to be cached for offline availability. We can comment lines by using a hash (#) at the beginning of the line:

```
CACHE MANIFEST
# This is a comment
ourscript.js
images/logo.gif
images/other_image.jpg
ourstyles.css
```

If more than one HTML page that the user browses points to the same manifest URI, the manifest package will be reused and all the HTML files browsed will be added implicitly to the manifest as "master resources." That is, after a package has been installed, if the user browses to another page that points to the same manifest, all the resources will already be available offline.

Accessing Online Resources

If our application attempts to access any resource that was not originally defined in the manifest file, the process will fail because the application is sandboxed offline. By default, all the resources are declared in an implicit `CACHE:` section.

If we need information from the web—as we probably will—we can define it in the manifest file in a special section called `NETWORK:`. (To define a section, we just end the line with a colon.) So, if we want a *countries.json* file to always be delivered from the server, we can change our manifest to:

```
CACHE MANIFEST
# Resources that should be installed on the user's device

CACHE:
ourscript.js
images/logo.gif
```

```
images/other_image.jpg
ourstyles.css
# Resources that should always be downloaded from the web

NETWORK:
countries.json
```

Then, *countries.json* will not be downloaded with the other resources and instead will be accessed online every time the application needs it. If there is no Internet connection, we will not get this file unless the browser has a cached version (using the typical web cache, not the application cache).

In the NETWORK: section, we can use wildcards, such as *, or folders; every resource in these folders will be accessible from the web while we are in an offline operation mode.

So, if we want to have an offline application that can access the full web if the user has a connection, we can just use:

```
NETWORK:
*
```

With this configuration, only files listed before the NETWORK: section will be loaded from the offline package; every other resource will be loaded from the web.

Fallbacks

The application cache has a mechanism to access external online resources but at the same time provide a fallback to avoid errors if the user is offline: the FALLBACK: section. In this section, we provide two URLs, space-separated; the first one can use wildcards while the second one should be a specific URL.

For example:

```
FALLBACK:
images/profile.png noconnection.png
```

In this example, when the web app tries to get *images/profile.png*, it will bring it from the server if the user is online and will return *noconnection.png* as a fallback file if the user is offline. The fallback image is stored in the application cache package implicitly.

Updating the Package

We've said that when the package is installed, all the resources—including the main HTML document—will always be loaded from the local storage and not from the web. Therefore, it's fair to ask: how can we update a resource? What happens if we want to update the theme CSS file, change an image, or add a new page link in the HTML document?

One part of the picture that I omitted earlier is that every time the user opens a cached web app, while the app is always loaded from the local storage, in the background the browser tries to get an updated manifest file from the server. If there is no Internet connection, nothing happens, and the local version is used. If there is a network connection available, the browser downloads the manifest file from the server and does a byte-by-byte comparison of the new version of the file with the local version from the original web app download. If even one byte has changed, the entire cached manifest is invalidated and every resource is downloaded again, using the new manifest file.

Go back to the previous paragraph and read it again. Done? OK, let's take another look at what's happening. If we change the contents of a CSS file but do not change the name of that file, the manifest will be the same, so the downloaded files will not be updated. This is an important point—we need to change the manifest itself for the web app to receive the update.

How should we change the manifest when we make an update to any of the listed resources? The change can involve something as simple as adding a space, changing the resource name (versioning it), or even including a comment line at the start of the manifest file containing a random value or the last-modified date, as in:

```
CACHE MANIFEST
# webapp updated 2016-10-01
```

If we make a single change—for example, the date—the whole manifest will be invalidated and the platform will download all the files again. (Yes, all the files—with this API we can't update just one resource.)

Remember that the resources in the manifest will not be downloaded again until we update the manifest file or invalidate the application cache.

There's another unpleasant problem that arises when dealing with manifest updates: if there is an update, the platform downloads all the resources in the manifest again, but this download process is done in the background while the previous files are on the screen. This means the user will not see the newly downloaded versions of the resources until he reloads the application.

In other words, if we change the manifest, the user must load the page twice to see the new version. As we'll see shortly, we can use events to handle this situation.

Several bugs in some browsers and the inability to partially update the package make the Application Cache API problematic at times. That's why Google has created the service workers spec to replace, over time, the usage of this API. If you want to read more about this, check out Jake Archibald's "Application Cache Is a Douche-bag" (*http://alistapart.com/article/application-cache-is-a-douchebag*).

The JavaScript API

There is a global JavaScript object that helps us to know the status of the application cache. The object is `applicationCache`, and it has a `status` property that can have one of the values listed in Table 7-2.

Table 7-2. Status of the applicationCache object

Value	Constant	Description
0	UNCACHED	This is the first load of the page, or no manifest file is available.
1	IDLE	The cache is idle.
2	CHECKING	The local manifest file is being checked against the server's manifest file.
3	DOWNLOADING	The resources are being downloaded.
4	UPDATEREADY	The cache is ready.

If the application cache status is 0, our document is loaded from the network; otherwise, it is loaded from the application cache.

We can use constants to ask about the current status. For example:

```
if ('applicationCache' in window) {
    // The API is available
    if (applicationCache.status==applicationCache.UPDATEREADY) {
        // There is an update waiting for reload
    }
}
```

The `applicationCache` object has the methods `update()`, which will force an update check, and `swapCache()`, which will swap from the older cached versions of the resources to the newly downloaded versions (if the object is in the `UPDATEREADY` state).

However, the HTML document and all resources already in memory will not be updated until we do a full page reload (such as with `location.reload()`).

Cache Events

The `applicationCache` object dispatches events that we can handle to manage every situation. For example, if the user is accessing our website for the first time, we can show a "Downloading app" message while the resources are downloaded so the user will wait, increasing the probability of a complete download. This is particularly useful for offline experiences, but if we are using the application cache for perception of performance, it's probably better to not add any visual indication of the download.

The possible events that we can bind to are as follows:

checking
: The browser is checking the manifest.

downloading
: The browser has started downloading the resources listed in the manifest.

progress
: A resource has been downloaded (this event is fired for every resource, so we can create a progress bar). The current HTML page and the manifest file count as resources, so this event will be fired $n+2$ times, with n being the number of files in the `CACHE:` and `FALLBACK:` sections.

cached
: The first download process has finished properly.

noupdate
: The cached manifest has been compared with the version on the server, and no update is available.

updateready
: There was an update, and the new resources have been downloaded properly and are waiting for a reload.

error
: There was an error downloading a resource.

obsolete
: When checking for an update, it was determined that the manifest is no longer valid, so the web app has been deleted from the storage and will not be available offline the next time the user attempts to use it.

We can bind to these events using `addEventListener`. For example:

```
if ('applicationCache' in window) {
    // The API is available
    applicationCache.addEventListener('updateready', function() {
```

```
            // There is an update waiting for reload
        if (confirm("There is an update ready. Do you want to load it now?")) {
            history.reload();
        }
    }, false);
}
```

The previous code will ask the user if she wants to use the update right away by reloading the page.

Compatibility and Limits

Fortunately, application cache compatibility is good in the mobile web, but on some platforms issues do arise that are difficult to debug. Cloud-based browsers do not support this ability, as they need an Internet connection to parse the website in the cloud.

Chrome for Android, Android Browser (since 2.1—effectively, all users today), Internet Explorer on Windows Phone, Edge, Opera Mobile, Firefox, BlackBerry Browser, Samsung Internet Browser, and Amazon Silk support the Application Cache API.

Even if the package was installed properly, most browsers, including Safari on iOS (see Figure 7-2) and Chrome for Android, allow users to delete all that data via the Settings app (Advanced→Website Data). There are no public stats about how many users access that Settings feature, but my guess is that most people will ignore it and never delete a website's data.

One of the biggest problems with the specification is the lack of a limit definition. How much space can we allocate for an offline web app? Is there any limit? If so, is it per URL or per domain? Usually, up to 5 MB there are no big issues on any platforms and the user will not receive any notifications or be asked for permission. On iOS, we can store up to 25 MB without the user's permission and up to 50 MB with the user's permission.

If we are using the application cache to increase performance's perception on next visit, we should keep the app's package as small as possible to increase probability of installation.

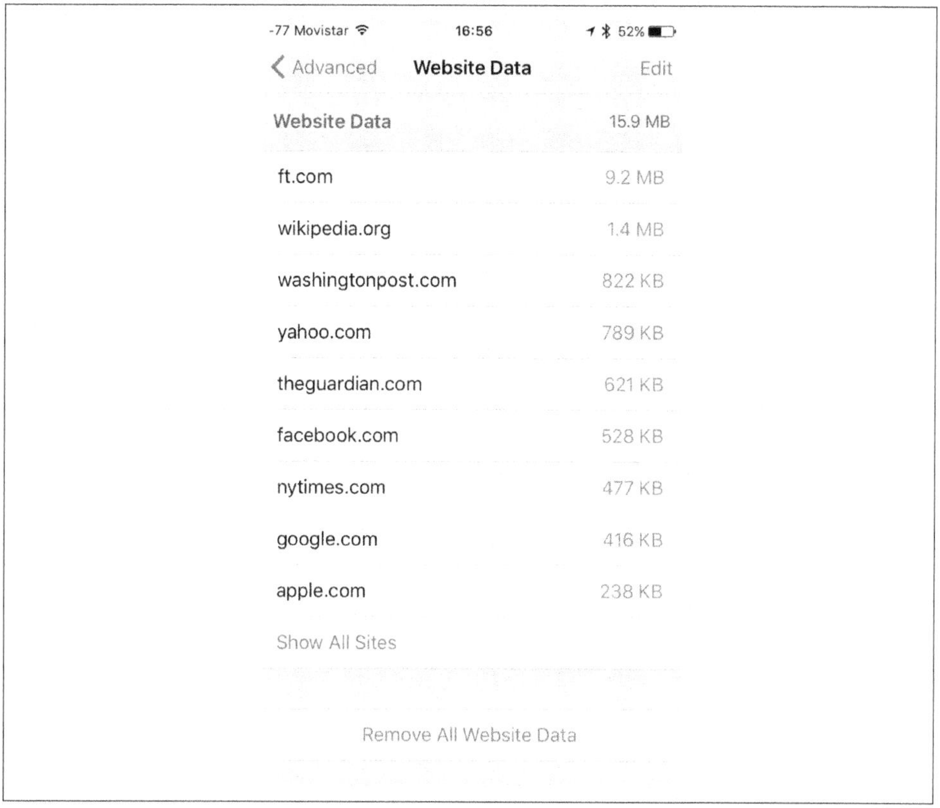

Figure 7-2. Safari on iOS users can see and delete data from websites via the Settings app (Settings→Safari→Advanced→Website Data)

Debugging the Application Cache

To debug the application cache, we can bind to the JavaScript events and log them to the console on every platform. Using Chrome for Android or Safari on iOS, we can use the Remote Inspection tools to check that console and to see the current state of the application cache.

Chrome will send debug messages to the console while the application cache is being generated or updated, as we can see in Figure 7-3, so we don't even need to log those messages.

To see if the application cache is stored and the current status, we can use the Remote Inspector, found on the Storage tab in Safari on iOS and under Resources→Application Cache in Chrome on iOS, as we can see in Figure 7-4.

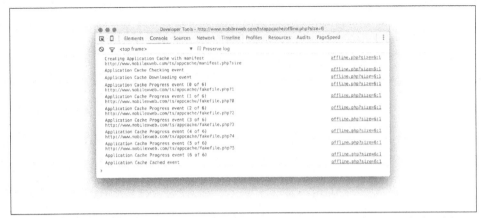

Figure 7-3. Chrome sends messages about the application cache to the console for debugging purposes

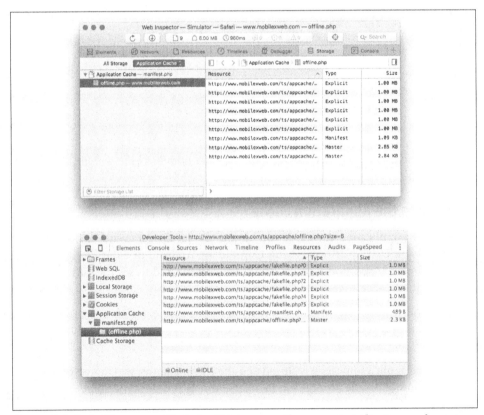

Figure 7-4. Both Chrome and Safari will let you see the current application cache status when connecting your device via a USB cable and using the Remote Inspector

Service Workers

Because the application cache can be buggy sometimes, it's not suitable for multipage solutions, and it will update every resource even if we change only one of them. In 2013, Google started work on a new specification that is now a W3C working draft: service workers (*http://www.w3.org/TR/service-workers*).

A service worker is a JavaScript process that will be executed outside of the scope of a browser's tab, and it can do different things while in the background. The first thing that a service worker can do is to hook itself into network requests and route requests to a custom cache, so it can replace the application cache completely.

It's similar to a shared worker—a web worker shared between two pages—in that it's not tied to any web page and it runs in its own scope, but it has more abilities, such as being event-driven so it can be executed automatically when some low-level event happens (such as a push message being received from the operating system).

While in this book we cover service workers for performance improvement usage only, the spec will allow several other interesting use cases for the mobile web, such as geofencing, beacon discovery, and OS integration.

A service worker is a JavaScript Web Worker, meaning it runs in its own thread and it can't access the DOM directly. At the time of this writing, only Chrome for Android, Opera Mobile, Firefox, and Samsung Internet Browser 4.0+ support service workers. Safari and Edge will add support for it in the future; check Mobile HTML5 Compatibility (*http://mobilehtml5.org*) or Can I Use Service Workers? (*http://caniuse.com/serv iceworkers*) for updated information.

In terms of performance, we can use service workers to create a custom cache and decide when to access the network and when to use a local resource on a JavaScript-based proxy hooked to network events. We can even emulate the application cache, because we can also subscribe to the initial HTML URL fetch.

Service workers make heavy use of ECMAScript 6 promises, so you should be familiar with this new way to use asynchronous code in JavaScript. Jake Archibald from Google has written a great article on JavaScript promises (*http:// www.html5rocks.com/en/tutorials/es6/promises*) you might want to check out.

Service workers work only over TLS-based connections, so your server must have a secure certificate and must be serving files through HTTPS. The only exception is through http://localhost, which is available for testing purposes.

When using service workers with a custom cache, we have to decide which fetch/cache policy we are going to use, such as:

- Caching everything after installation and then serving from the cache
- Caching only after fetching the resource from the network for the first time
- Always using the network (updating the cache) and only falling back on the cache when the fetch operation fails
- Always using the network and falling back to an alternate cached version when offline

 If you are not using HTTPS today and you want to start doing that without buying costly TLS certificates, you can start with free certificates from *https://letsencrypt.org*.

Service workers are available in Chrome for Android as of version 40, and the full Cache Storage API mentioned later in this section is available as of version 46. There is a Cache Polyfill (*https://github.com/coonsta/cache-polyfill*) available if you still have Chrome for Android users between versions 40 and 46.

Installing the Service Worker

To install a service worker in the user's browser, we first need to register it through JavaScript. This is usually done on the first page load. The service worker is a separate *.js* file that we will register through a `navigator.serviceWorker` public interface, as in the next example:

```
// We first check compatibility
if ('serviceWorker' in navigator) {
    navigator.serviceWorker.register("serviceworker.js")
                        .then(function(registration) {
                            // Worker successfully registered
                        })
                        .catch(function(error) {
                            // Error has occurred
                        });
}
```

We don't need to worry about registering a service worker that has been registered before. The browser will take care of that and it won't register it again, so we can call this method on every page load.

The location of the service worker will define its scope and what resources it can detect. If the service worker is in a subfolder of our domain, it will have permission to hook into URL requests under that folder. If it's located in the root folder, it'll have the power to work with the entire domain.

Caching Files

Now that we've installed the service worker, we can work with the *.js* file. That file is not connected to the DOM in any way, and it has the `self` special object pointing to the worker itself. The worker has several events that we can bind to, such as `install` to detect that the worker was successfully installed and `fetch` to detect a network fetch request from any page in the worker's scope.

When we are working with service workers for cache purposes, we usually bind to the `install` property and we cache the files there using the Cache Storage API available in service workers, as shown here:

```
var urls = ['/',                // Home page
            '/styles.css'       // Main CSS file
            '/images/logo.png'  // Images
           ];

self.addEventListener('install', function(event) {
    // The worker is now installed in the browser
    event.waitUntil(caches.open('my-app-cache'))
                    .then(function(cache) {
                        return cache.addAll(urls);
                    })
                );
});
```

In this example, we define an array of files to cache and then we use the global `caches` object in the service worker through a promise. We open the cache, named `my-app-cache` in our case, and then we use the `addAll` method of the `Cache` object that we receive by argument in the `open` event.

Google has created a Node.js module to easily cache files using service workers. You can download `sw-precache` from GitHub (*https://github.com/GoogleChrome/sw-precache*).

Because we are using `event.waitUntil()` inside the `install` event handler, we are guaranteeing that all the files are cached properly. If caching any of the files fails, then the whole installation event will fail and the worker will not be installed.

We can create as many caches as we want using different names.

You can download resources from your same origin (protocol+host+port) or resources from third-party origins if they support cross-origin resource sharing (CORS) (*http://www.w3.org/TR/cors*), where HTTP headers in the response allow cross-domain access. If you want to bypass the CORS rule, you can download resources to the cache from any source, creating an opaque response (meaning that you won't be able to know if the request was successful or not). To do this, you need to slightly change the way requests are to added to the cache, using:

```
cache.addAll(urls.map(function(url) {
  return new Request(url, { mode: 'no-cors' });
}));
```

Serving Files

Now we have a cache of files locally stored in the browser. How can we serve them? The service worker acts as a network proxy in its URL scope, using the `fetch` event. Every request to the server that the browser initiates within this scope will first go through our event handler. Then we can decide whether to deliver a file from the cache or fetch it from the network, as expressed in Figure 7-5.

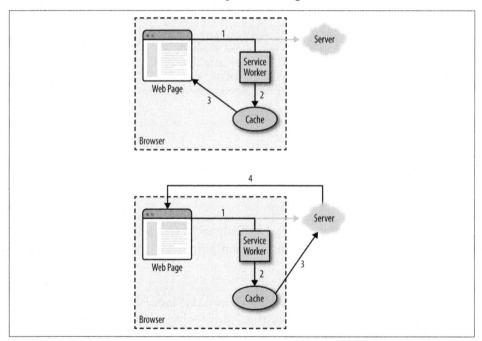

Figure 7-5. A service worker can intercept every request from the web page and deliver files from the cache when they're there (top diagram) or make a fetch request when they're not (bottom diagram)

To make this work, we need to bind a listener to the fetch event and use promises to return a result to the browser when requested:

```
// ... Rest of the service worker here ...

self.addEventListener('fetch', function(event) {
  event.respondWith(
    caches.match(event.request)
        .then(function(response) {
            if (response) {
                // It's in the cache, so we use it
                return response;
            } else {
                // It's not in the cache, so we fetch it
                return fetch(event.request);
            }
        })
  );
});
```

We can use event.request.url inside the respondWith promise to make decisions locally about what to do with the request. The respondWith promise is usually answered with caches.match(request) if we find a request in the cache, fetch(request) to make the HTTP request to the server, or mock manual responses using the Response constructor.

 The service worker's fetch method doesn't include any credentials or cookies by default when making the request. If we want to add them, we should use fetch(url, {credentials: 'include'}).

To create mock HTTP responses, we can set just a string response and, optionally, HTTP headers, such as:

```
self.addEventListener('fetch', function(event) {
  if (event.request.url=="/") {
    event.respondWith(
      return new Response("This is a fake response to every request");
    );
  else {
    event.responseWith(
     return new Response("This is a fake <b>HTML response</b>",
       { headers: { 'Content-type': 'text/html'}}
     )
    );
  }
});
```

You can decide to deliver fake responses or alternate precached responses if the user is offline or if the fetch operation failed. In the following example, we verify that the current fetch is for an HTML page (not some other resource) and then try to fetch it, as we always want to have fresh HTML. If the fetch doesn't work, we deliver a previously cached offline HTML file:

```
function isAnHTMLRequest(request) {
  // Searches for HTML MIME type in HTTP headers
    var mimeTypes = request.headers.get('Accept').split(',');
    var acceptHTML = mimeTypes.some(function (mime) {
      return mime=='text/html';
    });
    return acceptHTML;
}

self.addEventListener('fetch', function (event) {
    var url = new URL(event.request.url);
    if (isAnHTMLRequest(event.request)) {
        event.respondWith(
                fetch(request)    // We try with a network fetch
                .catch(function () {
                    // The network fetch failed!
                    // We return a precached file
                    return caches.match('/offline.html');
                })
        );
    } else {
        // It's not HTML, so we check the cache
        event.respondWith(
            caches.match(request)
                .then(function (response) {
                    if (response) {
                        // It's in the cache
                        return response;
                    } else {
                        // It's not in the cache, so we fetch it
                        fetch(request);
                    }
                })
        );
    }
});
```

 A service worker can add requests to the cache, remove them, or update them at any time.

Fetching and Caching

When you fetch a URL that is not in the cache, you can optionally add that request to the custom cache for future usage, such as in:

```
// ... Rest of the service worker here ...

self.addEventListener('fetch', function(event) {
  event.respondWith(
    caches.match(event.request)
        .then(function(response) {
            if (response) {
                // It's in the cache, so we use it
                return response;
            } else {
                // It's not in the cache, so we fetch it and cache it
                return fetch(event.request).then(function(response) {
                    cache.put(event.request, response.clone());
                    return response;
                });
            }
        })
  );
});
```

The Cache Storage Interface

Now that we know the basics of installing a service worker and using its events, it's time to talk more about the CacheStorage interface available through the global caches object inside a service worker.

The caches object is of type CacheStorage and it represents a collection of Cache objects created by the developer. The CacheStorage interface has the following useful methods:

open(name)
: Opens a Cache object by name. If it doesn't exist, it creates one.

delete(name)
: Deletes a Cache object by name with all the requests cached there.

match(request)
: Searches every Cache object for a request and returns a promise that can be used to get its cached response

keys()
: Returns all the available Cache names.

has(*name*)

Tells you if a cache is available by name.

If you are planning to have only one group of files cached in your service worker, you can use a version number as the Cache name, such as 'v1'.

Cache objects are represented by a user-generated string name and a collection of key/value pairs, with the key being an HTTP(S) request and the value an HTTP(S) response.

The caches object is available inside service workers and also inside the window object of the DOM in a normal script if it's served on HTTPS. The cache storage will include files cached by the author only; it won't include any files cached by the browser.

To get a Cache object by name with a promise, we just use the following code inside a web page or inside a service worker:

```
caches.open('my-cache').then(function(cache) {
    // We have the Cache object in the argument
});
```

The Cache object has the following methods, driven by promises:

add(*request*)

Fetches a request and adds it to the cache.

addAll(*requests*)

Fetches a collection of requests and adds them to the cache.

put(*request, response*)

Adds an already-fetched request with its response to the cache.

delete(*request, [options]*)

Deletes a request from the cache.

keys([*request, [options]*])

Gets requests from the cache (all of them or filtered by arguments).

match(*request, [options]*)

Finds one request in the cache so we can get its response.

```
matchAll(request, [options])
```
Finds several requests in the cache so we can get their responses. Usually used when the requests have the Vary header.

Every method accepting requests will accept string values as URLs or DOM Request (*https://fetch.spec.whatwg.org/#dom-request*) objects (having a URL, method, headers, etc.).

Updating Cache

With the application cache, the cache is automatically replaced when the manifest changes. There is no such autoupdate mechanism when using service workers and the Cache Storage API. Therefore, updating the cache is a manual operation that we have to do using JavaScript. The advantage is that we are fully in charge, meaning that we can update the cache partially, as needed.

One strategy to follow with some resources that might get updated in the future but where it's not so important to always have the most up-to-date version is to always deliver from the cache but fetch the new version at the same time from the network to update the cache. Therefore, the next time the user will get the updated version:

```
// ... Rest of the service worker here ...

self.addEventListener('fetch', function(event) {
  event.respondWith(
    caches.match(event.request)
        .then(function(response) {
            // Even if the response is in the cache, we fetch it
            // and update the cache for future usage
            var fetchPromise = fetch(event.request).then(
                function(networkResponse) {
                    cache.put(event.request, networkResponse.clone());
                    return networkResponse;
            });
            // We use the currently cached version if it's there
            return response || fetchPromise;
        })
  );
});
```

Another mechanism involves defining a custom versioning system, such as injecting an array of resources and their version numbers (or timestamps) inside the main document, and then querying on every load to see if the versions in the cache are up to date. If we find a resource that needs updating, we can then fetch it in the background:

```
cache.matches(urlToUpdate).then(function(request) {
    fetch(urlToUpdate).then(function(response) {
        cache.put(request, networkResponse.clone());
```

```
        });
    })
```

The previous code can be executed in the main page or within the `activate` event of the service worker.

Updating a Service Worker

Every time a website registers a service worker that is already installed, the browser downloads the service worker's JavaScript file and compares it byte by byte to the previous version. If it has changed, then the new service worker is installed (firing the `install` event)—but it won't be in charge of future `fetch` events until every page that is using the service worker has been closed. Therefore, the previous service worker version will be in charge of the network proxy for a while.

 The cache is not deleted or replaced when a service worker is updated. If we want to replace it, we can use a different name—such as `cache-v2`—and then delete the previous one, or just replace the files inside the same cache storage.

Once the new service worker takes control (because every page using the old version has been closed), an `activate` event will be fired. The `activate` event is usually the place to upgrade your cache. If you are not versioning your cache storages, then using the `install` event on your new service worker for cache management will interfere with the cache that the old version is using, while it's using it.

 You don't know how much time has passed since the user's last visit to your website (it can be months). A service worker update might happen that skips several versions, so you should never expect the current cache to be the last version before the new one. Using a whitelist of caches that you want and deleting everything else might be a good idea.

In his article "Introduction to Service Worker" (*http://www.html5rocks.com/en/tutorials/service-worker/introduction*), Google developer Matt Gaunt suggests deleting any caches that are no longer going to be used in the `activate` event when updating a service worker:

```
self.addEventListener('activate', function(event) {

  // Array of caches that we will use in this version
  var cacheWhitelist = ['pages-cache-v1', 'blog-posts-cache-v1'];

  event.waitUntil(
    caches.keys().then(function(cacheNames) {
```

```
    return Promise.all(
      cacheNames.map(function(cacheName) {
        if (cacheWhitelist.indexOf(cacheName) === -1) {
          // Deletes the cache because we won't use it here
          return caches.delete(cacheName);
        }
      })
    );
  })
);
});
```

Debugging Service Workers

Because a service worker runs in its own thread, separated from a specific web page, we can't inspect it from the normal developer tools. In Chrome for Android, you can debug your service workers in a remote debugging session (for details on using the Remote Inspector, see Chapter 4).

To see all the service workers installed in the system, open a new tab and type *"chrome://serviceworker-internals"* in the address bar. All the service workers will be listed on this page (even those not running at that point), and you can delete them from there as well as starting them. You can also see the scope for each service worker, as we can see in Figure 7-6.

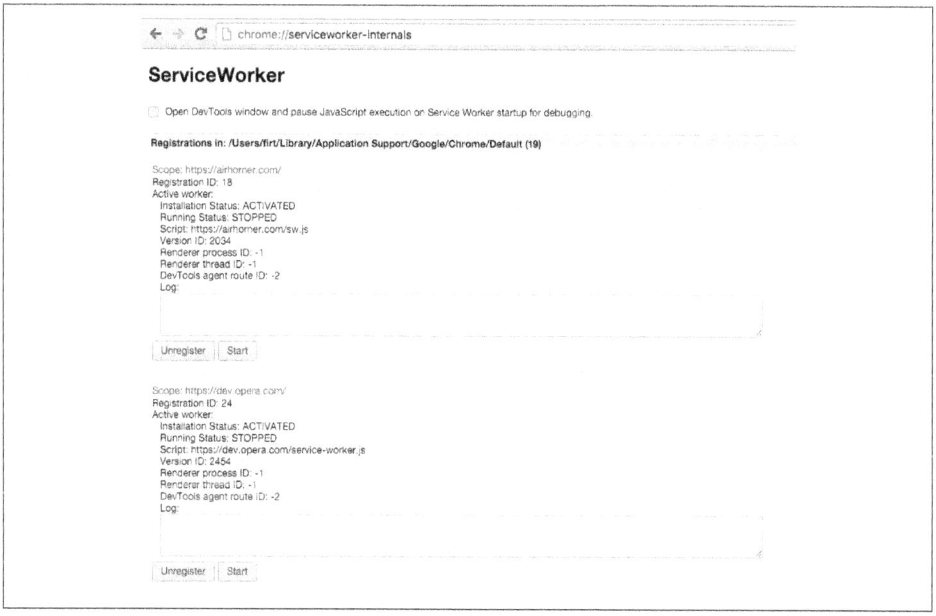

Figure 7-6. From the serviceworker-internals URL, you will be able to see every service worker installed on your Android phone in Chrome

To debug and inspect a service worker, it needs to be running first (you can use the Start button on the screen shown in Figure 7-6 if it's not running). Then, open *chrome://inspect* and check the service workers section; you will find here only currently activated service workers. You can kill them or inspect them (Figure 7-7) using the proper links.

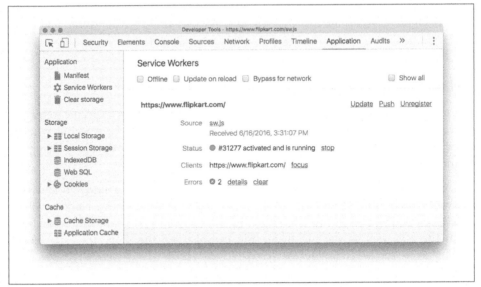

Figure 7-7. If a service worker is running—usually because an opened website from that scope has registered it—we can inspect it from the Remote Inspector and force some interesting scenarios, such as "offline" or "bypass for network"

Also, the latest versions of Chrome will let you see the current's page service workers from the Applications panel inside the Chrome Developer Tools.

When you inspect a service worker, you will be able to see the console, debug its JavaScript code, sniff the network, and profile the code, but most of the UI-related stuff in the Developer Tools will be disabled (such as Elements) as the service worker is not connected to any UI or web page.

From a service worker debugger tool, as well as from a normal web page, we can see and access the current caches available in the Application tab, as we can see in Figure 7-8.

If you are using Firefox, you can access a service worker debugging window through the *about:debugging#workers* URL.

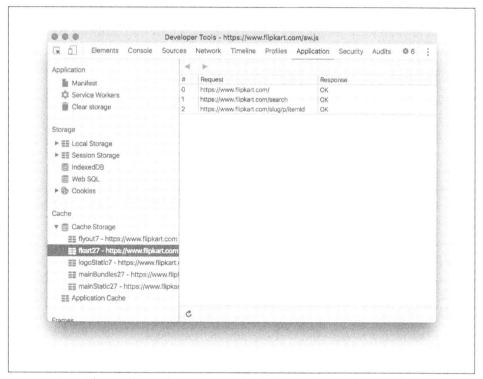

Figure 7-8. In Chrome for Android, we can check the Application tab (previously Resources) to see the current caches available and the resources inside

Background Sync

An extension to the service worker API has been proposed that lets the browser synchronize data and update information in the background. The API is known as Web Background Synchronization, or Background Sync.

This is particularly useful to create optimistic actions, such as liking a Facebook post offering the user immediate feedback about the action, even if the server isn't synchronized yet. With this API, even if the user closes the browser tab before the action is saved on the server, we will be able to do the sync in the background.

The Web Background Synchronization spec (*https://wicg.github.io/BackgroundSync/ spec*) is still an unofficial draft at the time of this writing, but it is available in Chrome for Android since version 49.

So how does it work? Instead of using Ajax or the Fetch API to save something to the network, we request a service worker background sync operation. That flag will make the browser execute the background sync event handler of our service worker as soon as possible when there is network availability.

Let's review some use cases. Let's say that the user has saved a form and we want to send that data to the server. If we use Ajax or the Fetch API, we will have the following problems:

- If the user has lost connectivity, the request will fail.
- If the user goes to a different page or changes the tab, the request will be aborted.
- If the user closes the browser or is out of battery, the request will never reach the server.

If we use a background sync request, the browser will process that request through our service worker, which is not attached to the page—so no matter what happens with the tab or the browser itself, the service worker will still be ready to execute the request.

If there is no connection at the time, the browser will defer the background sync until the connection is restored in the future. If there is a connection but your code can't save the data on the server for whatever reason, then the background sync will still be marked as pending, so the browser will retry executing your service worker's event handler in the future.

Let's see some code to register a background sync operation:

```
// We register a background sync within a service worker context
navigator.serviceWorker.ready.then(function(registration) {
  registration.sync.register('save-form-data').then(function() {
    // registration succeeded
  }, function() {
    // registration failed
  });
});
```

Then, inside our service worker file:

```
self.addEventListener('sync', function(event) {
  if (event.tag == 'save-form-data') {
    event.waitUntil(new Promise(function(resolve, reject) {
      // saveData is a function that we need to create
        saveData(function(ok) {
          // This is asynchronous
          if (ok) {
           resolve();
          } else {
              reject();
          }
      });
    }));
  }
});
```

You can use IndexedDB to store pending data in the main thread that will be accessed by the service worker later.

You can find out more about this API in the WICG article "Background Synchronization Explained" (*https://github.com/WICG/BackgroundSync/blob/master/explainer.md*).

Background Periodic Sync

This API will improve the perception of performance, as the data will be there when the user accesses our website. We will be able to define when to do a sync operation, such as only when the user is on WiFi and when the device is being charged, so we don't consume data or battery for this purpose.

At the time of this writing, Chrome is working on periodic sync for a future version, so it might be available in Chrome after version 54 at some point. The API will require permission from the user, as it might be doing stuff in the background without the user's intervention.

Just to give you some hints here of what the API looks like, take a look at the following sample, which will register a periodic sync on a web page:

```
navigator.serviceWorker.ready.then(function(registration) {
  registration.periodicSync.register({
    tag: 'download-new-stuff',      // default: ''
    minPeriod: 12 * 60 * 60 * 1000, // default: 0
    powerState: 'avoid-draining',   // default: 'auto'
    networkState: 'avoid-cellular'  // default: 'online'
  }).then(function(periodicSyncReg) {
    // success
  }, function() {
    // failure
  })
});
```

Then, a service worker will have its `periodicsync` event fired when the appropriate time and situation comes. For example:

```
self.addEventListener('periodicsync', function(event) {
  if (event.registration.tag == 'download-new-stuff'') {
    event.waitUntil(fetchLatestNews());
  }
  else {
    // It's an unknown sync request
    event.registration.unregister();
  }
});
```

In Chrome, service workers can also be used for push notifications (*https://developers.google.com/web/updates/2015/03/push-notifications-on-the-open-web*). While this doesn't have a direct relationship to performance, it can help us keep our users engaged with our content, and in the future we might be able to start a service worker from the server with silent notifications.

Future Visits Are an Opportunity

In Chapter 6, we saw how to optimize the first visit. In this chapter, we focused on how to take advantage of that visit to optimize the next ones as an opportunity to improve the experience.

We have two kinds of future visits to cover in terms of performance improvement: the content immediately accessed after the first visit, and separate visits in the near or far future. To improve performance we have to:

- Define a cache policy for the browser's cache using HTTP headers.
- Prefetch content and network-related stuff, such as DNS prefetching using meta tags or custom solutions.
- Use the application cache and service workers with the Cache Storage API to provide a better experience on next visits and to improve usage while the user is offline or has a bad connection. While the application cache might be deprecated in service worker–compatible browsers, it will still be necessary for other browsers.

In Chapter 8, we will start looking at how to improve responsiveness after the requested content has been loaded.

Optimizing Responsiveness and the Post-Loading Experience

When we think about web performance optimization, we usually think about initial load times, but performance improvement also includes how the user perceives the whole experience (how fast users can achieve their goals) and the responsiveness of the content once it has been loaded.

In this chapter, we will analyze how to improve performance and perception of the whole experience, including providing immediate feedback and keeping a good frame rate consistently on animations and scroll operations.

Immediate Feedback

As we saw earlier, a user will perceive anything that takes more than 100 milliseconds. Therefore, if the user taps on a button and doesn't receive any feedback, such as a UI pressed state, within 100 ms, he will perceive the delay. One of the goals of RAIL, therefore, is to provide feedback within this time limit.

Let's review some techniques that we can use to keep the feedback within our goal.

Touch Delay

In 2007, Apple released the first touch-optimized browser for the mobile space: Safari for iOS. It was the first browser exposing a desktop viewport to classic websites that is zoomed out to fit on the small screen. We all know how this works: the idea was cloned in every other mobile browser from that time.

While multitouch screens allow us to zoom in and out freely, sometimes it's difficult to just focus on one paragraph and make the zooming and positioning gestures to read that zone comfortably. Therefore, Safari incorporated a double-tap gesture to smartly zoom into a paragraph-based HTML element.

You are probably thinking, why are we talking about this in a performance book? Well, let me tell you that this particular gesture has damaged mobile web performance badly when talking about immediate feedback. When the user taps on any element on the screen—an input, a link, a button—the browser waits around 300 ms to see if a second tap will be made for the double-tap gesture. Therefore, if a user clicks on a link, the request operation will start 300 ms later—and that is clearly outside of our goal of 100 ms.

This behavior is also available in other mobile browsers, but fortunately for us, some browsers have started to solve the problem. When you have a mobile-optimized viewport declaration, such as:

```
<meta name="viewport" content="width=device-width">
```

Or when you disable zooming with a viewport declaration of user-scalable=no or other mechanisms, there is no point in waiting for a double-tap gesture, as there will be no zoom operation. Therefore, some browsers, such as Chrome for Android, remove the 300 ms delay, and they will fire the click operation immediately.

From iOS 9.3, Safari also removes the 300 ms delay when you have a mobile viewport such as the one just described or when the container where the links or tappable elements are located has the CSS touch-action: manipulation declaration, such as in:

```
body {
    touch-action: manipulation;
}
```

To remove the delay in browsers without support for autoremoval based on the viewport or CSS, the solution involves the use of touch events (such as touchend) instead of click events.

For example, a quick solution to progressively enhance <a> elements will look like:

```
var links = document.getElementsByTagName("a");
for (var i=0; i<links.length; i++) {
        links[i].addEventListener("touchend", function(e) {
                // we first prevent the click being fired in 300 ms,
                e.preventDefault();
                // then we go to the original link
                location.href=this.href;
        });
}
```

There are a couple of other situations we must handle also, such an abort operation when the user taps on a link then changes her mind and releases outside of the link, or multi-browser hacks such as letting the default behavior take precedence in browsers that already manage the problem for us.

Because Safari on iOS 9.3+ and Chrome from v32 don't add the 300 ms delay when using CSS or a mobile viewport, using frameworks or JavaScript-based solutions to remove the delay as a general rule is not a good idea anymore.

I suggest you use the open source framework FastClick (*https://github.com/ftlabs/fast click*) from the FT Labs on noncompatible browsers.

JavaScript Tasks

One of the usual reasons for not achieving feedback within 100 ms is JavaScript code in event handlers. We've already seen that JavaScript code executes by default in the main UI thread, the same thread that the browser uses to calculate styles and to render changes on the screen. If your JavaScript code is taking longer than 50 ms, you have a good chance of not reaching the feedback goal of 100 ms.

Therefore, our aim will be to release the main UI thread as soon as possible in an event handler, such as for a click or touch event. Typical code looks like this:

```
myElement.addEventListener("touchend", function(e) {
        // Long operation
});
```

Only after the long operation has finished, does the browser have the ability to calculate and render changes on the screen, such as returning a button state to nonpressed.

 If you are perceiving a feedback delay, you can use your browser's developer tools to profile that case from your phone and find the code that is responsible.

There are several solutions available to solve this problem, varying in compatibility.

Defer code

The simplest and most compatible solution is to set a timer that has already expired (with a time of 0 milliseconds), which will defer the execution. After the code finishes, the browser will update the UI, and when it's idle it will look for expired stored code to be executed, so it will then execute our long operation.

The code will look like:

```
myElement.addEventListener("touchend", function(e) {
    setTimeout(function() {
        // Long operation
```

```
        }, 0);
    });
```

This is the oldest solution, and the most widely compatible one, but not the best one to take advantage of newer browser execution engines. The upcoming `setImmediate` and `requestIdleCallback`, covered in Chapter 5, will provide a better alternative.

 Even if you are using a deferred execution technique, if your code takes too much time (more than 100 ms) it might be a good idea to split it into smaller pieces that will be called separately to reduce the probability of using precious time that the browser needs to keep the UI updated.

Debouncing and throttling

Debouncing and throttling are two design patterns that we can use to reduce the execution of too many event listeners when it's not really necessary; for example, when the user is scrolling the page, we might not need to update something on every `scroll` call. With debouncing, we group several calls to the same events into one; with throttling, we are forcing our call to be executed no more than once per time period, such as a maximum of once per 400 ms.

You can learn more about these practices in the CSS-Tricks article "Debouncing and Throttling Explained Through Examples" (*https://css-tricks.com/debouncing-throttling-explained-examples*).

Good-bye DOM, hello Canvas

In 2015, Flipboard (*http://flipboard.com*) rethought how to achieve the goal of 60 fps on a mobile website: using Canvas to provide an app UI. The developers have released an article describing what they've done for the mobile web (*http://engineering.flipboard.com/2015/02/mobile-web*); they have also released the React Canvas framework (*https://github.com/flipboard/react-canvas*), which lets you render React.js components to a Canvas context instead of the DOM.

Passive event listeners

Passive event listeners (*https://dom.spec.whatwg.org/#observing-event-listeners*) are a new way to bind events where we don't have the option of preventing the default operation. This technique is pretty useful while scrolling, because we don't have the option to cancel the default scroll: the browser can do the scrolling even if we are executing some JavaScript code.

You can make an event listener passive with an optional fourth argument:

```
myElement.addEventListener("touch", function(e) {
    // Your event handling code
}, true, { passive: true });
```

At the time of this writing, this possibility is available in Chrome for Android from version 51.

In Chrome for Android, you can enable a flag through *chrome:// flags* to force passive mode on every event listener. While it can break some websites, it will let you see the performance improvement.

Web workers

If a long operation involves calculations and operations that don't need to work with the DOM or UI other than to get an input before starting and to show the output at the end, we can consider using web workers.

Web Workers (*https://www.w3.org/TR/workers*) is a W3C specification that allows JavaScript to create working threads instead of executing all the code in the main UI thread, shared with the browser's rendering engine.

The specification defines two kinds of workers: workers and shared workers.

We covered service workers in Chapter 7. Service workers are not part of the initial Web Workers specification; they have their own spec, although they are also web workers.

Creating a worker allows a script to create an isolated thread that can communicate bidirectionally with the opener script and that has its own isolated context. A shared worker can be accessed by different scripts in the same domain that are working in different contexts, such as different tabs, windows, or iframes. Using the idea of ports, the shared worker can communicate with different executing scripts at the same time.

Shared workers don't have much usage in mobile browsers because, as we have seen, usually only one window or tab is active and running. Therefore, the need for shared workers is low, although they may sometimes be useful if we are using scripts in iframes.

Workers are not available in Android Browser up to version 4.1, or Internet Explorer up to version 9. Support has been incorporated in Safari on iOS from version 4.0, Internet Explorer from version 10, Edge, Chrome for Android, Firefox, and others.

A worker is always an external JavaScript file that will be executed in an isolated thread, and that means the worker can't access any DOM objects (such as document) or UI features (such as alerts). Using workers is especially important for performance purposes to avoid blocking the UI on long calculations and operations, such as a long parsing process.

 Because web workers run in a different thread, they release the main UI thread to update the UI as soon as possible.

While a worker can't access the DOM, it can send and receive information to/from the main thread though the Post Message API.

To create a worker, we just instantiate it:

```
myElement.addEventListener("touchend", function(e) {
    setTimeout(function() {
        // Long operation is inside worker.js
        var worker = new Worker('worker.js');
    }, 0);
});
```

In order to enable bidirectional communication, we use the message event and the postMessage function:

```
// Capturing messages from the worker
worker.addEventListener(function(event) {
    // event.data has the information sent by the worker
});

// Sending messages to the worker
worker.postMessage(dataToSend);
```

The message can be a basic data type such as a string or a number, an array, or an object containing other serializable data types. We can't pass native objects, such as document or window, through the communication channel. Objects being transferred are copied and not shared, so your object will be duplicated on the other side.

Using an object with JSON syntax, we can create our own communication protocol between the main thread and the worker, using different properties to define what we need.

The worker is an external file that has a special `self` object referring to the worker itself. It uses the same messaging API, including the `message` event and `postMessage`, to communicate with the main thread, using `self` to reference itself:

```
// worker.js

// Capturing messages from the main thread
self.addEventListener("message", function(event) {
    // event.data has the information sent by the main thread
})

// Sending messages to the main thread
self.postMessage(dataToMainThread);
```

With a nonstandard feature, some browsers allow the execution of a worker using a data URI or a blob element (binary data of a script) that can be created dynamically from a string file. Therefore, we can avoid the usage of an external file; however, this hack is not safe for mobile browsers.

A worker can load external files using the `importScripts` function and it can be terminated at any time using the `terminate` method.

Frame Rate

Another of the goals of RAIL is to keep a consistent animation frame rate of 60 fps. While we can have CSS, SVG, or JavaScript-based animations in our mobile web experiences, the most typical animation that we have is scrolling. When the user scrolls the website (a common scenario on not-so-large mobile devices), we should try to keep frame rate consistent. In some browsers, we can activate an FPS meter while doing remote debugging, so we will see the current frame rate on the screen. We can then start animations, scroll the page, and do other stuff and see if the frame rate drops or not.

Scrolling Experience

You may be wondering, what harm can it do to the experience if the scrolling is managed by the browser? Well, there are a couple of situations that will definitely harm scrolling performance.

Chrome Developer Tools includes a tool (see Figure 8-1) that will let us see which areas of the screen are being repainted when scrolled.

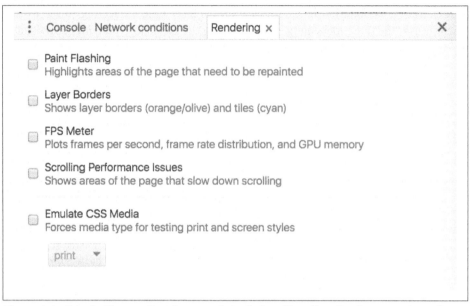

Figure 8-1. Google Chrome Developer tools include a "Scrolling Performance Issues" option that will help you finding code and features that are affecting the frame rate while scrolling

The first typical mistake is to use a JavaScript framework for scroll hijacking or scroll replacement, such as via iScroll. These frameworks were used a lot in the first years the iPhone was on the market, but they should be avoided at all costs today. They use JavaScript to detect low-level touch events, creating the scroll behavior entirely in JavaScript. The usual experience is bad, because too much JavaScript code needs to be executed on every finger move, leading to a frame rate drop and weird usability experiences.

 Some older browsers, such as Android Browser and Safari on iOS up to 7.x, pause all paint operations while the user is scrolling to avoid performance issues. Therefore, your JavaScript might be changing styles during scrolling without any result until the scroll has finished.

The second usual mistake that will harm scrolling experiences is to attach event listeners to the scroll event on window. While in some situations it's acceptable (such as for parallax effects), as a general rule we should avoid doing stuff in the main thread while the user is scrolling.

Some mobile browsers—typically older ones—won't even fire your scroll events while the user is scrolling and will fire just one event after the scrolling animation has ended. The same happens with UIWebView and home screen web apps on iOS, even in newer versions.

 Parallax websites frequently use scroll hijacking to provide a different experience when scrolling the page. Be careful and use this with care on mobile devices.

Also, using passive event listeners, as stated before in this chapter, can significantly improve the scrolling experience in compatible browsers.

Momentum-based scrolling areas

If you have small scrolling areas, such as block elements with the style `overflow: scroll`, you may notice that they don't scroll with momentum following the scroll on the page. They have a hard scroll: the user releases his finger and the scroll suddenly stops, with bouncing or momentum applied.

A hard scrolling behavior feels slow on a mobile device, so it's a good idea to improve the perception of performance by applying momentum. Some browsers allow us to define this through a CSS extension:

```
.scroll-area {
        overflow: scroll;
        -webkit-overflow-scrolling: touch;
}
```

This extension is compatible with Safari for iOS, Chrome on Android, and other modern Chromium- or WebKit-based browsers. The speed and duration of the continued scrolling (momentum) is based on how vigorously the scroll gesture was done by the user.

Avoid Large JavaScript Code

If you have timers that will execute code frequently, and that code takes more than 50 ms to execute, you might have performance issues if the user is scrolling the website or if there is an animation going on the screen. If you find animation glitches while scrolling the page with your finger, you should profile the moment and verify what's happening at the CPU level. It might be JavaScript code that is taking too much time not letting the browser update the UI fast enough.

Avoid Repainting

When the browser needs to repaint on each frame you usually have a frame rate drop, and your goal is to get 60 fps. Therefore, you should avoid repainting.

You should promote layers that you will animate to the GPU, through the CSS style `will-change` or the JavaScript version `element.style.willChange`. You define which property you are going to animate, as in the following example, and most browsers will take that as a flag saying that the element should be promoted to the GPU:

```
.fadedElement {
        will-change: opacity;
}
.transitionedElement {
        will-change: transform;
}
```

CSS Will Change (*https://drafts.csswg.org/css-will-change*) is still in draft but at the time of this writing is supported in Safari on iOS 9.3+, Chrome for Android, Opera, and Firefox.

 At CSS Triggers (*https://csstriggers.com*), we can see which CSS properties will need layout and paint operations from the browser that might affect animation performance. For transitions and animations, we should always pick properties that don't require layout or paint operations.

Also, we should emulate game programming with a game loop. In a game loop, we don't move elements on the screen—such as a character—when there is a user interaction (i.e., the user presses a key); we only render or change states on each frame. When a user interaction happens, we signal the change in state by setting a flag or variable, and this is taken into consideration on the next frame rendering.

CSS Containment

With CSS Containment (*https://drafts.csswg.org/css-containment*), we can limit the browser's ability to style, layout, and paint on certain areas of our document. Defining this limit can increase performance by avoiding styling, layout, and painting operations when they are not needed.

When we have a complex web design and we use JavaScript to manipulate elements in the DOM, the browser needs to recalculate styles, redo the layout, and repaint even elements that didn't suffer any change. This is because of the nature of CSS selectors, where a new element on the screen can affect others (such as sibling selectors, descendant selectors, and *n*th-child pseudoselectors).

The specification defines a `contain` property accepting the following values (space-separated if multiple):

none
: No effect (default browser behavior)

size
: Ensures that the containing element can be laid out without needing to examine its descendants

layout
: Ensures that the containing element is totally opaque for layout purposes; nothing outside can affect its internal layout, and vice versa

style
: Ensures that, for properties that can have effects on more than just an element and its descendants, those effects don't escape the containing element

paint
: Ensures that the descendants of the containing element don't display outside its bounds, so if an element is off-screen or otherwise not visible, its descendants are also guaranteed to be not visible

content
: Equivalent to `contain: layout style paint`

strict
: Equivalent to `contain: size layout style paint`; it's the most restrictive value as its contents are guaranteed to have no effect on the rest of the page outside the element's bounds, and it must have a size defined beforehand.

 CSS Containment defines a boundary between a DOM container and the rest of the document with a similar effect as when using an iframe for a rectangular area of a page. The boundary establishes a new layout root, so mutations in the sub-elements of that container never trigger reflows in the parent document.

The best option is to use `contain: strict` because the element's content will have no effect on the rest of the page, but most of the time we don't know exactly the size of the container ahead of time, so `contain: content` will usually be the default option to use.

At the time of this writing, Firefox and Google Chrome since version 52 support this property; it will be ignored by all other browsers without doing any harm.

Network Communication

Communication with the network is usually one of the operations that every web app or website uses while the user is interacting with the content. Typically, Ajax requests are used to achieve the results; however, mobile browsers offer other techniques that will improve perception and performance.

Fetch API

The Fetch API is a very simple API that is replacing typical XMLHttpRequest (also known as Ajax) operations. From a performance point of view, it generates an HTTP request as fast as with XHR, so we don't have any advantage but a cleaner API.

The Fetch API is available only in Chrome for Android, Firefox, Edge 14+, and Samsung Internet Browser 4.0+ at the time of this writing, and it's based heavily on promises.

The following is a simple example of using the Fetch API:

```
fetch('/api/my-url').then(function(response) {
        // Do something with the response
}).catch(function(error) {
        // Error
});
```

The Response object we receive on the then promise will have handy methods to get and treat the data as different formats, such as json() for JSON and blob() for binary data.

One of the advantages of the Fetch API over XHR is the ability to customize the Request object, such as forcing a request even if there is a valid entry in the browser's cache:

```
var request = new Request('/api/my-url', {
        method: 'GET',
        cache: 'no-cache'
});
fetch(request).then(function(response) {
        // Do something with the response
}).catch(function(error) {
        // Error
});
```

On the other hand, the Fetch API doesn't let us know about progress events in the case where we need to update the UI, which might be useful in some situations for the perception of performance.

Server-Sent Events

Server-Sent Events (*https://www.w3.org/TR/eventsource*) (SSE, also known as `Even tSource`) is a network specification draft for enabling web apps to use HTTP for uni-directional real-time communication from the server to the browser. Basically, it's like an Ajax request that doesn't close the connection, so the server can send pieces of information to the client whenever it needs to.

This API aims to replace the long-polling Ajax techniques, sometimes known as Comet techniques, which are not standard and may not work properly on mobile devices.

If for some reason the client or the server closes the connection, the browser starts a polling mechanism, opening the connection again.

At the time of this writing, SSE is compatible with Safari on iOS (since 4.1), Google Chrome, Amazon Silk 2.0, Opera, and Firefox. It's not available in Android Browser, Microsoft-based browsers (IE and Edge), or proxy-based browsers (such as Opera Mini).

 Because SSE doesn't close the connection between the client and the server, it allows the server to send data immediately when it needs to without waiting for an Ajax request from the client for that data. The experience is then improved, as the user will receive the data sooner.

To create an SSE request, we must instantiate an `EventSource` object with the script URL using a Messaging API event mechanism, as follows:

```
var request = new EventSource("/mySSEscript");

request.addEventListener("open", function() {
    // An HTTP request has been opened; it can be called more than
    // once if the connection drops
});

request.addEventListener("error", function() {
    // Something went wrong or the connection has been dropped (and
    // it will try to reconnect)
});

request.addEventListener("message", function(event) {
    // The server has just sent a message through the connection and
    // it's available in the data property
    var data = event.data;
});

// If we want to close the connection later, we call request.close()
```

Every time the server sends a message, we will receive a `message` event handler call. The message data can only be a string.

Server side

Usually this kind of real-time communication mechanism requires a server-side platform prepared for this kind of work (clients connected for long periods of time), so web servers like Apache or IIS may not be well suited to it. Solutions such as Node.js are much more optimized and prepared.

However, SSE can be implemented with any server-side HTTP platform —even PHP, as it's mounted over HTTP.

To answer an SSE request, we must use the MIME type `text/event-stream` and follow the SSE protocol.

The basic protocol involves answering with `data: <data>` and a line break. We replace *<data>* with the message we want to send to the client, which will be received in the `message` event. After sending a message, instead of closing the connection, the server should keep waiting in an event loop for new messages to send. Therefore, the server and the client are permanently connected, like a server that is taking a long time to respond and periodically flushing small pieces of information.

Besides the `data:` line, we can also define an ID that will be used by the client when the connection drops to recover the same session.

In PHP, we can do something like:

```php
<?php
header('Cache-Control: no-cache');
header('Content-Type: text/event-stream');
$end = false;
while (!$end) {
    // Wait for some external event here
    // that will update the $end variable
    echo 'data: Hello from the server';
    echo '\n\n'; // Newline
}
flush();
?>
```

We are using an $end Boolean variable here that we need to set to `true` when we want to end the connection. In the meantime, we should wait for something to happen. If you just want a heartbeat, you can use the `sleep` PHP function to send messages to the client every *x* seconds. In our example, the `message` event will receive the "Hello from the server" data string.

WebSockets

While SSE is great for real-time apps, it has a big problem: the communication can't be done bidirectional, such as from the client to the server. WebSockets solve this problem, enabling bidirectional, full-duplex, real-time communication between the browser and a web server.

WebSockets involve two specifications: the WebSocket API (*http://https:// www.w3.org/TR/websockets*), which defines the JavaScript API, and the WebSocket network protocol. Because of their bidirectional nature, WebSockets do not use standard HTTP messages, and therefore a special server is required.

There are some Apache-based projects to add WebSocket protocol supports, such as Apache WebSocket; on the Microsoft side, this protocol was added in IIS version 8 in conjunction with ASP.NET 4.5.

 Before it was finished by the IETF organization under RFC 6455, different browsers implemented different versions of the spec, known as hixie-75, hixie-76/hybi-00, hybi-07, and hybi-10. If you want to support WebSockets on older browsers, you'll need to test which version of the spec they implement.

At the time of this writing, the WebSocket API is available in Safari on iOS (since 4.2), Google Chrome for Android, Amazon Silk (from 2.0), Internet Explorer (since 10), Edge, Samsung Internet Browser 3.0+, and Firefox.

We define WebSocket URLs using the *ws://* protocol definition.

From an API perspective, using WebSockets is easy: we just instantiate a `WebSocket` object and use the `message` event and the `send` function to receive and send information from/to the server. When we create a WebSocket connection, we can optionally define the protocol name as the second argument:

```
var socket = new WebSocket("ws://myserver.com");
socket.addEventListener("open", function() {
    // The connection was opened
});
socket.addEventListener("close", function() {
    // The connection was closed
});
socket.addEventListener("message", function(event) {
    // We have just received a message from the server
    // We may send messages back
    socket.send("Hello server!");
});

// We can close the connection from the client
socket.close();
```

The WebSocket API is not like low-level socket implementations in other languages, such as C or Java. It supports only string messages, although there is a nonstandard extension supporting binary JavaScript data that works in some browsers.

Server side

We need to provide a server solution for our WebSockets. There are frameworks available for almost any server-side language and platform, but remember that WebSockets are more suitable for event-driven platforms that can maintain several connections at the same time instead of closing the connection after the response.

Socket.IO

Socket.IO (*http://socket.io/Socket.IO*) is a powerful open source client- and server-side framework, based on Node.js. Created by Guillermo Rauch (*https://twitter.com/rauchg*), it offers socket abilities using different techniques transparently to the client and server developers, through a very simple but unique API.

It provides a simple-to-use API both client- and server-side to send messages from the client to the server, from the server to each client, or from a server to every client via broadcast messages.

The Post-Loading Experience Is Also Important

When we are shipping high performance mobile web solutions, the experience of interacting with the content and its responsiveness are as important as the initial loading experience.

In this chapter, we covered several techniques that will help you in improving in the experience, including:

- How to keep a good frame rate while scrolling
- How to reduce network latency for after-load operations
- How to deliver immediate feedback after user intervention

In Chapter 9, we will enter the world of responsive web design and see what its relationship is with web performance.

Responsive Web Design

You resize the browser window and a smile creeps over your face. You're happy: you think you are now mobile-friendly, that you have achieved your goals for the website. But there's an ugly truth here: you will lose users and probably money if responsive web design is your entire goal and your only solution for mobile. The good news is that you can do it right, and this book is full of ideas for how to do this, such as not relying just on CSS and using server-side techniques in some situations.

In this chapter, we'll cover the relationship between the mobile web and responsive design, starting with how to apply responsive design intelligently, why performance is so important in the mobile world, and why responsive design should not be your website's goal, and ending with the performance issues of the technique to help us understand the problem.

The Problem

Designers and developers have been oversimplifying the challenges of mobile development since 2000, and some people now think that responsive web design is the answer to all of our problems.

We need to understand that, beyond any other goal, a mobile web experience must be lightning fast. Delivering a fast, usable, and compatible experience to all mobile devices has always been a challenge, and it's no different when you are implementing a responsive technique. Embracing performance from the beginning is easier.

Responsive web design is great, but it's not a silver bullet. If it's the only weapon in your mobile arsenal, then a performance problem might be affecting your conversion rate. With just a basic understanding of the problem, however, you can minimize this loss.

You are probably thinking at this point: "but mobile websites are from the past! Everybody is doing responsive design now." I'm not saying that you should not design responsively or that you should go with an *m.** subdomain. In fact, with social sharing everywhere now, assigning one URL per document, regardless of device, is smart. But this doesn't mean that a single URL should always deliver the same document or that every device should download the same resources.

Let me quote Ethan Marcotte (*http://www.abookapart.com/products/responsive-web-design*), who coined the term "responsive web design," from his book by that name:

> Most importantly, responsive web design isn't intended to serve as a replacement for mobile web sites.

Ethan continues:

> Responsive design is, I believe, one part design philosophy, one part front-end development strategy. And as a development strategy, it's meant to be evaluated to see if it meets the needs of the project you're working on. Perhaps there's a compelling reason to keep your site's desktop and mobile experiences separarte, or perhaps your content would be better served by a responsive approach. Only you and your users know for certain.

 Some people think that Google expects a responsive website to improve mobile SEO performance, but it's not true. While responsive is one of the most important techniques, creating mobile-specific experiences or hybrid experiences is also possible. What Google wants is a good experience; you can use any technique you want. Just look at the AMP Project we will discuss in Chapter 10: it was promoted by Google and it's leaving RWD from a one-code-fits-all perspective out of the discussion.

Responsive design usually entails delivering the same HTML document to all devices and using media queries to load different CSS and image files. You might have a slightly different idea of what it means, but that is usually how it is implemented, and how most people understand it.

We know from previous chapters that mobile cellular networks have higher latency, and that is something important for performance.

Responsive web design on cellular networks

Consider a real case. Keynote, a company that offers performance solutions, has published data on the website performance of top Super Bowl 2014 advertisers (see Figure 9-1). The data speaks for itself: on a wired or WiFi connection, the loading times range from 1 to 10 seconds, while on a cellular connection, the loading times range from 5 to 60 seconds. Think about that: one full minute to load a website being advertised during the Super Bowl!

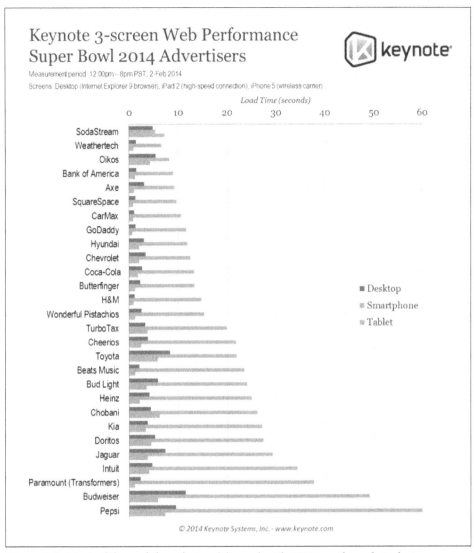

Figure 9-1. Most of the mobile websites delivered with RWD as the only technique are not well optimized for performance

The same report shows that 43% of those websites offer a mobile-specific version, with an average size of 862 KB; 50% deliver a responsive solution, with an average size of 3,211 KB (nearly four times larger); and 7% offer only the desktop version to mobile devices. So, by default, responsive websites are larger than mobile-specific websites.

You can definitely create a good, performant responsive-only website, particularly if you have been following along with this book. But if your website is complex, you will probably need a mixed technique. Just look at the strategy being used by most of the media and newspaper websites; they know that performance means money.

Of course, responsive design can look different, but unfortunately, the average responsive website out there looks like these ones of the Super Bowl advertisers.

One HTML for all

A typical responsive design delivers a single HTML document to all devices: TVs, desktops, tablets, smartphones, and feature phones. It sounds great, but we live in a world that has cellular and other problems. Your responsive HTML might render correctly on mobile devices, but it's not as fast as it should be, and that is affecting your conversion rate.

If a single `display: none` appears in any of your CSS, then your website is not as fast as it could be. Of course, you can decide to make exceptions when performance is not affected, but it's better to work on exceptions than to take `display: none` for granted as a general rule without performance impact.

On a website that has been designed from scratch to be semantic, the responsive overload will be almost nil; on a website whose HTML includes 40 external scripts, jQuery plug-ins, and fancy libraries, mostly for the benefit of big screens, the responsive overload will be at the high end. When the same HTML is used, the same external resources will be declared for all devices.

This isn't to say that responsive design alone can't be done, just that the website won't be optimized by default. If you are sensitive to performance, then your responsive solution might look different than the usual. Let's review the Starbucks website. Its home page is responsive and looks great in the three viewports I tested (see Figure 9-2). But upon checking the internals, we see that all versions load the same 24 external JavaScript files, 3 CSS stylesheets, and 70 images. Should a mobile device with 3G latency be expected to load 97 external files just to get the view shown here?

You might be thinking, "Hey, blame the implementation, not the technique" (*http:// timkadlec.com/2012/10/blame-the-implementation-not-the-technique*). You're right. This book is not against responsive web design. It's against aiming for responsiveness in a way that leads to a weak implementation, and it's against prioritizing responsiveness over performance, as we see with Starbucks. It looks great when you resize the browser, but that's not all that is important. Performance matters even more to mobile users.

If your responsive website has performance problems, then the fault may lie with how you've framed the goal. If you have the budget for responsive design, then you must also have the budget for performance.

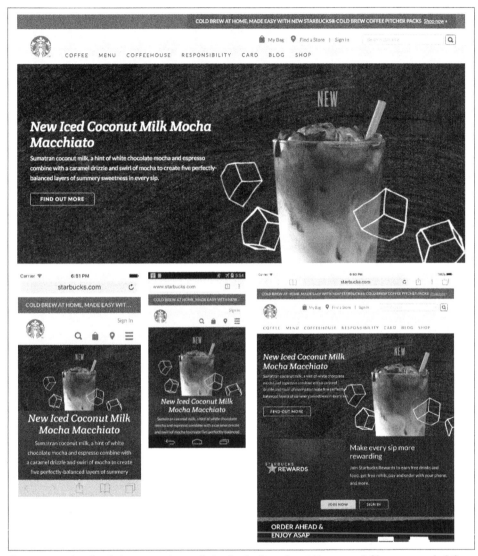

Figure 9-2. Starbucks's responsive website looks fine, but 97 external files are needed for every screen

Loading resources

Media queries are implemented in different ways, usually as one of the following:

- A single CSS file with multiple `@media` declarations
- Multiple CSS files linked to from the main page via `media` attributes

In the first case, every device will load the CSS intended for all devices because there is just one CSS group. Hundreds of selectors that will never be used are transferred and parsed by the browser anyway.

You might think that multiple external files are better because the browser will load the resources based on breakpoints. After all, tutorials in blogs, magazines, books, and training courses teach us to write code like this:

```
<link rel="stylesheet" href="desktop.css"
  media="(min-width: 801px)">
<link rel="stylesheet" href="tablet.css"
  media="(min-width: 401px) and (max-width: 800px)">
<link rel="stylesheet" href="mobile.css"
  media="(max-width: 400px)">
```

Well, you'd be wrong. All browsers will load all external CSS, regardless of context. Figure 9-3 shows an iPhone downloading all of the CSS files excerpted in the preceding code, even ones not intended for it.

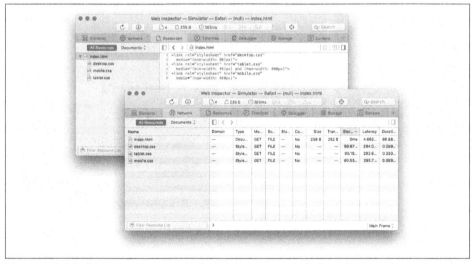

Figure 9-3. The basic responsive web design techniques will force the browser to download all the versions of CSS that you've defined in media queries

Why do browsers download all CSS files? Suppose you have one CSS file for portrait orientation and another for landscape. You wouldn't want browsers to load CSS on the fly when the orientation changes, in case a couple of milliseconds go by without any CSS being used. You'd want the browser to preload both files. That's what happens when you define media queries based on screen dimensions.

Can the dimensions of mobile browsers be changed? For the most part, not yet, but vendors are preparing their mobile browsers to be resized like desktop browsers, which is why the browsers usually load all CSS declarations regardless of whether their width matches the media query.

While stretchable viewports don't usually exist on phones, some viewports resize in certain situations:

- When the orientation changes in certain browsers
- When the viewport declaration changes dynamically
- When offset content is added after `onload`
- When external mirroring is supported
- When more than one app is open at the same time on Android 7.0+ and some Samsung Android devices (in multi-window mode)
- When (on some newer iPads) the user uses Side View and changes the size

Browsers that are optimized for these changes in context will preload all the resources that they might need.

While browsers might be smarter about this in the near future, we're left with a problem now: we are delivering more resources than are needed, and thus penalizing mobile users for no reason.

The Real Problem: Responsive Design as a Goal

As Lyza Danger Gardner says in "What We Mean When We Say 'Responsive'" (*http://alistapart.com/column/what-we-mean-when-we-say-responsive*), designers define "responsive" differently, which can lead to communication problems.

Let's get to the root. The term responsive web design first appeared in a 2010 post by Ethan Marcotte (*http://alistapart.com/article/responsive-web-design*), followed by a book with the same name. Ethan defines it as providing an optimal viewing experience across a wide range of devices using three techniques: fluid grids, flexible images, and media queries.

Nothing is wrong with that definition. The problem is when we set it as the goal of a website without understanding the broader goals that we need to achieve.

When you set responsive design as a goal, it becomes easy to lose perspective. What is the real problem you are trying to solve? Is being responsive really a problem? Probably not. But do you understand "being responsive" to mean "being mobile-friendly"? If so, then you might be making some mistakes.

The ultimate goal for a website should be "happy users," which will lead to more conversions, whatever a conversion might be (getting a visitor to spread the word, providing information, or making a sale). Users won't be happy without a high-performing website.

The direct impact of performance on conversions, particularly in mobile, has been proven many times.

When you know your goals, you can decide which tools and techniques are best to achieve them. This is when you analyze where and how to use a responsive approach. You use responsive design—you don't achieve it.

Responsiveness Versus Users

The *New York Times* redesigned its website (*http://www.nytimes.com/redesign*) recently, with the goal of keeping "you in mind." Meanwhile, thousands of other big companies present their new responsive websites with pride.

The *New York Times* website follows responsive design in different ways, but some people complained that it still uses a separate mobile version, instead of adapting the layout based on the same HTML (for more information, see "The Latest New York Times Web App Misses the Point of Responsive Design" (*http://readwrite.com/ 2013/12/05/new-york-times-responsive-web-app-todays-paper*)).

Who said that responsive web design means supporting all possible screen sizes with the same HTML? Sure, this is a common understanding, but that rule isn't written anywhere. It's just our need to simplify the problem that has led to it.

In recent months, companies have said things along the lines of, "We've applied a new responsive design, and now our mobile conversions have increased by 100%." But did conversions increase because the website was made to be responsive, or are users realizing that the website is now responsive and so are happier and convert more?

People convert more because their experience on mobile devices is now better and faster than whatever solution was in place before (whether it was a crude mobile version or a crammed-in desktop layout). So, yes, responsiveness is better than nothing and better than an old mobile implementation. But a separate mobile website with the same design or even a smarter solution done with other techniques would achieve the same conversion rate or better.

Alternatives

Server-side feature detection and decisions are not new to the mobile web. Libraries such as WURFL (*http://www.scientiamobile.com*) and DeviceAtlas (*https://deviceatlas.com*) have been on the market for years.

Mixing responsive design with server-side components is not new either. Known sometimes as *responsive design with server-side components* (RESS) (*http://www.lukew.com/ff/entry.asp?1392*) and sometimes as *adaptive design*, it improves responsive design in terms of speed and usability, while keeping a single code base for everyone server-side.

> According to the Q1 2016 Mobile Overview Report (*http://data.wurfl.io/MOVR/pdf/2016_q1/MOVR_2016_q1.pdf*), less than 20% of mobile-friendly sites are using just classic responsive web design techniques, without the use of JavaScript or server-side libraries. 54% of top websites are using *m.** (a separate website) or an adaptive technique.

Unfortunately, these techniques haven't gained much traction in the community over the last few years. Just look at any blog or magazine for developers and compare mentions of "RESS" and "adaptive" to "responsive." There's a reason for that: we are frontend professionals. Anything that involves the server looks like a problem to us, and we don't want that.

In some cases, the frontend designer will be in control of a script on the server; in other cases, a remote development team will manage it, and the designer won't want to have to deal with the team every time she wants to make a small change to the UI. I know the feeling.

That's why it might be time to think of a new architecture layer in large projects, whereby a frontend engineer can make decisions server-side without affecting the backend architecture. Node.js is an excellent candidate for this platform, being a server-side layer between the current enterprise backend infrastructure and the frontend.

In this new layer, the frontend engineer would be in charge of decisions based on the current context that would make the experience fast, responsive, and usable on all the devices, without touching the backend architecture.

The Solution: Responsive and Fast

We can gain the benefits of responsive design without affecting performance on mobile if we use certain other techniques as well. Responsive web design was never meant to "solve" performance problems, which is why we can't blame the technique itself—and why believing that it will solve all of your problems, as many seem to do, is wrong.

Designing responsively is important because we need to deal with a range of viewport sizes across desktop and mobile devices. But thinking only of screen size underestimates the problems with mobile devices. While the line between desktop and mobile is getting blurrier, different possibilities are still open to us based on the device type. And we can't decide on functionality using media queries yet.

Some commentators have called for "responsible responsive web design," while others talk about responsive web design with a modern vision. Without getting into semantics, we do need to understand and be aware of the problem.

While there is no silver bullet and no solutions that can be applied to every type of document, we can use a couple of tricks to improve our existing responsive solutions and maximize performance:

- Deliver each document to all devices with the same URL and the same content, but not necessarily with the same structure.
- When starting from scratch, follow a mobile-first approach.
- Test on real devices what happens when resources are loaded and when `display: none` is applied. Don't rely on resizing your desktop browser.
- Use optimization tools to measure and improve performance.
- Consider different image loading techniques, including `srcset`, `<picture>`, and JS-based options when new specs are not available.
- Load only the JavaScript that you need for the current device with conditional loading, and probably after the `onload` event.
- Inline the initial view of a document for mobile devices, or deliver above-the-fold content first.
- Apply a smart responsive solution with one or more of these techniques: conditional loading, responsiveness according to group, and a server-side layer (such as an adaptive approach).

Remember that a responsive website is not a different world; everything we've covered since Chapter 6 applies here.

Conditional Loading

Don't always rely on media queries in CSS, because as we saw earlier, browsers will load and parse all of the selectors and styles for all devices (more on this later). This means that a mobile phone will download and parse the CSS for larger screens. And because CSS blocks rendering, you will be wasting precious milliseconds over a cellular connection.

Replace CSS media queries with a JavaScript matchMedia query on devices whose context you know will not change. For example, we know that an iPhone cannot convert to the size of an iPad dynamically, so we can just load the CSS for the device that we really need. In some cases, when a resize operation is being triggered, we can load the new CSS asynchronously using a framework such as loadCSS (*https://github.com/filamentgroup/loadCSS*); in situations where the new CSS is taking a while, you need to balance initial loading when using too many media queries with low execution probability.

Another solution for JavaScript-based media queries is Enquire.js (*http://wicky.nillia.ms/enquire.js*). You can also mix techniques using cloud-based solutions such as Wurfl.js (*http://web.wurfl.io*) to make smart decisions on the fly based on the current device's capabilities.

 This trick is useful when you find that serving one HTML version for all screens is good enough. Typically, if more than 10% of your HTML is hidden on one kind of screen, you might want to separate it server-side.

Responsive from Big to Small

When we are rendering a website in a desktop browser, or even on a tablet, there is a possibility—small, but it exists—that the user might resize the browser to a very narrow window. In these cases, we might want to load different CSS—preferably using async techniques—and readapt the layout in a responsive way, instead of preloading all the CSS as in a typical RWD classic solution.

However, that might be a problem in the other direction, from small to big. If the page was loaded for a narrow-screen device—typically a mobile phone—the probability of going wider is near zero today, so there is no need to load that content. Therefore, the server might be serving different HTML for phones that will never load different CSS.

Responsiveness by Group

While we can rely on a single HTML base and responsive design for all screens when dealing with simple documents, delivering the same HTML to desktops and smartphones is not always the best solution. Why? Again, because of performance on mobile.

Even if we store the same document server-side, we can deliver differences to the client based on the device group. For example, we could deliver a big floating menu to screens 6 inches and bigger and a small hamburger menu to screens smaller than 6 inches. Within each group, we could use responsive techniques to adapt to different scenarios, such as switching between portrait and landscape mode or varying between iPhones (320, 375, and 414 pixels wide), 5-inch Android devices (360 pixels), and phablets (400 pixels and up).

More Complex Scenarios

On the other hand, the web space is getting more complex every day, adding new challenges. I'll discuss here two cases that are adding more complexity to the responsive web design discussion.

iOS and Android Split Modes

Since iOS 9, the iPad Air and iPad Pro have had Side View and Split View modes allowing us to open two apps at the same time, sharing the screen 2/3 and 1/3 or 1/2 and 1/2 (see the example in Figure 9-4).

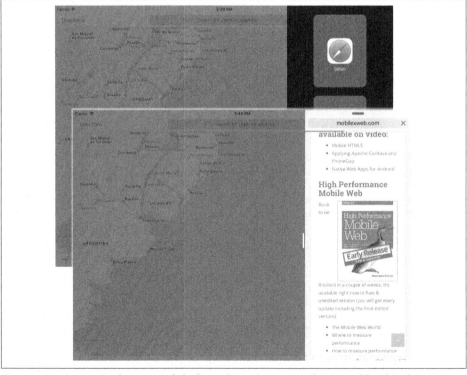

Figure 9-4. On an iPad, we can slide from the right a second app and load Safari content inside that it emulates a "phone" viewport

Safari and Chrome for iPad can work in this mode meaning that our website can be rendered with a viewport of a full iPad, half an iPad, one-third of an iPad or two-thirds of iPad, with the addition of portrait and landscape options in every mode.

Also, starting with iOS 10 Safari itself has a split-view mode where you can open two websites side by side, each with 50% of the screen.

In Figure 9-5, we can see how complex viewports on iPads are today, which may make us again think that responsive web design is the best solution—and in an ideal world it is. However, in reality, we know it may harm performance, so we need to think about how to solve the problem.

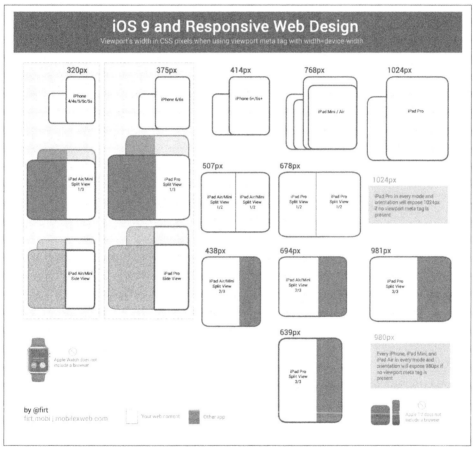

Figure 9-5. Since iOS 9, we have too many viewport sizes available. This makes us wonder about the solution from a responsive and performance point of view.

Up to Android 6, there is no split mode that can cause a resize operation on our viewport, but it's available since Android 7 as multi-window mode, shown in Figure 9-6. Furthermore, some manufacturers—primarily Samsung but also LG and HTC—have changed the Android core to support two running apps at the same time side by side or in picture-in-picture mode, even on Android 4.x, 5, and 6. Therefore, Chrome, Android Browser, and/or Samsung Internet Browser can be running while sharing the screen with another Android app.

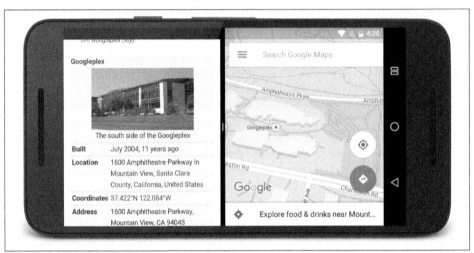

Figure 9-6. Since Android 7, multi-window mode lets us open two apps at the same time, such as in this example, which shows Google Chrome and Google Maps open simultaneously

It's not practical (or necessary) to create different versions per viewport. But if you have already analyzed the use of one HTML for all and it's not suitable for the performance of your website, you might consider asking the user if she wants to reload the site (or app) to load the right resources for the new situation—for example, when the website was loaded in 1/3 mode (using the phone version) and then it's resized to full iPad mode.

Another option to consider is using RWD techniques from big to small, but not from small to big. That means that the HTML that you are serving to iPads and desktops can contain media queries for phone-sized viewports, but not vice versa. Therefore, a phone will always get the most optimized version. This is an effective approach because we know the phone's screen won't become larger (at least, in most iOS and Android situations today…just wait for the next section).

Windows 10 Continuum

Windows 10 Mobile has a feature known as Continuum (*http://windows.micro soft.com/en-us/windows-10/getstarted-continuum-mobile*) that lets you use your phone like a PC, connecting it to an HDMI monitor, keyboard, and mouse.

In this case, you can have a web page loaded into an unresizable viewport in the Edge browser on a phone, with a phone user agent, and suddenly it can get an upgrade to a desktop Edge browser in a desktop's window, without a reload.

For these situations, if you are using only classic and basic responsive web design techniques, you might want to consider a reload operation (probably with the user's intervention) when you detect with JavaScript that the context has changed from a desktop to a mobile device, and vice versa.

Responsive as a Strategy

If you understand responsive web design as a strategy to cover every device with an optimal design based on one set of code, we agree. However, your technical solution to achieve that strategy might move beyond the classic responsive web design techniques—that is, you might use a mix of approaches, including server-side solutions that can make decisions to deliver the fastest possible experience for the current device.

In this case, the goal is to avoid having to maintain separate versions. In the following chapters, we will talk about some alternate mobile content versions, such as Google's AMP, that might force us to have a separate version.

Does RWD Matter from a User's Point of View?

Responsive web design is a great tool for improving the user experience, but it's not the only tool available to us and it's definitely not a silver bullet. Every project today will probably involve the usage of RWD techniques, but that doesn't mean it's the only option, or the only thing we need to do.

Also, responsive web design is an invisible attribute, from a user's point of view. As Brad Frost put it:

> Your visitors don't give a sh*t if your site is responsive.

Brad is completely right. Users want something fast and easy to use. They don't usually resize the browser on a mobile device, and they probably don't even understand what "responsive" means. Of course, we need to manage what happens when the browser is resized; I'm not saying you should stop doing that, but always check the cost.

The quote is a bitter truth, and it doesn't quite apply to all websites. But it's better than thinking, "We can relax. Our website is responsive. We've taken care of mobile."

Sometimes, even when not relevant to the situation, saying that responsive design is "bad for performance" can be good because it helps to spread the word on why performance is so important. But technically, responsive web design is not bad or good for performance, because it's a technique with a different goal.

The *New York Times* is right: the goal is the user. It's not a tool or a technique or even the designer's happiness. If you can provide good performance with responsive web design only, then do it. If not, remove your "responsive goal" and just create the best and fastest experience you can. Nobody but you will care if it's responsive or not (from a technical perspective).

We've been talking about lots of problems and how to solve them in terms of performance. Just remember them, and that responsive web design is not a different world; it's the same mobile web world we've been talking about throughout this book.

To achieve good web performance on responsive sites, you need to:

- Remember everything we've covered since Chapter 6
- Not rely just on CSS media queries
- Use server-side techniques—adaptive design—when possible
- Use responsive images (as covered in Chapter 6)

In Chapter 10, we will be talking about some extreme techniques that we should analyze to get the most performant solution.

Extreme Mobile Web Performance

In previous chapters, we have explored several techniques that can be used to improve the performance and perception of our mobile websites. In this chapter, we will talk about how to mix these techniques and add some other ideas to achieve extreme performance with probably more effort and more architectural changes than with the classic techniques we've seen so far.

To achieve extreme web performance, we first must implement some of the techniques we've covered in previous chapters, such as:

- No HTTP redirects—not even one
- No app banners
- Gzipped response
- No sync `<script>` tags
- Reduced usage of data URIs
- Reduced usage of web fonts

Some approaches—such as using responsive web design without any server-side techniques—might be harmful to achieving extreme performance on mobile devices, as we covered in Chapter 9. This is not written in stone, and there are some situations where RWD won't harm extreme performance for mobile websites and apps, but as a general rule, it holds.

Mobile Web Alternatives

Because mobile web performance is so important and it is hurting conversion rates, Google and Facebook have been looking into alternatives to the typical mobile web that will help them get more users engaged with content—which, in other ways, will let them make more money.

Facebook has come up with Facebook Instant Articles and Google—with support from other vendors, such as Twitter and LinkedIn—has started the Accelerated Mobile Pages (AMP) Project. These systems appear to be alternative ways to deliver web content for mobile devices; the content is precached on Facebook or Google's servers so the final experience will be faster.

Later in this chapter, we will explore the technical implications of both platforms.

The Lucky Numbers

We have already mentioned several important numbers for web performance, such as the RAIL idea of response in 100 ms, animation frame rate of 60 fps, idle execution time of 50 ms, and load time of 1 second.

Now we will focus on the last one: loading in 1 second. The idea is to load the page in an average mobile browser, through an average mobile cellular connection, in just 1 second. That is our budget: only 1 second.

Even with all the techniques that we've covered in Chapters 6 and 7, achieving a load time of only 1 second seems a lot to ask, right? The situation is even worse, as Figure 10-1 illustrates.

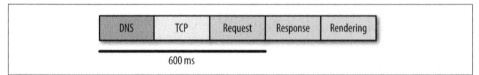

Figure 10-1. An average 3G connection leaves us only 400 ms for server delivery and client render

Figure 10-1 shows a typical page load over a 3G cellular network for the first time:

- 200 ms for the DNS lookup
- 200 ms for the TCP connection (and optional TLS handshake)
- 200 ms for the HTTP request

Therefore, in an average scenario, we will have only 400 ms left of our one-second budget to transfer the contents from the server and render them on the screen. We might split those 400 ms into two equal parts to simplify the problem: 200 ms to send everything to the client and 200 ms for rendering.

You might be thinking I'm crazy and that this is an impossible mission.

Well, it's difficult but not impossible. And we will use some magic tricks. We don't need the whole page to be loaded in 1 s; we can trick the user and create the perception of loading within 1 second.

14 KB

Even if you are not an expert in network communications, you probably have heard about TCP splitting data into packages, known as TCP packets. If your HTTP response from the server is big enough, it won't fit in one TCP packet, meaning that more time will be needed before rendering content.

Therefore, our goal is to send everything we need to render the page in one TCP packet. How big is a TCP packet? While it's a complex answer, it gets simpler when we talk about the first packet. Because we are talking here about the first load, it will be the first TCP packet sent from that server, and because of a TCP rule known as *slow start*, the first TCP packet has a maximum size of around 14.6 KB. In other words, if your HTTP response for the first HTML is 14.7 KB, it will fit in 2 TCP packets and another 200 ms will be used for the second TCP connection.

14.6 KB? Doesn't seem like enough for the whole page. Well, if you read Chapter 6, you are for sure sending the response using *gzip*. The 14.6 KB is calculated after the GZIP operation and it equates to around 70 KB of uncompressed text-based file, such as HTML.

If you are using the new Brotli compression engine (*https://github.com/google/brotli*), it can be even more—around 85 KB for compatible browsers.

The exact uncompressed size of the HTML response to achieve 14.6 KB compressed will depend on your contents, so you should always test it using the Network tools of your browser.

Even with 70 KB available, we must use that data and only that data to render the contents—if we need external JavaScript code or CSS code, it will need additional HTTP requests (and possibly TCP requests), and we don't have any budget left for it.

If your entire web content—HTML, CSS, and JavaScript—fits in around 70 KB, then you are ready. Just embed the CSS and Java-Script in the HTML, don't use external resources, and you'll be done. You can also embed images using data URIs but only if they fit in the 14.6 KB compressed.

How can we fit all the HTML, CSS, and JavaScript for our initial web page into just one HTML file of around 70 KB? Well, we need to start thinking about the Above the Fold pattern, to separate what we really need to render in the "above the fold" part of the website—that is, what the user is really seeing in the first view—and lazy load the rest of the content that will be available after the user scrolls.

The ATF Pattern

The Above the Fold pattern involves separating out what is most important for the initial load: what the user will see in the first viewport rendering process. If we can serve everything there in 1 s, then the user will perceive it as a fast website. While the user's brain is scanning the page and reading what is on the screen after this content is loaded, we can download the rest of the content we need. Figure 10-2 shows a full page load and the above-the-fold section that is rendered before the first scroll.

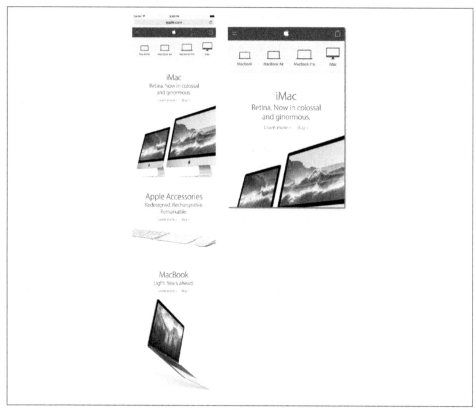

Figure 10-2. In a long website, the above-the-fold content (ATF) is what you see without any scrolling (as in the image on the right)

Therefore, we must fit into one TCP packet (~70 KB uncompressed) at least:

- The HTML for rendering the initial view
- The critical CSS styles, embedded in a `<style>` element, to define layout and styles for ATF content (also known as the critical-path CSS)
- The JavaScript code—if needed—embedded in a `<script>` element
- The logo in data URI (for bitmaps), embedded in the HTML or CSS or in an inline SVG

At *https://github.com/addyosmani/critical-path-css-tools* you can find an updated list of tools that will help you in determining what parts of the CSS you should separate from the ATF content.

Additionally, and only if we still have room, we can add into the HTML:

- Data URI–embedded small images that are mandatory for the UI
- A low-resolution, data URI–embedded main photo

We need to remember that images are nonblocking resources by default. If they fit in our first TCP packet, then great. If not, it's better to keep them as additional resources that will be loaded after the page is rendered, so they don't harm our loading perception trick.

The logo is necessary to give the user the perception of the content being loaded. If the user sees just placeholders, she might think the website is not ready. The logo should be as optimized as possible, using one or more of the following techniques:

- Use an 8-bit optimized PNG
- Use an SVG scalable logo, embedded in an HTML5-compatible `<svg>` tag

If you are using bitmap-based logos, you probably have different versions for different resolutions. For the ATF version, you should deliver the low-resolution version even if it's not the best experience for the user. You can later upgrade it with a high-resolution version, after loading the ATF content in 1 second.

Mobile Viewport

ATF content will be different based on the viewport size. In other words, the same website on different devices will probably render different ATF content, as they will have more or less space available on the screen.

Because we are targeting mobile devices in this book, we will probably be optimizing for mobile phones with a mobile viewport. A tablet has a viewport similar to desktop, so achieving an ATF load in 1 second is much more difficult.

But even if we are focusing only on mobile phones, several form factors are available. My recommendation is to take the ATF content of a phablet, such as a Galaxy Note or an iPhone 6+, with a viewport of around 450 px wide and, 800 px high to be safe. If your website is a blog or an article-based page, it usually means you are serving in the ATF content the logo, a menu, and two to three articles with images.

You can use Chrome Developer Tools to set a viewport of any size using the Mobile Emulation tool, as seen in Figure 10-3.

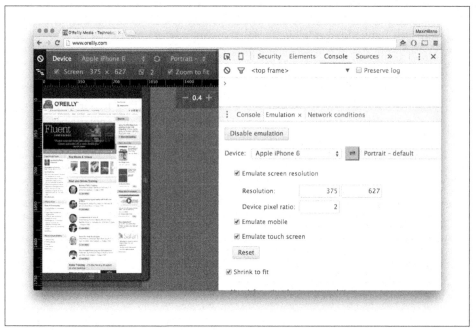

Figure 10-3. Google Chrome Developer Tools allow us to define any viewport in the mobile emulation mode

Critical CSS Extraction Tools

One of the easiest tools available to extract and inline the ATF CSS is Critical (*https:// github.com/addyosmani/critical*), a script that will take the viewport width and height as arguments so you can create one or more versions of it based on different resolutions.

Other tools available are CriticalCSS (*https://github.com/filamentgroup/criticalCSS*) and Penthouse (*https://github.com/pocketjoso/penthouse*).

We can run these scripts manually or add them as Gulp tasks.

Lazy Loading

Once you've loaded the ATF content within 1 second, you are ready to load the rest of the content. To do that, you can inject the CSS and JavaScript in the DOM and/or use XHR to inject the rest of the HTML content below the ATF content.

Images

We talked about image optimization in Chapter 6, but now it's the turn of extreme techniques for images, including image decoding and using today's alternative formats.

Extreme Responsive Images

In Chapter 6, we covered several new formats available today for getting the most out of compression methods and achieving better compression rates compared to JPEG and PNG, such as WebP and JPEG-XR. Also, for some images it's possible to use SVG. The problem is that not every browser supports every format. However, we can have the advantages of modern image formats and faster responsive images using the <picture> element. For example, we can serve several versions of the same image using the type attribute:

```
<picture>
    <source type="image/webp" src="image.webp">
    <source type="image/vnd.ms-photo" src="image.jxr">
    <source type="image/jp2" src="image.jp2">
    <source type="image/svg+xml" src="image.svg">
        <img src="image.png" alt="description">
</picture>
```

The problem appears when we add art direction or different versions for different screen sizes or resolutions, because the amount of different file URLs or <source> elements becomes too big. We will have as many file URLs as formats × size versions × art direction versions.

For example, let's say we want to support WebP for Android users, JXR for Windows users, and JP2 for iOS users, while having a fallback version in PNG. Then we want to have three art direction versions: phone portrait, phone landscape, and tablet. And finally, we are going to serve three densities. The final count will be 4 formats × 3 art direction versions × 3 densities, which gives us a total of 36 different URLs we need to define in the markup. It doesn't make too much sense, right?

In Chapter 5, we covered the new Client Hints spec that will let us know on the server side some information about the client, such as the DPR or viewport width. Also, by reading HTTP headers, we can detect if, for example, WebP or JPEG-XR is supported. Mixing everything together, we can determine on the server side which is the best format and the best image size to deliver, and do it automatically.

To do this, we first need to opt in Client Hints as a meta tag in the <head>:

```
<meta http-equiv="Accept-CH" content="DPR, Viewport-Width, Width">
```

and then use <picture> without specifying srcset options for DPR or file types:

```
<picture>
  <source media="(orientation: landscape)" sizes="50vw" srcset="images/myimage">
  <source media="(orientation: portrait)" sizes="100vw" srcset="images/myimage">
  <img sizes="100vw" src="images/myimage">
</picture>
```

As you can see, we always point to "images/myimage". Note that we are not defining a file extension or image density. That's because the server will have the intelligence to determine that information.

Also, using service workers, we can intercept the request before it hits the server and add our own additional data to Client Hints, such as current network conditions. You can see more about this trick at "Automatic Resource Selection with Client Hints" (*https://developers.google.com/web/updates/2015/09/automating-resource-selection-with-client-hints*).

Finally, if we don't have Client Hints information, we can fall back to device libraries, such as WURFL by ScientiaMobile (*http://scientiamobile.com*), where—based on the User-Agent—we will determine the best format and size.

Nonblocking Image Decoding

By default, when you define an <img> element with a URL, the browser will download the file through the network and then decode the image into a memory bitmap on the main thread. But that decoding process takes some milliseconds that can be used for other processes in the main thread.

The solution is to decode the image in a web worker—a separate thread—through `createImageBitmap` (*https://html.spec.whatwg.org/multipage/webappapis.html#dom-createimagebitmap*) and then draw it on a canvas.

You can learn more about this trick at Paul Lewis's blog (*https://aerotwist.com/blog/the-hack-is-back*).

At the time of this writing, this works only in Firefox and is available in Chrome under a flag, but it may be more widely supported by the time you are reading this.

Low-Resolution Images

A good trick to increase perception of performance is to include low- or very low-resolution images in the HTML itself that are then replaced with high-resolution versions after the ATF content is loaded.

For example, if an image for a mobile viewport has 300 × 300 CSS pixels (in high resolution, this may be up to 1,200 × 1,200 physical pixels, based on pixel density), we can set an `<img>` tag with that picture embedded but reduced to 30 × 30 physical pixels and highly compressed if using JPEG. Because we are reducing the image's dimensions, the file size is really small (near 400 bytes), and when converted to Base64 it can be embedded in the initial ATF HTML without any problems.

Medium (*https://medium.com*) uses a similar technique; in Figure 10-4, we can see what the user sees while the image is in very low resolution and how it looks after a couple of milliseconds. In this case, if you want to see "big pixels" instead of a bicubic resize operation (softened) the trick is to use a `<canvas>` element: using the Canvas API with JavaScript, you can take every pixel of the low-resolution image and draw it much bigger.

Facebook's developers have also tested this approach and published the results in "The Technology Behind Preview Photos" (*https://code.facebook.com/posts/991252547593574/the-technology-behind-preview-photos*). They've found great performance improvements: "For people on a slow connection, this helped speed up profile and page loads by 30 percent. Even on the fastest connections, this ensured that people would always see a cover photo preview immediately, making their overall experience more seamless."

The trick involves compressing every JPEG photo into a super-low-resolution version of a maximum of 200 bytes, reducing it to 42 × 42 pixels, trimming the JPEG header, and then appending the header again client-side while applying a blur effect in a `<canvas>`. This creates a really fast preview of the image, as we can see in Figure 10-5, while the normal-resolution version is being downloaded, creating a really good experience.

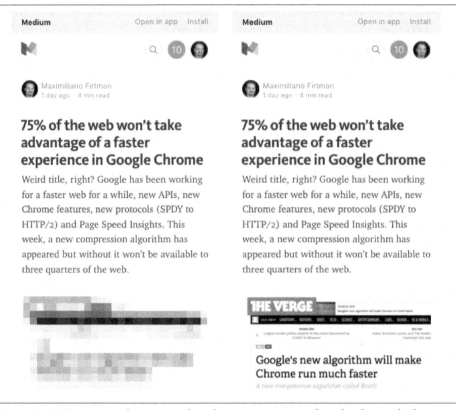

Figure 10-4. To increase the perceived performance, you can download or embed a very tiny version of the image that can then be resized, before downloading a full image

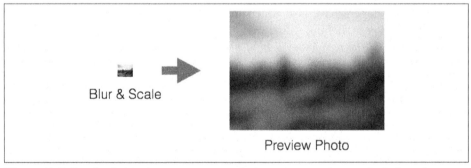

Figure 10-5. Facebook is using an extreme technique to create impressively fast photo previews just with 200 bytes

JavaScript Only as Dessert

We know now that JavaScript defers parsing by default, and when we are counting milliseconds as gold, using the main thread to parse and execute JavaScript code doesn't sound like a good idea.

To get extreme performance, we should eat JavaScript only as dessert, which is to say at the end. If we do that, the browser will have enough time to download, parse, and render the most critical parts: the HTML and CSS.

Avoid Big Frameworks

A big framework is any one bigger than 10 KB. That includes most of them, even jQuery. Avoid loading them, at least in the first load, by not using them for the ATF content load.

Avoid Client-Side Rendering

Client-side rendering is also a problem for performance in mobile browsers if we want to achieve the goal of 1 second. Client-side rendering frameworks are frameworks that render the final HTML and CSS from JavaScript; therefore, the users see nothing (or partial content) until the JavaScript framework has been downloaded, parsed, and executed and generates the render.

In this category, we have several frameworks with different levels of impact on performance, such as jQuery Mobile, Sencha Touch, Ionic, Angular.JS, and React.

Back in 2012, the Twitter home page was using client-side rendering. When you loaded *twitter.com*, it was an empty shell with some JavaScript code that was responsible for loading the first *n* tweets, which were injected into the HTML.

Twitter developers realized that they could improve performance, reducing load times by one-fifth, if they changed the client-side rendering to server-side rendering, at least for the first *n* tweets.[1]

 Even if you are using a client-side rendering framework, such as Angular.JS, you may be able to take advantage of server-side rendering for the ATF content by using a server-side version of the framework. These usually run on Node.js, such as Angular.JS-Server (*https://github.com/saymedia/angularjs-server*)

---

1 You can read more about this at "Improving Performance on twitter.com" (*https://blog.twitter.com/2012/improving-performance-on-twittercom*).

Try to generate the HTML and CSS for your ATF content from the server, already prerendered. Then use whatever JavaScript mechanism you want to load the rest or to interact with the user, after you've achieved the RAIL goals.

SD/HD Pattern

If you are a YouTube or Netflix user, you probably know that they offer an SD/HD experience (standard and high quality) based on current network conditions. We can use all the APIs seen in Chapter 5 to do something similar for text and content, including the Save-Data Client Hint that we can receive from the server. We can define more than two quality levels that we can determine when the initial page has loaded and let the user changes it if necessary.

Google offers a very basic 305-byte version of its logo when the user is in a bad situation.

We need to remember our primary goal: to offer the best possible experience for the user in order to improve engagement and conversion rates. If the user is in a bad situation (bad connection, old device), we should deliver the best possible experience for those conditions. If the user moves to a better situation, we can then upgrade the experience.

The PRPL Pattern

The Polymer Project team (*https://www.polymer-project.org/1.0/blog/2016-05-19-Polymer-IO-2016*) has developed a new design pattern for web performance, known as *PRPL* (Push, Render, Pre-Cache, Lazy Load). PRPL is based on the use of the latest technologies, including the Web Components, HTTP/2 Server Push, and service worker APIs.

The pattern stands for:

- Push critical resources for the initial route
- Render the initial route quickly
- Precache remaining routes
- Lazy load and create remaining routes on demand

The Polymer App Toolbox (*https://www.polymer-project.org/1.0/toolbox/server*) is one of the first solutions using these techniques; it will help you serve files using any server technology you want through command-line interface (CLI) tools.

The (Near?) Future

On the extreme side of web performance optimization, we also have some clever ideas that are emerging. In this section, we will analyze web streams and WebAssembly.

Web Streams

Streams (*https://streams.spec.whatwg.org*) is a new API for creating, composing, and consuming streams of data. These streams are designed to map efficiently to low-level I/O primitives, and allow easy composition with built-in backpressure and queuing.

The whole idea of streams is that we can manage low-level data as soon as it becomes available, meaning that we don't need to wait for all the response to be received. If we mix web streams with service workers, we can render content on the screen in the fastest possible way.

To learn more about web streams, I recommend you read Jake Archibald's blog post (*https://jakearchibald.com/2016/streams-ftw*) on the topic. At the time of this writing, web streams are only available under an experimental flag on Chrome Canary.

WebAssembly

Because performance is so important for the web, a new project was started in 2015: WebAssembly (*https://github.com/WebAssembly*), also known as *wasm*. WebAssembly is a portable syntax that is designed to be faster to parse than JavaScript, as well as faster to execute inside the browser. Its initial aim is to support compilation from C and C++, but other languages may be added later, including JavaScript.

The project is a work in progress, but teams from Google, Mozilla, Microsoft, and Apple are preparing the spec, so we may see initial support sooner rather than later.

AMP

The Accelerated Mobile Pages (AMP) Project (*http://ampproject.org*) is an open source initiative originally promoted by Google but supported by many other technical providers (Vimeo, Twitter, Pinterest, Medium, LinkedIn) and by dozens of media publishers worldwide. It's just getting started, and it's still unclear how big the impact will be in the mobile web space. The lead quote on the project's website describes its goals quite succinctly:

> For many, reading on the mobile web is a slow, clunky and frustrating experience—but it doesn't have to be that way. The Accelerated Mobile Pages (AMP) Project is an open source initiative that embodies the vision that publishers can create mobile optimized content once and have it load instantly everywhere.

The idea is to offer a mobile web alternative for HTML-based content that is proven to be as fast as possible and that will have some important advantages besides performance, such as precaching on Google's servers, while letting the publisher maintain complete control over analytics, ads, and content. The project is a response to the bad performance of the mobile web and a lot of publishers, ad agencies, user trackers, and other providers are supporting it.

AMP pages are suitable only for publishing-type content (e.g., magazines, newspapers, blogs, etc.), supporting text, images, video, galleries, audio, ads, and a short list of other content types. We can't use the format for web apps, forms, or ecommerce as we can't leave the AMP scope if we want to take full advantage of it.

 AMP pages are web-based, so every browser will load them, but they use web components to force the designer to keep the performance under control, using extreme web performance techniques like the ones we've been seeing in this chapter.

AMP pages are just HTML5 files that go through an AMP validator. If you follow the rules and your HTML page is a valid AMP page, then you will get the benefits. If not, it's just an HTML page, so it will still work as a normal page in any browser.

 AMP is an open source initiative, so everyone can participate. If you want to get involved, check out "How to Contribute to AMP" (*https://www.ampproject.org/docs/support/contribute.html*).

Benefits

Using AMP pages instead of normal HTML pages will give you the benefit of better performance, as you will only use techniques that are well known as being good for performance.

But it doesn't end there. The idea is that if your page is AMP-valid, then some providers can do something on top of that, such as precaching the page to improve the user experience.

Since 1Q 2016, Google has been using AMP pages as a way to increase visibility and enhance the user experience when searching for articles. If your content is crawled by the Google Spider and you provide an AMP page, then Google will cache it in its own servers free of charge.

Google says that if you AMP-ify your pages, it will cut down load time by as much as 85%.

Besides being stored in the cache, your AMP pages will appear in a Carousel in Google's search results (as seen in Figure 10-6) with an AMP icon. If you click on one of those results, you will end up browsing the precached articles inside Google.com, where you can swipe right–left to change search results.

At the time of this writing, this is the best example of the benefit of taking advantage of this format, but other providers can expose similar solutions. For example, Twitter can precache an AMP page when you browse through your timeline so if you click on a link it loads quickly from the cache. A non-AMP page will suffer from a normal load process through a web view or a browser.

Figure 10-6. In Google's search results, you can see the benefits of AMP pages in action when you search for content articles using a browser on iOS or Android

Controversy

AMP is still controversial in the web community, as it tries to narrow web compatibility and recalls the XHTML Mobile Profile subset of the 2000s. However, it appeared on the market as a subset with fixed rules for a greater good. The controversy is not typically about the goals, but about how it takes over some of the browser's responsibilities, such as loading of resources, with a JavaScript implementation of that process (meaning the browser cannot use its intelligence—and new algorithms in future versions—to improve performance); how it does the validation; and that, while it's open, providers (analytics, tracking pixels, web fonts, and ad agencies) need to be whitelisted in the system and there is no open way to manage this.

Tim Kadlec has proposed an alternative and more standard solution, Content Performance Policies (CPP) (*https://timkadlec.com/2016/02/a-standardized-alternative-to-amp*), that takes the good part of AMP (performance rules) and shifts responsibility to its enforcement to the browsers.

Also, at the time of this writing, Facebook—the other big IT company behind browsing web content on mobile devices—hasn't mentioned AMP support; it's still using Facebook Instant Articles, its own private similar solution, which we will look at later.

Discovery of AMP Pages

You can serve AMP pages as your mobile web version, or you can have a normal HTML solution (responsive or not) and an alternate set of AMP pages. In the latter case, you can tell search engines and other apps, such as Twitter, that you have an AMP version using a `<link>` element in your normal HTML with a `rel="amphtml"` attribute:

```
<link rel="amphtml" href="full-url-to-amp-version">
```

In your AMP version, you can also add a `<link>` pointing to your normal HTML using `rel="canonical"`:

```
<link rel="canonical" href="full-url-to-classic-version">
```

AMP-HTML Template

An AMP HTML page is just an HTML5 file based on a template you must follow:

```
<!doctype html>
<html ⚡ lang="en">
  <head>
    <meta charset="utf-8">
    <title>First Example of AMP</title>
    <link rel="canonical" href="url-to-classic-version" />
    <meta name="viewport"
        content="width=device-width,minimum-scale=1,initial-scale=1">
    <script type="application/ld+json">
      {
        "@context": "http://schema.org",
        "@type": "NewsArticle",
        "headline": "Your Title",
        "datePublished": "2016-10-07T12:02:41Z",
        "image": [
          "logo.jpg"
        ]
      }
```

```
    </script>
    <style amp-boilerplate>body{-webkit-animation:-amp-start 8s steps(1,end) 0s
1 normal both;-moz-animation:-amp-start 8s steps(1,end) 0s 1 normal both;-ms-
animation:-amp-start 8s steps(1,end) 0s 1 normal both;animation:-amp-start 8s
steps(1,end) 0s 1 normal both}@-webkit-keyframes -amp-start{from{visibility:hid
den}to{visibility:visible}}@-moz-keyframes -amp-start{from{visibility:hid
den}to{visibility:visible}}@-ms-keyframes -amp-
start{from{visibility:hidden}to{visibility:visible}}@-o-keyframes -amp-
start{from{visibility:hidden}to{visibility:visible}}@keyframes -amp-
start{from{visibility:hidden}to{visibility:visible}}</style><noscript><style
amp-boilerplate>body{-webkit-animation:none;-moz-animation:none;-ms-
animation:none;animation:none}</style></noscript>
    <style amp-custom></style>
    <script async src="https://cdn.ampproject.org/v0.js"></script>
  </head>
  <body>
    <h1>Your first AMP Template</h1>
    <!-- The rest of the content here -->
  </body>
</html>
```

Analyzing the template, we find that it includes the following:

- A special attribute in the `html` element: the lightning-bolt Unicode character, ⚡ (or `<html amp>` if you don't like the character)

- A `<link>` with `rel="canonical"` that can point to a classic HTML version of the page, or if not available, the URL of that same AMP page

- Schema.org data in JSON for Linking (*http://json-ld.org*) data format

- A `<style>` declaration with the `amp-boilerplate` attribute that must not be changed

- An optional `<style>` declaration with the `amp-custom` attribute where you can add your own styles

- An async `<script>` tag that will load the AMP framework from the CDN; the script file is around 40 KB in size and is served compressed

The AMP HTML template might change with time, so check "Create your First AMP Page" (*https://www.ampproject.org/docs/get_started/create_page.html*) for updated information.

An AMP file is just an HTML file, so it usually uses the *.html* syntax for static files. To semantically define that we are using AMP pages, we can use the *.amp.html* double extension.

If your page doesn't follow every rule of AMP, it will work in every browser anyway, and you will probably get some performance enhancement, but you won't get the special benefits from different providers, such as in Google's search results.

You can find examples of using every feature of AMP at AMP by Example (*http://ampbyexample.com*).

Requirements

An AMP page has a suite of requirements that might change with time. The first version of the spec has the following restrictions:

- You can't load any JavaScript of your own on the main page
- You can load custom JavaScript code in sandboxed iframes if they are `async`
- External resources (images, videos, ads, iframes) must have the size statically defined to avoid repaints or more than one HTTP request for rendering
- Your CSS must be inlined in the HTML's `<head>` through one `<style>` decalration (no external stylesheets), and it has a maximum size of 50 KB; the `style` attribute is forbidden
- If you use CSS animation or transitions, they can only animate the `transform` or `opacity` properties to guarantee GPU-accelerated animations
- Some CSS declarations are forbidden, such as `!important`, the `*` selector, the `not` selector, and the `filter` property
- AMP controls every resource load, so you can't use any HTML code that generates a download operation, such as `<img>`, `<video>`, `<link>`, and so on. AMP will provide you alternatives that will guarantee performance
- If you are using web fonts, they can be loaded only from whitelisted providers; at the time of this writing, only Google Fonts and Fonts.net are approved

As you can see, AMP pages are basically normal HTML pages using web components with specific restrictions aimed at providing the fastest possible experience.

Custom Components

You can use most of the semantic HTML elements with no problems. The only elements that are forbidden are the ones involving external HTTP requests and complex components that will expose mobile-optimized behaviors, such as galleries.

To embed images, you use `<amp-img>`, which takes the standard `<img>` attributes. For example:

```
<amp-img src="logo.png" width="100" height="40">
```

It can be extended with responsive image support using `srcset`. Similarly, instead of `video` you use `amp-video`. Ad banners must be served through HTTPS using the `<amp-ads>` tag with several attributes available.

The basic components are included in the main AMP JavaScript core file, and extended components must be installed as a separate `<script>` element that will define the file to load asynchronously and the custom element.

For example, to embed Facebook posts, we must add this in the `<head>`:

```
<script async custom-element="amp-facebook"
        src="https://cdn.ampproject.org/v0/amp-facebook-0.1.js"></script>
```

On the UI side, extended components (*https://www.ampproject.org/docs/reference/extended.html*) today include Pixel Tracking, Accordions, Analytic Support, Animated Image, Carousels, Custom Fonts, Lightboxes, Service Worker, Lists, User Notifications, and more.

Several providers are supported for embedding content in our AMP pages, such as Facebook posts, tweets, YouTube videos, and Pinterest widgets.

For example, to show a YouTube video after installing the component, we must use code like the following:

```
<amp-youtube
    data-videoid="mGENRKrdoGY"
    layout="responsive"
    width="480" height="270"></amp-youtube>
```

Custom components can be styled with CSS using standard selector techniques.

Everything else that we want to add must be served through an `<amp-iframe>` and should not be part of the ATF content unless we are providing a placeholder text alternative. With AMP we can also set up a service worker that will be installed in the browser and can be used to precache content to improve performance on the link the user will follow next. At "From AMP To PWA" (*https://greenido.wordpress.com/2016/06/07/from-amp-to-pwa/*), we can see how we can start the initial load with an AMP page and then upgrade the experience to a Progressive Web App.

More information, including examples, experimental components, and API documentation, is available at *https://www.ampproject.org/docs/*.

Validation and Debugging

To validate that our AMP pages follow every rule so we can get the full benefit, we must run the AMP validator.

The AMP validator runs directly on top of the AMP page itself as JavaScript code, with the output shown in the Developer's Console.

To run the validator, you first need to serve the files through a web server. Running them locally through the *file://* protocol might trigger some XHR request errors. To run the validation and see warnings or errors, you must add *#development=1* to the URL; for example, *https://mydomain/myfile.amp.html#development=1*.

When you add the development hash and you open the Developer's Console in your browser, you will see an "AMP validation successful" message, as illustrated in Figure 10-7.

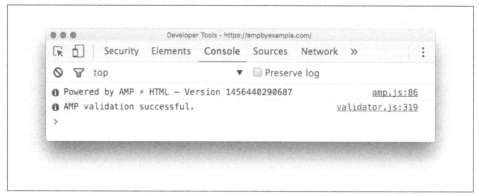

Figure 10-7. AMP will validate your code to match the spec if you enable developer mode

If you have errors in your AMP validation, you will see the list with some suggestions in the console, as you can see in Figure 10-8.

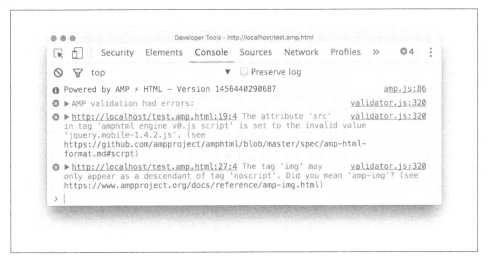

Figure 10-8. If you are not following the AMP validation rules, you will find messages about the errors in the console after activating developer mode

Facebook Instant Articles

Facebook, in pursuit of its goal of offering better and faster services to users, has created Instant Articles (*https://instantarticles.fb.com*) to offer content publishers an alternative way to deliver articles to Facebook users.

When someone shares a link, scripts on Facebook's servers will verify if there is an Instant Article alternative. If that's the case, then Facebook users on the mobile app will use that version instead of the web version. The Instant Article will be precached on Facebook's servers so it will appear immediately to the user after clicking on the link.

While AMP pages render in any browser, Instant Articles will render only in the Facebook native apps for iOS and Android, instead of the Facebook web browser or the default web browser.

> According to Facebook, an Instant Article will load as much as 10 times faster than the standard mobile web version.

The Technical Side

The Instant Articles documentation (*https://developers.facebook.com/docs/instant-articles*) provides all the technical information on how to create Instant Articles.

An Instant Article is an HTML5 document that is optimized for fast delivery and can't use CSS for styling. The template will include some metadata and semantic HTML, such as:

```
<head>
  <meta charset="utf-8">
  <meta property="op:markup_version" content="v1.0">

  <!-- The URL of the web version of your article -->
  <link rel="canonical" href="http://example.com/article.html">

  <!-- The style to be used for this article -->
  <meta property="fb:article_style" content="myarticlestyle">
</head>
<body>
<article>
    <header>
      <!-- The cover image shown inside your article -->
      <figure>
        <img src="http://mydomain.com/path/to/img.jpg" />
        <figcaption>This image is amazing</figcaption>
      </figure>

      <!-- The title and subtitle shown in your article -->
      <h1> Title </h1>
      <h2> Subtitle </h2>

      <!-- A kicker for your article -->
      <h3 class="op-kicker">
        This is a kicker
      </h3>

      <!-- The author of your article -->
      <address>
        <a rel="facebook"
           href="http://facebook.com/brandon.diamond">Brandon Diamond</a>
      </address>

      <!-- The published and last modified time stamps -->
      <time class="op-published"
            dateTime="2016-12-11T04:44:16Z">December 11th, 4:44 PM</time>
      <time class="op-modified"
            dateTime="2016-12-11T04:44:16Z">December 11th, 4:44 PM</time>
    </header>
  </article>
</body>
```

To style your content, you use a rich editor inside Facebook that will let you customize colors and other formatting styles.

Besides images and videos, there are some interactive elements that are supported, such as tap to expand, tilt to explore, 3D rotating maps, geotagging, and embedding web content as a mini-web view inside your article.

To publish your Instant Articles to Facebook, you must provide an RSS file that will point to every article available. The RSS URL must be provided inside Facebook's portal, and they will pull the file every three minutes to see if there is any new content that needs to be cached by Facebook (only 100 articles per fetch).

> The Facebook team must approve your Facebook Instant Articles RSS feed. Therefore, you must follow their rules if you want to support this feature.

Facebook will use the Instant Article instead of your website when the user clicks on a link to your site, if the `<link rel="canonical">` tag of your Instant Article matches the URL of the page to be loaded.

If you change an article, Facebook will reload it from your server only if the RSS file has updated the modified time.

Facebook also has a manual Instant Article editor where you can create articles or modify the ones that are loaded.

The Distribution Side

Starting in Q1 2016, every publisher can join Facebook Instant Articles and distribute content through it. The main difference from AMP is that we are talking about a private mechanism from Facebook that can't be used by other providers at least in its first stages.

You can use your own ads inside an Instant Article or participate in Facebook's Audience Network to use its monetization system.

To work with Instant Articles you will need a Facebook page associated with your website.

> Facebook Instant Articles appears to be Facebook's reaction to Google's AMP. The truth is that Facebook Instant Articles came first, and AMP was the reaction.

The Extreme Side Will Reward You

In this chapter, we've seen several techniques that we can apply to our websites that will increase the performance and perception of our web content. There is a cost—we will need to make some concessions, and we may need an architecture change—but the benefits are clear, as these techniques will increase our conversion rates. And that is, in the end, our ultimate goal.

We've covered:

- The 14 KB approach to achieve one-second load times
- Separating ATF content from the rest
- How to serve extremely fast images, including fast previews
- JavaScript techniques and how to avoid stop signs
- A possible future with web streams and WebAssembly
- Alternatives with AMP and Facebook Instant Articles

Extreme techniques also need more attention, as they might change with time and we should always retest whenever a new browser version appears on the market.

In Chapter 11, we will get into the native world when it's mixed with the web, including web views and Cordova solutions.

The Native Side of the Web

The web is not just about browsers today. We've already seen during this book that a big percentage of users are browsing the web from native apps that are not marketed as browsers, such as Facebook and Twitter, or using web views such as Firefox and Chrome on iOS.

A lot of web content is executed inside native apps, to show rich content or to create hybrid or native web apps, such as Apache Cordova (PhoneGap) apps.

In this chapter, we will talk about the situations that might affect performance inside web views, such as using old versions or printing solutions.

The first thing to mention is that most of the techniques that we have seen for browsers will apply in web views too (or at least they won't harm performance if they are ignored).

 Most modern web views allow you to attach remote inspectors and use all the debugging techniques we've already mentioned for websites.

Web Views on iOS

If you are using web views on iOS, you will first want to upgrade to WKWebView (as mentioned in Chapter 1), because it has better performance than UIWeb View, and then apply some tricks to improve the user's perception of the experience.

Goodbye UIWebView

From iOS 2.0, UIWebView has been the web view control available in the UIKit framework. Starting with iOS 9, we can fully use the new WKWebView in the WebKit framework to load web or local content.

UIWebView is deprecated, and unless you still need to support users on iOS 7 and/or iOS 8 (for local content only) you should consider migrating to WKWebView. While the migration should be simple, you need to verify all the documentation—the new web view does not inherit from the old one, so the API is not the same.

> Starting in Q1 2016, Chrome on iOS has migrated to WKWebView as the engine inside the browser. It's a good signal that you should migrate too. The Chrome developers have said that the new version crashes 70% less than older versions.

The first big advantage of WKWebView in terms of performance is that we can use the JIT Nitro JavaScript compiler, improving JavaScript execution performance by 3x (that's 300% faster!). That usually has a total performance impact of around 20%.

Also available are the Navigation Timing API and many others that are not supported by UIWebKit.

Performance improvements happen on other levels, too; for example, with WebGL. According to the WebGL Performance Tester (*https://www.scirra.com/demos/c2/renderperfgl*), WKWebView shows more than 2x better performance with WebGL 3D code. You can find more insights about WebGL performance in the different iOS web views in @krisrak's blog post "WKWebView vs UIWebView" (*http://blog.initlabs.com/post/100113463211/wkwebview-vs-uiwebview*).

> If you want to compare UIWebView vs. WKWebView on any URL, you can download the free app available at *http://www.initlabs.com/projects/webview-app*.

WKWebView also offers a set of new classes that will help us measure the loading process and take actions on it, such as WKNavigation and WKNavigationResponse.

The final feature of WKWebView that can help us on the performance side is the ability to inject a WKUserScript in any web page loaded in the web view. The WKUser Script is JavaScript code that we create that can work with the page (e.g., talking to the Navigation Timing API).

Rendering as an App

One big difference between a native app and web content is incremental rendering. While a native app renders everything at once (and you see nothing or a loading screen in the meantime), the web content will render incrementally, actually showing how the content is being rendered in pieces.

When you are designing hybrid applications, you might want to emulate an app and disable the incremental rendering behavior. You can do that with both UIWebView and WKWebView. Here's how to do it in the latter using Swift:

```
let c = WKWebViewConfiguration()
configuration.suppressesIncrementalRendering = true

let webview = WKWebView(frame: CGRectZero, c: configuration)
// rest of the web view setup code
```

Web Views on Android

I've already mentioned in Chapter 1 how messy web views on Android are. In this section, we will see what we can do to improve performance when working with Android and web views.

Basic Setup

On modern Android devices (4.4+), the web view is already optimized.

For older devices (Android 2.x or 3.x), the first thing we can do to improve performance in a web view is to enable hardware acceleration in the activity that has the web view inside it. There are several ways to do that, with the simplest being to add an XML attribute in the *AndroidManifest.xml* file:

```
<activity android:hardwareAccelerated="true" />
```

Enabling hardware acceleration improves scrolling and the animation frame rate. GPU acceleration is enabled by default when targeting Android 4+. The only problem here was on older devices, where hardware acceleration was broken, which led to several UI glitches in the web view.

Up to Android 4.3 (WebKit-based web views), it was possible to set the render priority of the web view via `WebSettings.setRender Priority`. Today, the feature is deprecated and it won't be supported in the future.

Another trick to improve the performance of an Android web view is to disable the cache (useful when loading local files) or change the default cache behavior (you can set LOAD_NO_CACHE, LOAD_CACHE_ONLY, or LOAD_CACHE_ELSE_NETWORK):

```
myWebView.getSettings().setCacheMode(WebSettings.LOAD_NO_CACHE);
```

 From Android 5, the web view is updatable from the Google Play Store. If you want to play with future versions of the web view, you can participate in the WebView Beta community (*https:// plus.google.com/communities/105434725573080290360*).

Amazon WebView

Amazon WebView (AWV) is a Chromium-based web view replacement for 3rd- and 4th-generation Kindle Fire tablets that is already installed in the system and ready to use.

These devices were based on Android 4.0 without a Chromium web view. On newer Fire OS 5 devices, such as 5th-generation tablets (2015+), the Fire Stick, and Fire TV, the Android version is 5.x, so the standard Chromium web view is installed and we shouldn't use AWV anymore.

To get more information about how to use AWV, check the Amazon WebView SDK documentation (*https://developer.amazon.com/public/solutions/platforms/android-fireos/docs/building-and-testing-your-hybrid-app*).

Crosswalk

Because the Android web view world is so complicated, many native web apps are failing in offering a good and fast experience to Android users. That's why Intel has started a project to solve the problem: the Crosswalk Project (*https://crosswalk-project.org*).

With Crosswalk, you can embed a web view inside your Android native application. The Crosswalk web view is based on the latest versions of Chrome and it works from Android 4.0. Even on newer versions of Android with Chromium-based web views, such as Android 6, Crosswalk has better performance and API support than the native web view.

The main advantages of using Crosswalk are that we can normalize the execution engine across every Android device out there, and we will have the latest Chromium engine with better performance, bug fixing, and API support—including some APIs not available in the native web view, such as WebRTC and WebGL.

Crosswalk is available as a native component that you can use in your Android Java project to replace the web view or as an Apache Cordova plug-in that will automatically replace the default web view with the optimized one when creating Cordova/ PhoneGap applications.

Bigger APKs

The main disadvantage of using Crosswalk is that your Android app package (APK) will be bigger, because you are embedding the web engine in it. It'll add around 20 MB per architecture—such as Intel x86 or ARM—to your APK and 55 MB on the phone after installation.

To reduce this problem, Crosswalk has two separate subprojects that will let you get a more performant web view while not adding too much size to your native app:

Crosswalk Lite (https://github.com/crosswalk-project/crosswalk-website/wiki/Crosswalk-Project-Lite)
> This is a reduced version of the web engine (11Mb on x86, 9.6Mb on ARM) removing support of some features such as no remote debugger, QUIC protocol, WebRTC, or WebP.

Shared mode (https://crosswalk-project.org/documentation/shared_mode.html)
> The app won't include the web engine, but a simple library that will download the latest web engine from the repository (if not installed by any other app in the system). You must test your app for each version of Crosswalk, as you are not in control of the Crosswalk version that will execute your code.

Download mode (https://crosswalk-project.org/documentation/download_mode.html)
> When the app is first run on the device, the Crosswalk libraries are downloaded in the background from your server. You will need to host the files and the APK will just include some core libraries.

> If having a bigger APK is an issue for your app's distribution, you can evaluate the use of Download mode or Crosswalk Lite.

What Doesn't Work on Embedded Content

When you are loading HTML files that were embedded in your native package (such as when creating hybrid applications), there will be no network operations, so most of the tips that we have covered in this book won't apply. You won't find DNS queries, TCP connections, or HTTP requests and responses.

In these situations, files are loaded from the local filesystem of the mobile device, so that part is as fast as possible and some techniques need to be re-evaluated. For example, using CSS Sprites doesn't make any sense from a network-saving point of view, and it might be harming memory. On the other hand, precaching all the images you are going to use in memory can help performance, so it's a matter of testing in each situation.

 Typical web view performance tweaks involve using hardware acceleration as much as possible and minimizing reflows, DOM manipulation, and memory used.

When working with embedded content, you may want to focus your performance measures and improvements on the user experience, targeting areas such as scrolling and animation frame rate, and immediate feedback, using the tips we covered in previous chapters.

In-App Browsing

If you have a native app and you are currently using a web view for letting the user browse the web inside your app, you should know that there are better solutions available. The main problem with using web views is that the user will not browse the web with the same engine as the one in the usual browser on that same device, causing performance issues and user experience issues such as:

- No access to current opened sessions (i.e., social networks)
- No access to Read mode or Share actions normally available in the browser
- Still using old version of the engine, even if the user updates the browser
- No access to bookmarks or history

But you don't want to open the browser, because that removes the user from your app's experience. Fortunately, we now have a third solution that will solve the issue: we can ask the installed browser to open a browsing session within the context of our app. This solution is called Custom Tabs on Android and the Safari view controller on iOS. There is no similar solution for Windows at the time of this writing.

Custom Tabs on Android

Chrome Custom Tabs (*https://developer.chrome.com/multidevice/android/customtabs*) lets you open Google Chrome on Android devices in a special mode that can match the look and feel of your native app, including:

- Toolbar color
- Enter and exit animations

- Custom menu items in the Chrome Toolbar that will be executed back in your app
- Custom action buttons

The user must have Chrome 45 or newer to make it work. In Figure 11-1, we can see a Custom Tab in action.

The Custom Tabs protocol is open, so other browsers might implement it too in the future.

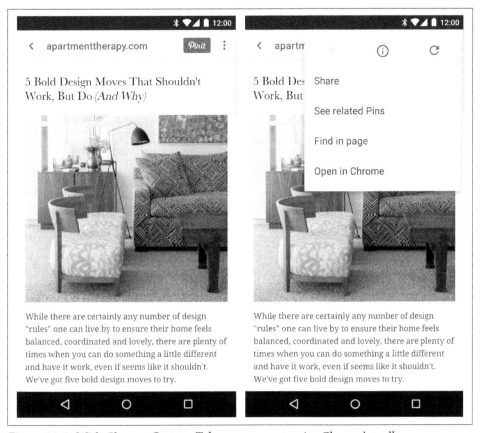

Figure 11-1. With Chrome Custom Tabs, we can customize Chrome's toolbar: we can add button actions (left image) and menu items (right image) that will be executed back in our app with the current web context

Warming up the browser

Chrome Custom Tabs has a great feature for web performance: we can talk to the browser before opening the Custom Tab so it can start preloading the website. Chrome will start the DNS resolution process and the TCP handshake, so when the tab appears on the screen it will have some work done ahead.

Also, we can tell Chrome a possible URL or list of URLs that the user might load later based on our data and perception. Chrome will keep that in mind for improving the user experience too, if some conditions are met (such as being on WiFi with enough battery).

 In case the user doesn't have Chrome or has a previous version of the browser, we should always have a fallback solution to open the browser in standard mode or using a web view.

Samsung Custom Tabs

Starting with version 4.0, Samsung Internet Browser has also included support for Custom Tabs. It supports customizing menu items and toolbar color, and warming up the browser. This browser is only available on Samsung devices, and version 4 has only been preinstalled since 2016. Previous devices shipped with an older version not compatible with Custom Tabs, and the user will have to update it manually.

Safari View Controller

The SFSafariViewController class (*https://developer.apple.com/library/ios/documen tation/SafariServices/Reference/SFSafariViewController_Ref*) provides a way to integrate Safari into your native iOS application as a view controller, starting from iOS 9. It will usually appear as a modal view controller (like a modal sheet), and it can load the URL you want with the advantages of sharing sessions with Safari, a Done button that will go back to your previous view controller, 3D Touch Peek support, and an Action button that will open a Share dialog where you can insert your own items.

Figure 11-2 shows how the Flipboard app uses a Safari view controller to show external web content using Safari without leaving the app.

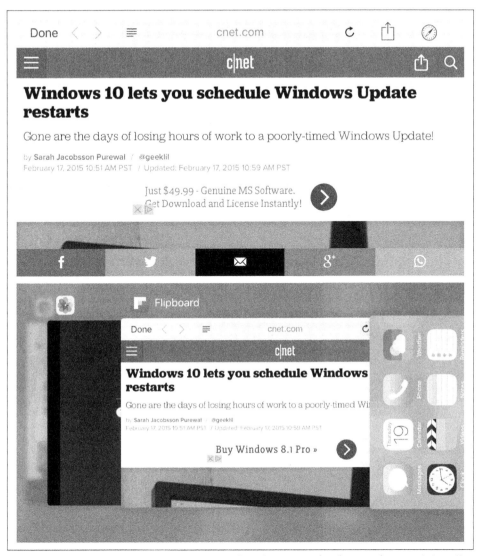

Figure 11-2. From iOS 9, native apps can take advantage of Safari rendering while still keeping the user inside the app using a Safari View Controller

The Same But Different

In this chapter, we've seen that the basic approach for applying web performance optimization to web views is the same as for the browser.

Additionally, we should:

- Use WKWebView on iOS whenever possible
- Use Crosswalk on Android if we want to have a fast web view on every Android device
- Use Custom Tabs or a Safari view controller when we want to offer an in-app browsing experience

Most of the techniques are used in this new context while we might not use some of the network-based practices when loading content locally. Now it's time to wrap up in Chapter 12 everything we learned in this book with the Mobile Web Performance Checklist.

Mobile Web Performance Checklist

We've covered a huge number of techniques throughout this book. Now it's time to see all of them at once, in the form of a checklist that you can use for every web project you are working on.

The checklist will be updated with more techniques over time on this book's website at *http://highperfmobile.com*.

Basic Data

In this section of the checklist, you will gather some metrics from different sources that will help you see later if you've improved the performance. If you look at Chapters 3 and 4, you will find details on how to get these metrics.

For a desktop viewport (>900 px):

- Time to first byte (ms)
- Start render (ms)
- Speed Index on initial view
- Speed Index on repeat view
- Page load time on initial view
- Page load time on repeat view
- Page speed insights score

For a tablet viewport (600–800 px):

- Time to first byte (ms)
- Start render (ms)

- Speed Index on initial view
- Speed Index on repeat view
- Page load time on initial view
- Page load time on repeat view

For a mobile viewport (320–400 px):

- Time to first byte (ms)
- Start render (ms)
- Speed Index on initial view
- Speed Index on repeat view
- Page load time on initial view
- Page load time on repeat view
- Page speed insights score

Also, it's important to see if you can create your own custom metric to get a "Time to First Meaningful Interaction" based on what that means for your content. In this case, you will define how to calculate that metric using the APIs we covered in Chapter 5.

For custom metrics, you will need the following:

- Name
- Description of the meaningful interaction
- Formula to measure

Network Checklist

This section lays out some things you should do on the network layer.

General technologies you should start implementing:

- TLS (HTTPS)
- HTTP/2
- Other mobile techniques rather than just responsive web design (RWD)

Features you must have:

- *gzip* enabled on *all* text files
- DNS queries kept to a minimum

- Keep-alive enabled
- No redirects

Features you should have:

- If serving on TLS, use HSTS
- Cookieless domain
- Small cookie size
- Flush HTML's `<head>` early from the server
- Static content with far-future expiration
- CDN for static content
- Domain sharding for HTTP/1.1
- If domain sharding enabled, disable it for HTTP/2 or use a multidomain certificate
- Don't rely only on CSS media queries for RWD; use JS or server-side libraries
- Don't set RWD as a goal for your project
- Use JavaScript measuring APIs to gather real-world data

Basic Optimizations

This section lists optimizations that you should implement most of the time.

Tips for initial loading:

- Don't use custom mobile app banners
- Don't use client-side rendering for the initial view
- Announce DNS as soon as possible with `dns-prefetch`
- Announce resources using Resource Hints
- Announce CSS ASAP
- Don't use blocking JavaScript
- Minify JavaScript
- Minify CSS
- Combine essential JavaScript in one file
- Combine essential CSS in one file
- Use on-demand code when possible
- Analyze usage of `defer` or `async` in every `<script>` element

- Use `DOMContentLoaded` instead of `load` for initialization
- Use HTTP/2 server push when possible

Tips on images:

- Don't use blocking images (Base64) as a general rule
- Resize images for the current device
- Apply responsive images with `srcset` and `<picture>`
- Use CSS Sprites on HTTP/1.1
- Use Base64 images in specific situations (only inside CSS or when loaded using prefetch techniques)
- Use SVG when possible
- Compress your images
- Replace animated GIFs with muted videos when possible
- Deliver hero images ASAP

Tips on web fonts:

- Use web fonts with a loader
- Use web fonts with a CDN
- Optimize web fonts, removing glyphs and unused characters

Tips for responsiveness:

- Verify that you don't have scripts running for longer than 50 ms
- Verify that all feedback is given within 100 ms
- Use a mobile viewport or `touch-action` CSS to remove touch delay
- Use passive listeners, debouncing, or throttling on scroll events
- Use web workers for long tasks
- Use momentum for small scrollable areas
- Use `will-change` on elements that will be animated to avoid repaint
- Use CSS containment to reduce browsers' useless recalculations
- Analyze using SSE or Web Sockets for some situations
- Use the browser's developer tools to turn on an FPS meter and check that you are reaching your goal of 60 fps, mostly while scrolling or animating

Tips for native web solutions:

- Use WKWebView on iOS instead of UIWebView
- Use Crosswalk on Android as a web view replacement
- Use Custom Tabs on Android for in-app browsing
- Use a Safari view controller on iOS for in-app browsing

Extreme Optimizations

This section recaps possible extreme techniques that will lead to great performance but may require an architecture change in your implementation.

Network layer tips:

- Achieve your goal of 1 second ATF page load on 3G connections
- Implement Brotli compression encoding
- Use other alternative compression methods

Architecture tips:

- For users who are offline or on a bad network, offer an alternative experience through service workers or the application cache
- Separate out ATF content
- Try to fit all the ATF content in 14 KB (after gzipping)
- Don't use media queries for responsive web design
- Create AMP and Facebook Instant Article versions if applicable
- Use SD/HD techniques based on initial metrics
- Deliver a low-res version if the `Save-Data` flag is on within Client Hints
- Analyze the creation of a custom cache
- Predict near-future browsing with prefetching
- Use lazy loading for components
- Use service workers as a progressive cache mechanism
- Avoid big frameworks for initial loading
- If using a client-side rendering framework, analyze creating a server-side initial rendering for it

Image tips:

- Opt in to HTTP Client Hints for server-side responsive images
- Use server-side libraries to help with HTTP Client Hints
- Use alternative image formats: WebP, JPEG-XR, JPEG-2000
- Use image preview techniques

Measuring Improvement

After you apply one technique, it's a good idea to retest the metrics that you gathered in the first section of this checklist and see how much things have improved. You need to remember that sometimes one technique might not help in your particular case, so it's better to isolate each technique to get a conclusion per case rather than applying several techniques in a row without measuring.

You've Selected the Red Pill

Now that you've finished this book—you've taken the red pill—you can't ignore the new world that is now in front of your eyes. You have a lot of work to do, so enjoy your future fast website, and always remember that *performance matters*…a lot.

Index

Windows Phone, 23
Windows Phone Emulator, 43
Windows Simulator, 44
Windows Store apps, 146
wireless network latency, 6
WKWebView, 20, 278
workers (web workers), 111, 225-227

X

XMLHttpRequest, 119

Z

Zopfli, 134

About the Author

Maximiliano Firtman (@firt) is a mobile and web developer, trainer, speaker, and writer. He has written many books, including *Programming the Mobile Web* and *jQuery Mobile: Up and Running*, published by O'Reilly Media. He is the founder of ITMaster Academy and he has been doing training on native mobile, the web, and performance for 15 years in more than 30 countries.

Max has a blog about mobile web development at *www.mobilexweb.com* and he maintains the website *www.mobilehtml5.org*. He has created dozens of online training courses on Mobile HTML5, Apache Cordova, web performance, and native app development. He keeps an updated list of talks, training materials, and videos at *http://firt.mobi*.

Max is a frequent speaker at conferences, including O'Reilly's Fluent and Velocity Conferences, Google Developer Day, Frontend, JSConf, and many other events around the world.

He has received different recognitions, including Nokia Developer Champion, Adobe Community Champion, Microsoft IE User Agent, BlackBerry Elite developer, and a Google recognition for being one of the most innovative mobile developers.

Colophon

The animal on the cover of *High Performance Mobile Web* is a Red-throated Loon (*Gavia stellata*). It is a migratory aquatic bird found in the northern hemisphere; it breeds primarily in Arctic regions, and winters in northern coastal waters. In non-breeding plumage, its markings are nondescript, grayish on top with a white face, neck, chest, and belly. During the breeding season, the face and neck are gray with a brick-red patch on its throat.

The Red-throated loon is a swimming and diving bird. Its legs are set far back on its body making it unable to walk on land; it simply drags itself on its belly, pushing its body forward with its feet. Underwater it is very agile and can stay under water for more than a minute. It hunts by sight and its diet consists of mostly fish, but will also eat insects, amphibians, crustaceans, plant vegetation, and invertebrates. It is the only loon able to take-off directly from land or water. When it lands on the water, it slides in on its breast rather than its feet. When frightened, it prefers to dive quickly under the water rather than fly away.

A monogamous species, the Red-throated Loon forms long-term pair bonds. Both members of the pair help to build the nest, incubate the eggs (up to three per clutch) and feed the hatched young. The chicks are well-developed when they hatch and can swim within 12-24 hours. Both adults are very attentive, they feed the chicks for several weeks, sometimes making up to 11 food flights during a day. The chicks fledge in 49-51 days.

Many of the animals on O'Reilly covers are endangered; all of them are important to the world. To learn more about how you can help, go to *animals.oreilly.com*.

The cover image is from *British Birds*. The cover fonts are URW Typewriter and Guardian Sans. The text font is Adobe Minion Pro; the heading font is Adobe Myriad Condensed; and the code font is Dalton Maag's Ubuntu Mono.

Get even more for your money.

Join the O'Reilly Community, and register the O'Reilly books you own. It's free, and you'll get:

- $4.99 ebook upgrade offer
- 40% upgrade offer on O'Reilly print books
- Membership discounts on books and events
- Free lifetime updates to ebooks and videos
- Multiple ebook formats, DRM FREE
- Participation in the O'Reilly community
- Newsletters
- Account management
- 100% Satisfaction Guarantee

Signing up is easy:

1. Go to: oreilly.com/go/register
2. Create an O'Reilly login.
3. Provide your address.
4. Register your books.

Note: English-language books only

To order books online:
oreilly.com/store

For questions about products or an order:
orders@oreilly.com

To sign up to get topic-specific email announcements and/or news about upcoming books, conferences, special offers, and new technologies:
elists@oreilly.com

For technical questions about book content:
booktech@oreilly.com

To submit new book proposals to our editors:
proposals@oreilly.com

O'Reilly books are available in multiple DRM-free ebook formats. For more information:
oreilly.com/ebooks

O'REILLY®

©2014 O'Reilly Media, Inc. O'Reilly logo is a registered trademark of O'Reilly Media, Inc. 14373

Have it your way.

O'Reilly eBooks

- Lifetime access to the book when you buy through oreilly.com
- Provided in up to four, DRM-free file formats, for use on the devices of your choice: PDF, .epub, Kindle-compatible .mobi, and Android .apk
- Fully searchable, with copy-and-paste, and print functionality
- We also alert you when we've updated the files with corrections and additions.

oreilly.com/ebooks/

Safari Books Online

- Access the contents and quickly search over 7000 books on technology, business, and certification guides
- Learn from expert video tutorials, and explore thousands of hours of video on technology and design topics
- Download whole books or chapters in PDF format, at no extra cost, to print or read on the go
- Early access to books as they're being written
- Interact directly with authors of upcoming books
- Save up to 35% on O'Reilly print books

See the complete Safari Library at safaribooksonline.com

©2014 O'Reilly Media, Inc. O'Reilly logo is a registered trademark of O'Reilly Media, Inc. 14373

Lightning Source UK Ltd.
Milton Keynes UK
UKOW04f0113210916

283412UK00004B/4/P